AQA A2 Economics

Chris Vidler
Charles Smith

Heinemann is an imprint of Pearson Education Limited, a company incorporated in England and Wales, having its registered office at Edinburgh Gate, Harlow, Essex, CM20 2JE. Registered company number: 872828

www.heinemann.co.uk

Heinemann is a registered trademark of Pearson Education Limited

All text with the exception of Exam cafés © Chris Vidler 2008
Exam cafés © Pearson Education Ltd 2008

First published 2008

12 11 10 09 08
10 9 8 7 6 5 4 3 2 1

British Library Cataloguing in Publication Data is available from the British Library on request.

ISBN 978 0 435692 23 0

Edited by Bill MacKeith
Designed by Tek-Art
Typeset by Tek-Art
Original illustrations © Pearson Education Ltd 2008
Illustrated by Tek-Art
Cover design by Philippa Baile
Picture research by Maria Joannou
Cover photo/illustration © Alamy / Johnny Greig Creative
Printed in the UK by Scotprint

Websites
There are links to relevant websites in this book. In order to ensure that the links are up-to-date, that the links work, and that the sites are not inadvertently linked to sites that could be considered offensive, we have made the links available on the Heinemann website at www.heinemann.co.uk/hotlinks. When you access the site, the express code is 2230P.

Contents

About the authors

Chris Vidler is a highly experienced teacher, trainer, inspector and author of economics texts. He has taught in schools and colleges for more years than he cares to reveal, but has always remained an enthusiastic teacher who believes that learning economics helps students have a better understanding of the world and its problems. He has worked as an examiner and moderator for a number of awarding bodies.

Chris has always encouraged his students to look critically at what they read, what they hear, and what others say about economic issues. He is particularly interested in environmental and development economics and believes that all of us have a role in tackling global issues of inequality and climate change. Ten per cent of his royalties from writing this book will be donated to Oxfam to support their work in fighting global poverty.*

Dr Charles Smith is one of the most experienced examiners of economics in the country. He is a fellow of the Chartered Institute of Educational Assessors, a former chief examiner, and currently principal examiner for a major 'A' Level awarding body.

He has taught previously in secondary and further education and currently works at Swansea Metropolitan University. As a teacher trainer he has run workshops for economics teachers in nearly 20 countries around the world, covering all of the five continents.

He broadcasts regularly on economic matters on regional radio and television, and has served as an adviser to the Welsh Assembly Government on skills, training and employment.

His hobbies include swimming, cycling, visiting a holiday caravan in west Wales, playing the Irish whistle, and (most important of all) being a grandfather.

*Oxfam is a registered charity. The views expressed in this book are those of the author and should not be taken to represent those of Oxfam.

Acknowledgements

The author and publisher would like to thank the following individuals and organisations for permission to reproduce photographs:

AKG Images / RIA Novosti p 38; Alamy / Corbis Super RF p 86; Alamy / Janine Wiedel Photolibrary p 70; Alamy / Travelshots.com p 56; Alamy / Nik Wheeler p 41; Alamy / David Williams p 58; Corbis p 109; Corbis / Bettmann p 15; Getty Images / Peter Macdiarmid p 143; Corbis / Robert Wallis p 130; Fotolia / Philippe Minisini p 118; Fotolia / Daniel Tackley p 171; Getty Images / Scott Barbour p 145; Getty Images / Lambert p 115; Getty Images / Joy Tessman / National Geographic p 120; iStockphoto / David H Lewis p 68; iStockphoto / Lisa McDonald p 31; PA Photos p 3; PA Photos / AP Photo / Eckehard Schulz p 43; PA Photos / AP Photo / Richard Vogel p 63; PA Photos / Bifab 145486 / DPA p 84; PA Photos / Johnny Green / PA Archive p 8; PA Photos / PA Archive p 127; PA Photos / Andrew Parsons / PA Wire p 90; Photofusion / Paul Baldesare p 78; Photolibrary / Fresh Food Images / John Carey p 45; Photoshot / UPPA p 146; Rex Features p 160; Rex Features / John Powell p 154; Shutterstock / breezeart.us p 19; Topham Picturepoint p 61; Topham Picturepoint / UPPA p 177.

Crown Copyright material reproduced with permission of the Controller of Her Majesty's Stationery Office and the Queen's Printer for Scotland.

Every effort has been made to contact copyright holders of material reproduced in this book. Any omissions will be rectified in subsequent printings if notice is given to the publishers.

Introduction

Welcome to *AQA A2 Economics*. This book has been specially written for students taking the AQA course. This means that it:

- follows the AQA specification closely

- has been written to ensure that all concepts are clearly explained in terms understandable by students taking this subject for the first time

- includes plenty of advice from examiners to help you get the best possible grade.

This introduction is divided into three parts. First, the links to your AS work are made clear. This is followed by a more formal description of how the A2 part of your course is organised. Finally, you will be introduced to the special features of this book which have been designed to help you get the grade you deserve.

Your AS experience

How was it for you? We hope you got the grade you deserved. If you did not, think about a retake. Even if you scored well for AS, it can be worthwhile taking units again. It is easier to score marks for AS than it is for A2 and as the second year of your course involves more in-depth consideration of many of the topics you took in the first year you should get better and better at economics.

Having studied advanced economics for a year, you should be:

- familiar with the special technical language associated with economics

- able to use graphical analysis to show that you can predict the outcomes of changes in economic and other variables

- developing skills of analysis and evaluation.

Your AS programme consisted of two sets of learning. You probably tackled Unit 1: 'Markets and market failure' first and followed this with study about the national economy for Unit 2.

This structure is reflected in the A2 course. Unit 3, covered in Part 1 of this book, builds on Unit 1 and is designed to give you a deeper and more critical understanding of markets and market failure. In addition, you need to learn about labour markets and the distribution of income and wealth. Many students follow this structure, tackling Unit 3 in the autumn term of their A2 programme as this gives them the opportunity of sitting the Unit 3 examination in January. Success at this stage lessens the pressure in the final round of exams. Not getting the grade you wanted is not the end of the world as there is the opportunity of a retake in June.

Most students leave Unit 4, dealt with in Part 2 of this book, until last, taking the examination in June. You don't have to do things this way but you do need to be aware that the move up to A2 standard is quite significant – success at AS does not guarantee success at A2, especially in terms of achieving a top grade. Your school or college may not allow you to take exams in January. Whatever the constraints, it pays to plan ahead, especially to reduce pressure on yourself next May and June.

The main thing to know and never *never* forget is that examiners can ask questions based on both the AS and A2 parts of your course. Don't throw away your notes from last year and don't forget to revise basic stuff like elasticity and aggregate demand and supply for your A2 examinations.

Moving up to A2

Most students find the second year of the course much more demanding than AS. You have to know more; and questions are less straightforward and require longer, more detailed answers. This is because a higher proportion of marks is awarded for showing that you have the higher-order skills of analysis and evaluation. The good thing about economics is that once you have mastered a particular topic it should stick in your brain.

As already indicated, Unit 3: 'Business economics and the distribution of income' is advanced microeconomics and consists of three linked elements:

● theory of the firm

● labour markets

● market failure and government intervention.

The theory of the firm involves a deeper understanding of revenue and costs faced by firms operating under different market conditions. This links directly to a consideration of why markets might be considered to fail, and possible strategies for government intervention, which themselves might fail. Parallel to this is an element about how labour markets work and how this might explain differences in income and wealth. This theme also links into market failure/government intervention/government failure.

Unit 4: 'The national and international economy' – the advanced macro module – also consists of three linked elements:

● economic growth and inflation

● government policies

● international economics.

The first two of these involve a much more detailed consideration of what you did in Unit 2 for AS but the final part on the international economy is likely to be new to you. It involves looking at the costs and benefits of international trade, balance of payments and exchange rates.

There is a special emphasis in A2 on two contexts in which you are expected to apply your understanding of economics concepts and theories. You need to have an understanding of two major influences on both the micro- and the macroeconomy of the UK:

● the EU

● globalisation.

This requires a basic understanding of how the EU has developed and its main institutions, together with an appreciation that we are all part of a global economy in terms of the production and sales of goods. The global economy is not static: some argue that economic power is shifting away from the USA to the rapidly growing economies of China, India, Russia and Brazil – a change which is likely to be very significant in your lifetime. It will pay you to have an understanding of these important changes. A good move is to collect a file – electronically or on paper – of major European and global issues. This should contribute to your confidence in discussing such issues, which will be part of your economics classes.

Collecting such a file will also help in your examinations, as in both Unit 3 and Unit 4 you will have a choice of stimulus response questions – one chosen from a European context and one chosen from a global perspective. If you have built up an understanding of major issues, the chances are that you will be familiar with the issues chosen by the examiner.

Finding your way

The text of *AQA A2 Economics* is set out in a similar fashion to that of the AS student book. The major difference is that the individual sections within each chapter are longer, to give enough space to develop the more detailed treatments required for A2.

The central body of text is designed to explain the key concept(s) featured in each section. There are Activities designed to help you consolidate your learning. Throughout the book you will find Learning tips designed to help your learning.

At the start of each chapter and other key points, you will find a heading 'Building on AS', which points out the links to the work that you did for AS, with the suggestion that you should revise some basic concepts introduced then. This is followed by 'Stepping Up to A2', which outlines the additional learning required for examination success at A2.

Each chapter contains a number of Economics in context texts designed to help you apply the economics you have learned to current economic issues; some of these have a global or a European focus.

If you are going for a top grade, look out for the 'Stretch and challenge' activities, which usually go beyond the requirements of A-levels to give you a taste of what higher study of economics might be like.

You will find definitions of key concepts. You must know these and get into the habit of defining the main terms you use in all your exam answers.

At the end of Part 1 and Part 2 there is a section called the Exam Café, devoted to exam preparation. It consists of advice, from examiners who work for AQA, on good practice when it comes to exams. It will give you a feel for what examiners actually look for when it comes to marking your work.

Finally, there are sample questions and answers and further examination style questions for you to develop the skills that will be tested at the end of your course.

In doing the Activities and following Stretch and challenge items, the following websites will be useful to you (to access them, go to www.heinemann.com/hotlinks and enter the express code 2230P). The first two are specifically designed to meet the needs of students of A-level economics and the third is the best and most comprehensive link to a wide range of other sites:

- bized
- tutor2u
- economicsnetwork

That's about it for now – time for proper studying.

Good luck.

Business economics and the distribution of income

Welcome to Part 1 of A2 Economics. This introduction includes:

● an overview of what you can expect to study

● a look at the relationship between what you have studied for AS and the requirements of A2

● global and EU contexts.

Overview of Unit 3

Part 1 of your A2 text is devoted to covering all that you need to know to succeed in the examination based upon the AQA specification for Unit 3: 'Business Economics and the Distribution of Income'. It is synoptic, which means it draws on material learned for AS, especially material in unit 1. Unit 3 consists of five different but overlapping areas:

● *theory of the firm* – this includes detailed treatment of costs and revenue, which you need to know to be able to predict how firms are likely to behave in relation to three key variables: price, output and profits. This will involve you using graphical analysis to aid your understanding of how firms might behave.

● *market structures* – this builds on theory of the firm and consists of three different models: perfect competition, monopoly and oligopoly.

● *the labour market* – you are required to develop a more detailed understanding of how factor markets work, concentrating on markets for labour. As with the other areas of Unit 3, you have to learn a series of graphs and how they might be used to explain differences in wages and incomes between different groups. Examining labour markets provides a good example of the possible limits to the usefulness of economics in understanding complex human institutions.

● *distribution of income and wealth* – another separate but related topic, designed to help you understand how income

and wealth are very unequally distributed in UK society, leading to problems of poverty for a significant minority of the population.

● *government intervention* – this section explains how and why the government intervenes in all the different markets identified above. It uses a mixture of graphical and written analysis that you need to develop to show you have reached the A2 standard.

AS and A2

You should quickly appreciate that much of the content of Unit 3 is similar to what you learned for AS in Unit 1: 'Markets and market failure'. For example, for AS, you will have dealt with competitive and concentrated markets. For A2, a deeper theoretical understanding is required. Another way of seeing the difference is that for AS most of your treatment of markets was descriptive, whereas at A2 you are required to use graphs and be more precise in your analysis.

At AS you would have touched on factor markets, but not in the depth required for A2. Thus, the term 'marginal revenue product' (MRP) will be new to you, as will consideration of inequalities in income and wealth.

Finally, government intervention in these markets builds and develops on the work that you did for AS.

Global and EU contexts

There is a special emphasis in A2 on the application of economic concepts to global contexts, including an assessment of the impact of multinational companies and major environmental issues such as global warming. Similarly, you will be expected to have an understanding of the impact of EU policies, especially those relating to agriculture, migration and competition.

1 The firm: objectives, costs and revenues

On completion of this chapter you should be able to:

- understand the significance of the objectives of firms
- explain the possible separation of ownership from control in large businesses
- distinguish between returns in the short and the long run
- calculate, draw and interpret cost curves
- apply the concepts of economies and diseconomies of scale
- evaluate the impact of technological change on production, efficiency and costs
- calculate, draw and interpret revenue curves.

This chapter is divided into seven sections, each relating to different elements of the AQA specification:

- The objectives of firms
- Ownership and control
- Short- and long run-returns
- Costs of production
- Economies and diseconomies of scale
- Technological change
- Revenue.

The objectives of firms

BUILDING ON AS

This topic was touched on in the beginning of your AS course. You should know that, although there are many different types of firms and businesses in the private, public and voluntary sectors, all need to ensure that they make some amount of profit. Businesses operating in more competitive markets will be under a greater incentive to make profits, while those in less competitive markets may have the opportunity to pursue other objectives.

You will further develop the understanding introduced at AS of economies and diseconomies of scale.

STEPPING UP TO A2

As far as A2 is concerned, you need to have a deeper knowledge of how economists treat the objectives of firms. You need to have a good understanding of what is meant by profit maximisation, and by the end of this chapter you should have a sufficient understanding of both revenue and costs, which you will use later to analyse and explain the behaviour of firms operating under different market conditions.

The classification of objectives

Economists use the term **objectives** to refer to the overarching business aims of firms. These are not always explicit, as firms are often sensitive to their public image and it is not likely that a publicly known business will openly say that they wish to 'crush' all competition, or charge customers as much as possible or pay suppliers as little as possible. This means that economists sometimes have to closely examine the actual behaviour of firms in order to try to clarify their objectives. These may include:

- survival
- profit maximisation
- sales maximisation
- social and community objectives
- building shareholder value
- growth and expansion.

SURVIVAL

The drive to ensure business **survival** is probably most important for small businesses. The survival rate of newly established businesses is not very high and many struggle to stay afloat. Competition is often intense and new businesses are often under-capitalised, which means they often have insufficient financial backing to survive unforeseen events.

Getting through the first year of trading is a difficult objective, and one that is likely to dominate the actions of owners of small businesses. Inexperience can lead to business mistakes, and HM Revenue and Customs have a reputation for not being very forgiving if tax returns and VAT payments are not made in time. Estimates vary, but around one in ten of new businesses do not survive the first year of operation and the success rate drops to around 65 per cent for the first three years of trade.

However, it is not just small and new businesses that have to fight to survive. Established UK companies like Somerfield, and Cable and Wireless have struggled to survive and, like their smaller counterparts, will do virtually anything to stay in business.

If both large and small companies faced with bankruptcy don't minimise losses and don't strive to

DEFINITIONS

Objectives: the basic goals that a firm sets itself

Survival: avoiding bankruptcy

ECONOMICS IN CONTEXT

BUSINESS SURVIVAL

Sock Shop was started in 1983 by the husband-and-wife team Sophie Mirman and Richard Ross (above) with a bank loan of £45,000 under the government Loan Guarantee Scheme. The first small booth was in Knightsbridge tube station.

Only four years later, in 1987, Sock Shop went to the Unlisted Securities Market (USM) of the London Stock Exchange. The 5p shares were offered at a premium of 120p each – an issue price which valued the company at £27.5 million. The share offer was oversubscribed 53 times. In the hectic trading that followed, shares changed hands for as much as 295p. For Sophie and Richard the launch marked a public recognition of their commercial partnership and marked them out as, arguably, even more successful than their friends Anita and Gordon Roddick, founders of Body Shop.

However, in 1990, an even shorter three years later, the shares were suspended at only 34p as the company went into administrative receivership. Sophie and Richard were blamed for the collapse, as the spectacular success story of the 1980s, often held up as evidence of the new 'enterprise culture', became one of the first casualties of the harsh trading conditions of the early 1990s. More than half of Sock Shop stores were closed and the company was sold, although it continues to trade in its shrunken form.

Hindsight makes it much easier to see why Sock Shop failed. Expansion in the UK and USA was funded by increased borrowing. In the early 1990s recession hit and interest rates rocketed. The combination of falling demand and increasing costs was a killer blow. The original backers of the project, Barclays, pulled the plug and put the company into administrative receivership.

make as big a profit as possible, they probably won't survive.

PROFIT MAXIMISATION

Profit maximisation means doing everything possible to ensure that profits are as large as possible. This can lead to similar behaviour to those businesses striving to survive, indeed it is a similar objective to survival. It means that a business is as prepared to cut production as it is to expand, and it means that chasing profits is more important than any other objective. As will be shown on pages 21–22, a firm that wishes to maximise profits will go on expanding production and sales until the last unit sold adds as much to its revenue as it does to its costs. In this way a profit-maximising firm will always ensure that its profits are as large as possible.

SALES MAXIMISATION

Sales maximisation is a similar concept and applies to firms that sell as much as they can while still covering their costs. A sales-maximising firm is likely to want to produce more than a profit-maximising firm and will go on producing and selling until the price that it receives for the last unit sold is the same as its cost of production. There is a subtle difference between this and profit maximisation, as will be explained in more detail on pages 21–22.

learning tip

Sorting out the objectives of firms is not always easy. In large companies it is not uncommon to find that different departments of the same firm would like to pursue different objectives. The production department may wish to produce at minimum cost, sales people will be interested in maximising sales, while those responsible for finance will consider data of financial performance in order to maximise profits.

SOCIAL AND COMMUNITY OBJECTIVES

Profits and sales are not always the most important objectives for organisations, especially those in the public and voluntary sectors, which may argue that meeting **social needs** is paramount. Schools may set out to get the best examination results, or to attract more and more students, and this can be more important than making as large a profit as possible.

Local councils will probably say that they strive to meet the needs of the local community, and many voluntary organisations will have similar socially directed objectives.

Meeting community and social needs is not confined to charities and public bodies. Most companies in the private sector claim to have wider objectives than merely the pursuit of sales or profit. As noted earlier, to say that you are relentlessly in pursuit of profit is not seen to be good for the image of large businesses. Hence, Tesco has run schemes to provide schools with computers, and more and more businesses are striving to be carbon neutral. The success of more ethical traders like Fairtrade is influencing some businesses to emphasise more altruistic objectives.

DEFINITIONS

Profit maximisation: gaining the maximum profit – shown where marginal cost is equal to marginal revenue, usually expressed as MR = MC

Sales maximisation: gaining maximum sales – shown where the volume of sales is as large as possible without making a loss, i.e. where AC (average cost) cuts AR (average revenue) at the highest possible level of sales

DEFINITION

Social needs: needs of society and special interest groups

ECONOMICS IN CONTEXT

TESCO AND THE ENVIRONMENT

Energy efficiency

Over the past year, we have spent £3.7 million on energy-saving schemes. This has included installing fan inverter drives in 91 stores. These reduce the speed of the fan motor in air-conditioning units, reducing the volume of air flowing into the store by 15–20 per cent, and reducing energy consumption by up to 50 per cent. We have also installed a further 104 'Intellihood' systems, to add to the 274 installed last year. This is an extraction system which roughly halves the amount of energy consumed by the extractor fans at in-store bakeries and staff restaurants – saving 15,777 MW of electricity worth £710,000 last year. We are working with the Carbon Trust to produce an energy-efficiency training video for staff.

Our Horsham store has been trialling a combined heat and power (CHP) unit since 2003, and has concluded that there are electricity savings to be made, despite a few problems. We are currently considering plans for future roll-out. We are also examining the potential of light-emitting diode (LED) lighting, which uses much less power, releases less heat into the refrigeration areas, and has lower maintenance costs.

Our drive for energy efficiency applies throughout the Tesco group. In Central Europe, we have dedicated energy managers responsible for energy saving. There are similar programmes in all our international businesses.

Emissions trading

Tesco supports the UK government's position on climate change and the Kyoto Protocol. We are participating in the UK Emissions Trading Scheme and Climate Change Levy. As part of the Trading Scheme, we are committed to an absolute reduction in greenhouse gas emissions over a five-year period at a control group of 118 stores, in return for a payment from the government which is invested in further energy-saving initiatives. Over the past year, growth in the sales areas at these control stores has required us to use up carbon credits we earned in 2003–4 from greater than expected cuts in energy consumption. We participated in the UK government's consultation on the EU Emissions Trading Scheme, and we expect to be part of the scheme when it is extended to retailers in 2007.

Renewables

In January 2004 we installed a solar-powered roof at our Hucknall store, in partnership with Solar Century and partially aided by a government grant. The system produced 4,854 kWh over a 15-week period, enough to light the petrol station building for 20 weeks. We expect the system to pay for itself within 13 years. Further roll-out is currently under review.

We are also investigating the potential held by geothermal heating and cooling systems, which use the earth's natural ability to store heat.

Source: Tesco Corporate Responsibility Review 2005

BUILDING SHAREHOLDER VALUE

Shareholder value and similar-sounding terms are often used in the UK by public limited companies (plcs) whose shares are publicly traded on the stock exchange. The value refers to the return, or profit, that shareholders receive from owning shares. This can be boosted by larger dividends and, most importantly, by higher share prices. The determination of share prices is a complex and, some would argue, an irrational process and large companies use a range of strategies to push up the price of their shares. In the USA, in recent years this has included the use of dubious and illegal accounting practices.

DEFINITION

Shareholder value: the price at which shares are traded at a given time

GROWTH AND EXPANSION

This is almost the opposite of survival, and many medium-size and large firms strive to grow and dominate the industry in which they operate. This is often described as gaining **market share** – that is, the proportion of total sales in a given market going to one particular firm – and can be achieved in two ways.

Firms can out-compete their competitors and build sales by selling at lower prices or by beating rivals in terms of quality. Or the same objectives can be achieved by merger and takeover of rivals or related businesses. Currently Vodafone has become the third largest UK company by its relentless acquisition of rivals both in the UK and abroad.

DEFINITION

Market share: the proportion of market in the hands of a given number of producers

ACTIVITY ····⫶

Find out about private equity groups. What are they? How might their objectives differ from those listed?

Reconciling competing objectives

Few, if any, firms are simple one-dimension organisations. Most follow a clutch of different, potentially conflicting, objectives. Sorting out which is most important can be difficult. Firms themselves are not always very clear about how they prioritise their objectives. Economists are often forced to make generalisations. At a very basic level, no organisation can survive if it fails to ensure that revenue equals or exceeds costs.

As will be shown on page 22, small businesses probably need to go for profit at the expense of other

objectives, and it is possible to argue that larger organisations should give greatest priority to building shareholder value.

Some businesses set minimum levels of profit or market share, which allows them to pursue other objectives. This is called '**satisficing**'.

DEFINITION

Satisficing: doing the minimum required – usually in the context of keeping dividends to shareholders to an acceptable minimum

Are objectives important?

The short answer is yes, especially to economists, but also to firms themselves. Employees of well run and organised firms will probably be more effective if they subscribe to meeting company objectives. Economists are able to model the likely behaviour of firms if they have a better understanding of business objectives. Finally, many economic models assume that profit maximisation is the most important objective for firms – the usefulness of their models will partly depend upon the validity of assumptions such as this.

For these reasons, economists have undertaken extensive research into trying to establish what motivators or drivers are most important in determining how firms actually behave. There is a lot of evidence to suggest that business behaviour is heavily influenced by the culture of different societies. Thus, traditionally, Japanese firms have put much more value on ensuring that a wide range of workers' needs are met – for example, health care, sport and recreation, child support and the like. US companies are often stereotyped as having a 'get up and go' attitude in which growth and expansion are highly socially valued.

In his book *The State We Are In* (1995), Will Hutton argued that British businesses are too short-termist, and that quick returns and profits rather than long-term investment are the expectation. Economists have to be careful to avoid making sweeping generalisations, but it is reasonable to assume that businesses planning long term might well adopt different priorities from those that focus on short-term goals.

ACTIVITY ⋯⋅⊱

How difficult might it be for firms to reconcile conflicting objectives?

ACTIVITY ⋯⋅⊱

Choose a well-known UK business and assess how far they can genuinely reconcile environmental or ethical objectives with those relating to profitability.

The divorce of ownership and control

Identifying the objectives of firms provides economists with a means of gaining a better understanding about their behaviour. It is also useful to determine how decisions are made within businesses. Decision makers are important **economic agents,** which is why it is important to try to gain a better understanding of their motivation.

The Canadian-born economist J.K. Galbraith explored decision making and argued that the growth of corporations in the USA had led to a breakdown in the traditional relationship between ownership and control of firms. When businesses are small, they are almost always controlled by their owners. Clearly this is the case with sole proprietors and partnerships. It is logical to argue that if people have put money into a business, they will run that business to ensure that they make reasonable profits. Ownership of the firm is likely to result in the pursuit of profit maximisation as the principal objective.

DEFINITION

Economic agent: an individual or institution whose decisions have an impact on economic issues

The dynamics of decision making are likely to change as businesses become larger. The growth of firms requires additional funds. In countries such as the UK, the stock market is an important source of finance. Shares are sold to raise capital, but they also indicate that ownership has passed from the few to the many. Technically speaking, shareholders own public limited companies. Thus, Marks & Spencer is owned by thousands of individual shareholders. Galbraith argued that these shareholders did not actively participate in decision making. As long as they received what they considered to be a reasonable share of profits – their dividend – he argued that their role would be passive. Decisions regarding company objectives would be left to paid employees: senior managers.

Galbraith argued that this group of people, whom we would now call *economic agents,* were strongly motivated by social status, and this was earned in the USA by being associated with a company that was growing and expanding. He suggested that such key managers would be more interested in boosting sales and achieving greater market share than they would be in chasing the highest possible profit. They would be foolish to totally ignore shareholders, but, as long as they were happy with their returns, managers would be left to get on with running the company.

ACTIVITY ⋯⋅⊱

Business objectives and their prioritisation will affect how firms behave, especially in terms of setting levels of output and/or price. Explain why one of the following is likely to set the lowest prices:

1 a profit maximiser
2 a sales maximiser.

STRETCH AND CHALLENGE
EVALUATING GALBRAITH'S ARGUMENTS

Galbraith's arguments about the divorce between ownership and control of large corporations have had a significant impact on how economists deal with large companies. Clearly, it is dangerous to automatically assume that all businesses are profit maximisers, but at the same time, companies that ignore the pursuit of profit are likely to find it difficult to survive in the long term.

It is possible to argue that widespread share ownership means that individual shareholders exert little power. This is not always the case: when large companies in the UK are faced with difficult times, it is common for the small shareholders to try to use their collective share ownership to bring about changes in the decision-making processes.

Many small shareholders were affected by the collapse of Northern Rock bank in 2007

Another factor to be taken into account is that the ownership of shares is not usually evenly distributed. Shares are not all owned by little old ladies living in Eastbourne. In the UK, it is very common for directors of public limited companies to also be major shareholders. Also other businesses controlling pension funds and the like are also often owners of large blocks of shares. These individuals and organisations are likely to regard themselves as both owners and decision makers.

The only way in which Galbraith's arguments and those who disagree can be properly evaluated is by undertaking empirical research designed to reveal how individual companies behave.

Short- and long-run returns

BUILDING ON AS

For AS you should have learned about the difference between the short run, during which time the input of one factor of production can be changed, and the long run, when all inputs can be changed.

The behaviour of costs in the short and long term can be illustrated using diagrams and the short-run cost curve for a firm is U-shaped, as shown in Figure 1.1. The point of optimum production where average costs of production are minimised is shown at *x* when output is *OA*. As you will have learned, average costs of production will increase as more and more workers get in the way of each other – this is known as the law of diminishing returns.

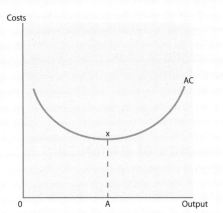

Figure 1.1 Short-run average cost curve

In the long run, increasing, decreasing, or constant returns to scale might apply, and these three possibilities are illustrated in Figure 1.2.

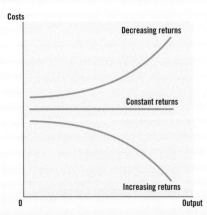

Figure 1.2 Long-run average cost curves

ACTIVITY ⋯⋯

Why doesn't the law of diminishing returns apply in the long run?

ACTIVITY ⋯⋯

Use average cost curves to illustrate:

- falling productivity per worker
- increases in business rates
- technological improvements.

Costs of production

All firms, regardless of their mission statements, objectives, ownership and what they might say about themselves, have to make decisions about two key factors: costs and revenue. If firms are going to survive, they need to ensure that, one way or another, their revenues are at the very least the same as their costs. Most businesses strive to ensure that **total revenue** exceeds **total costs.** This positive difference is described by economists as profit. Should costs exceed revenue, a loss is made.

It is important to note that economists include an element of profits within costs. It is argued that all businesses need to achieve some degree of surplus when total revenue is compared to total costs. These are described as **normal profits** and are defined as the level of profit which is required to keep a firm in an industry and to maintain its current level of production, that is, there is no incentive to increase or decrease production.

DEFINITIONS

Total revenue (TR): price × sales

Total costs: average cost × sales

Normal profit: level of profit required to keep a firm in a given market – neither expanding nor contracting

learning tip

Normal profits will not be the same in every industry – generally speaking if risks are higher, normal profits are greater, and vice versa.

Thus, understanding costs and revenue is important in helping you to develop a better understanding of the behaviour of firms. This applies just as much to organisations that are not primarily motivated to make profits – for example, government agencies and voluntary groups. The following section is devoted to developing an understanding of how economists look at average costs of production in the short run. This is defined as the time period in which it is possible to change the input of only one factor of production – usually labour. (The section on pages 13–18 is devoted to long-run costs, which occur when it is possible to change any or all factor inputs.)

Short-run costs of production

All payments made by a firm in the production of a good or provision of a service are called costs. Economists use the convention, followed by many businesses, of distinguishing between overheads and running costs.

Fixed costs

Overheads are costs of production that businesses have to pay regardless of their level of output. Such expenditures are defined as **fixed costs**. Thus, a bookstore is likely to be faced with bills for rent, business rates and repayment of loans, which will remain the same regardless of how many books are sold. These expenditures are classified as fixed costs and the convention is that these do not change in the short run, which is defined as that period of time in which it is not possible to change the quantity of an input of a particular factor of production (usually called factor input).

Variable costs

Payments which vary according to the sales and output of a firm are classified as **variable costs.** Thus running costs, such as payment of wages, stock purchases and the like, which will change as sales change in the short run, are classified as variable costs.

Classifying fixed and variable costs

In practice, it is not always easy to decide whether a particular cost should be classified as fixed or variable. For example, contracts and salaries might be agreed to cover a particular length of time, making them fixed, as they have to be paid regardless of output for a given time period. However, maintenance costs might change considerably as output changes making them variable.

Total cost

The addition of fixed to variable costs gives total cost, which includes all the costs faced by a firm in the production of a good or a provision of a service.

Average cost

The total cost divided by the output of the business gives the short-run average total cost, which is usually abbreviated to short-run average cost, or even just **average cost**. This is probably the most useful of these measures, as it indicates the cost of producing each item or providing a service. The average cost is also referred to as the *unit cost*.

Marginal cost

Finally, economists and business people make extensive use of the concept of the **margin**, by which they mean what happens to a dependent variable when the determining variable is changed by a small amount – usually one unit. Thus, if output is increased by one unit, the additional costs of production are called **marginal costs**. For example, if a clothing manufacturing company were to produce an extra suit, it would be faced with the costs of additional materials and labour, but would not have to pay out any more for design or machine-setting costs.

Marginal costs will differ according to the product or service that is produced. Thus the marginal cost of an additional passenger on an existing train or bus service is likely to be very low.

Economic analysis of the behaviour of firms focuses on either the short or the long run. In the short run, as has already been indicated, a firm will have at least one fixed factor of production. In the long run, a firm can change all its inputs. This section is concerned with the analysis of changes in the short run, and a series of logical deductions can be made on the basis of this classification. The data contained in Table 1.1 is based on the actual costs of running a bookshop and illustrates how short-run costs are calculated.

Table 1.1 shows it is easy to work out the monthly total costs (total variable cost plus total fixed cost) of running the bookshop (column 2 plus column 4). From this, it is possible to derive the average cost of

Fixed Costs	£	Variable costs	£
Rent	2,000	Purchase of new stock	2,000
Uniform business rate	1,000	Postage	300
Bank loan repayment	750	Telephone	200
Depreciation of computer and other equipment	50	Overtime	500
Insurance	50		
Wages	2,000		
Total fixed cost	5,850	Total variable cost	3,000
		Total cost £8,850	

Table 1.1 Calculation of short-run costs

Annual sales of lambs	Fixed costs £	Variable costs £	Total costs £	Average costs £
0	5,000	0	5,000	.
50	5,000	1,000	6,000	120
200	5,000	4,000	9,000	45
500	5,000	14,000	19,000	38
1,000	5,000	60,000	65,000	65
1,500	5,000	105,000	110,000	73

Table 1.2 Average costs of lambs

selling convenient bundles of books. In this example, 2,500 books were sold in March. If this figure is divided into the total costs of £8,850, the average cost of selling each book is £3.54.

Graphing average costs

By collecting cost data relating to different levels of output or sales, it is possible to construct graphs illustrating the relationship between costs and different levels of sales. To take an agricultural example, farmers are likely to have a fair idea of the best number of livestock to keep given the acreage and quality of their farmland. In Table 1.2, average costs of producing each lamb on a 250-acre farm are related to different 'outputs' of lambs.

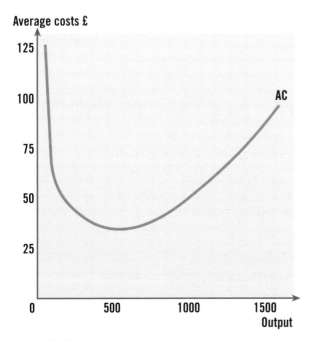

Average costs £

Figure 1.3 Average cost curve

Table 1.2 shows what a good farmer would know without having to make such calculations – that is, the most appropriate number of ewes to keep given the size of farm and cost of different factor inputs. In this example, if no lambs were sold, the farmer would still be faced with certain fixed costs which will probably be dominated by fencing, rent and repayment of loans.

A small flock of around 30 ewes might be expected to produce 50 lambs. Variable costs for feed, veterinary fees and the abattoir would be incurred. However, given the relatively high level of fixed costs, it would cost £120 to rear and slaughter each lamb. Production of 200 lambs would be more 'economic', as better use would be made of the available land. However, each lamb would still cost £45 to produce.

Increasing the flock to 300 ewes could produce 500 lambs and even better use would be made of the farm, giving an average cost of £38 per lamb. Continued expansion of the flock would, however, push up average costs to £65 a lamb when 1,000 are produced and £73 if 1,500 were raised. This is because breeding more lambs would put pressure on the available grass, leading to the purchase of more hay and concentrates, and probably a greater incidence of disease and loss of lambs.

In short, if this farmer wanted to be most efficient and keep short-run costs to a minimum, he or she should produce around 500 lambs a year.

The average cost data contained in the table is illustrated in Figure 1.3. Output is measured on the horizontal axis and average costs of production on the vertical. This (short-run) average cost curve is U-shaped. As output expands, efficiency increases and the short-run average cost falls. It reaches a minimum, or 'optimum', point beyond which short-run costs rise, indicating declining efficiency.

This will apply to the short-run costs of any firm and is known by economists as the **law of diminishing marginal returns**, which will always occur if the use of a variable factor is increased while another factor input remains fixed. In Table 1.2, more and more fodder and concentrates were purchased to feed an expanding flock of sheep, but the size of the farm remained the same.

Similarly, if a factory manager wanted to increase production in the short run, he or she would not be able to rapidly expand the size of the factory, nor buy new machines. Employees could be asked to work overtime and more workers could be taken on. If this process were to continue, a point would be reached when overcrowding and the sheer mass of workers would contribute to rising short-run average costs.

DEFINITION

Law of diminishing marginal returns: applies in the short run: if output is increased by using more and more of a variable factor, a point will be reached beyond which increased factor use will lead to smaller and smaller increases in output

Graphing marginal costs

As indicated on page 10, any change in costs brought about by changing production by an additional unit is described as a marginal cost. These costs can be calculated by looking at how total costs change according to changes in output. Table 1.3

Daily number of MoT tests	Total daily costs £	Average costs £	Marginal costs £
0	150		
1	150	150	150
2	180	90	30
3	196	65.3	16
4	211	52.75	15
5	224	44.8	13
6	236	39.3	12
7	247	35.3	11
8	257	32.1	10
9	266	29.5	9
10	274	27.4	8
11	280	25.4	6
12	285	23.75	5
13	292	22.5	7
14	301	21.5	9
15	311	20.7	10
16	331	20.7	20
17	355	20.9	24
18	385	21.4	30
19	423	22.3	38
20	471	23.6	48

Table 1.3 Average and marginal costs of producing MoT tests

relates to total costs incurred on a daily basis by a garage specialising in undertaking MoT tests.

The garage owner is faced with fixed costs of £150 a day – rent, business rates, wages, loan repayment and so forth. As more MoTs are carried out, resources are used more efficiently – reflected in both falling average and marginal costs.

As with the sheep farmer, the garage owner will find that average, or unit, costs will bottom out and then begin to increase. In this example, undertaking 16 rather than 15 MoTs causes a big rise in costs – perhaps extra labour is required. As work increases, the garage becomes more crowded and congested, and both average and marginal costs rise. This is illustrated in Figure 1.4. Marginal costs are plotted against the midpoint of each unit change in output, and the marginal cost curve will cut the lowest point of the average cost curve.

In the short run, average and marginal cost curves will always have the same relationship to each other. The application of the law of diminishing marginal returns means that any attempt to increase output by changing the use of one factor while the use of others remains fixed will initially lead to falling average and marginal costs. An optimum will then be reached, where average costs are at a minimum and, thereafter, growing inefficiency will lead to

rising average costs. This observation that short-run average cost curves are U-shaped is one with which all students of economics should become familiar.

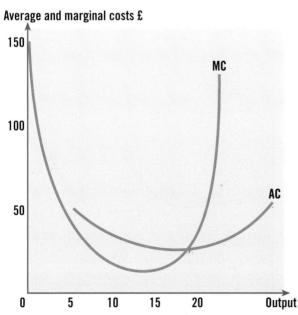

Average and marginal costs £

Figure 1.4 Marginal and average cost curves

ACTIVITY ⋯⋮

Assume that the Forest Bookshop is able to sell twice as many books in April 2008 as it did in March. Construct your own table of data reflecting these higher sales. What impact will increasing sales have on:

a fixed costs

b variable costs

c average costs

d marginal costs

e potential profits?

How might these changes affect the owners of the Forest Bookshop?

Economies and diseconomies of scale

The previous section focused on the relationship between costs of production and output in the short run. This section is devoted to the different relationships between output and costs that can apply in the long run. The long run is defined as that period of time in which it is possible for a firm to alter any or all of its factor inputs. Traditionally, economists have considered that the distinction between the long and the short term is very important in analysing costs and the behaviour of firms. There is now more debate about this approach, and at the end of this section there is an outline of alternative approaches. You need to understand both traditional and newer approaches to the analysis of costs.

Traditional theory

This builds on the analysis on pages 10–12. Thus, the long run is about the sheep farmer purchasing more land, the bookshop expanding its premises and the garage installing new car-testing machinery. The effect of expanding production on long-run average costs is likely to depend on a number of factors. The following three scenarios apply to the sheep farmer doubling the size of his or her farm.

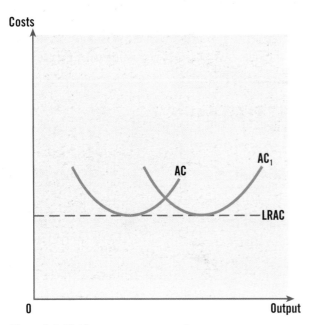

Figure 1.5 Flat long-run average cost curve

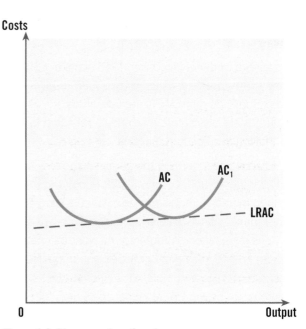

Figure 1.6 Diseconomies of scale

Constant returns to scale

Suppose the cost of a loan to purchase additional land is the same as was already being paid for the original 250 acres. Assume that there will be proportionately similar increases in costs for labour, winter feed, fencing and veterinary fees. In this situation, the average short-run cost of producing each lamb would not be very different from the short-run cost on the smaller farm.

This means that at the optimum level of output, each lamb would cost about £38 to produce. However, the farmer can now produce 1,000 lambs a year whereas on the smaller farm diminishing returns occurred if more than 500 lambs were produced. This is illustrated by Figure 1.5, which shows unchanged average costs of production and a possible long-run average cost curve.

Diseconomies of scale

The cost of borrowing additional money might be greater and a larger farm might be more difficult for one farmer to manage. In this case, long-run costs would be rising, as shown in Figure 1.6. At the farmer's optimum level of output, the short-run average costs of producing each lamb would be greater than was the case with the optimum level on the smaller farm, giving a rising long-run average cost curve. These are described as **diseconomies of scale**.

Economies of scale

In contrast to the previous scenario, the newly acquired land might be easier to manage. It may pay the farmer to transport his or her own livestock, and suppliers of winter feed might be prepared to supply larger orders at a discount. In this case, optimum short-run costs of production would fall. This means that not only would the farmer be able to produce more lambs, but also he or she would be able to produce each one more cheaply. Figure 1.7 clearly

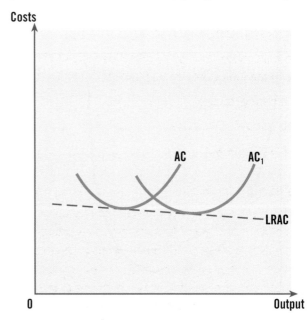

Figure 1.7 Economies of scale

indicates that long-run costs are falling – **economies of scale**.

Ford Motors pioneered mass production in the early twentieth century

Factors affecting returns to scale

Unlike short run-costs, there is no law or certainty governing the shape of the long-run average cost curves. Economists refer to the relationship between long-run costs and the increasing size of a firm as 'returns to scale'. Long-run costs can increase, decrease, stay the same or contain elements of each of these relationships. Economists usually distinguish between three scenarios:

● economies of scale

● diseconomies of scale

● constant returns to scale.

A number of factors will determine which relationship applies and these are further subdivided into internal and external returns to scale.

Internal economies of scale

Internal economies of scale relate to a growth in the size of the individual firm and include:

● technical factors

● organisational factors

● market power.

TECHNICAL FACTORS

As firms grow, producing and selling larger outputs can make it 'economic' to automate or mechanise particular stages of production in order to drive down costs. Henry Ford used production-line techniques to mass produce cars that were much cheaper than those produced more traditionally. Similarly, wide-bodied planes such as the Airbus 380 series have

lower running costs per passenger mile compared to a smaller aircraft such as the Boeing 747. Larger planes tend to be more fuel efficient.

In the same way, as manufacturing firms grow and produce larger saleable outputs, they are more likely to be able to afford more expensive but more efficient computer applications and automated production methods.

ORGANISATIONAL FACTORS

The growth of firms and production of larger outputs enables firms to apply the division of labour and principles of specialisation. Those who work for small firms may have to undertake a range of jobs, and will find it hard to develop cost-saving skills and expertise in particular fields. As firms grow, they can afford to employ specialists in finance and marketing and so on, and this can result in cost savings, leading to falling long-run average costs.

Growth and higher revenues can allow firms to invest more heavily in research and development. This is especially important in those industries in which the rate of change is rapid – for example, electronics and pharmaceuticals. These sectors of the global economy tend to be dominated by giant firms such as Sony and GlaxoSmithKline. Their growth leads to greater research efforts, which lead to the development of new products and the establishment of new sources of competitive advantage.

MARKET POWER

Firms that grow larger can exercise more power in the various marketplaces in which they operate. Expanding output can allow companies to negotiate larger discounts from suppliers. In the UK, the major supermarkets are said to be able to compel prospective suppliers of foodstuffs to accept ever-lower prices while maintaining ever-higher standards.

Larger, wealthier companies can afford to devote larger amounts of their resources to advertising, which is particularly important in branding and the development of global markets. Transnational companies have the power to influence governments and are in a stronger position than smaller companies to use bribery or take advantage of corrupt business practices.

Larger companies are also likely to have larger market shares and such monopoly power enables them to use different pricing strategies to limit competition. They are more likely to be able to cut prices to drive out smaller competitors.

External economies of scale

These can be very beneficial to some firms, as they can bring the benefit of long-run cost reductions without additional expenditure by individual firms. External economies of scale relate to changes in long-run costs that are associated with the expansion of a particular industry rather than an individual firm.

External economies of scale are often associated with the growth and concentration of particular industries in defined geographical areas. This can attract related businesses, reducing transport costs and making collaboration more possible. Local schools and colleges are more likely to provide relevant vocational training, which will also benefit local businesses, helping them to reduce long-run average costs. These factors help to explain why biotech businesses are attracted to the Cambridge area in the UK and software manufacturers to Silicon Valley in California.

Diseconomies of scale

However, there are factors that can lead to the increasing size of firms being associated with rising long-term costs. Such diseconomies of scale can also be both internal and external to the firm in question.

INTERNAL DISECONOMIES OF SCALE

These can be classified in the same way as economies of scale. Technical diseconomies of scale often relate to technological constraints. For example, ships that are built beyond a certain size require different methods of construction, which can result in increasing average costs. Their size might be such that ports and particular routes are no longer usable.

Organisational diseconomies are probably relatively more significant as the growth in size of businesses is often associated with increases in red tape and bureaucracy. Companies employing tens of thousands of workers are more difficult to manage, communications can be slower and less effective, and both workers and managers might be less motivated. All these factors might contribute to rising long-run costs.

Growing size does not automatically bring greater market power. Large, dominant companies might be slower in responding to market trends. They are likely to be more distant and less responsive to the demands of their customers. There are many examples of companies that have expanded and lost touch with their customers. Xerox was once the world leader in the photocopier market but it is now struggling to survive. In the UK, businesses such as Marconi and ICI have been forced to demerge and downsize in order to try to survive.

EXTERNAL DISECONOMIES OF SCALE

In the same way that particular geographical areas can be associated with the complementary growth and development of related businesses, the decline of particular firms and industries can drag down the fortunes of others. Some of the worst social and economic problems in the UK are associated with the failings of particular industries – the decline of shipbuilding on the Mersey and Clyde and coalmining in South Wales, Yorkshire and Nottinghamshire are two obvious examples where many small businesses have not survived because of external changes.

Modern theories of the firm

Some economists have questioned the wisdom of making a rigid distinction between short- and long-run costs, while others have studied the actual nature of costs faced by firms in different industries. This research shows that in many modern businesses, flexible working and modern technological developments mean that the distinction between the short and the long run can become blurred. Thus, modern technologies can link factories in one country to others across the world. If more machine parts are needed, it is not necessary to construct a new factory or plant; new orders can very easily be subcontracted to other suppliers in some other part of the world. Similarly, improvements in the transportation of materials mean that individual components can be shipped around the world quickly and relatively cheaply. These developments are related to the globalisation of production and businesses.

Research also shows that many firms find that initial growth in output and sales is accompanied by dramatic cost savings – that is, economies of scale are significant. Thereafter, unit or average costs remain similar, regardless of output, until a point is reached at which average costs rise dramatically.

If these two sets of research findings are applied to traditional approaches of classifying costs, they have a significant effect on how the behaviour of firms is

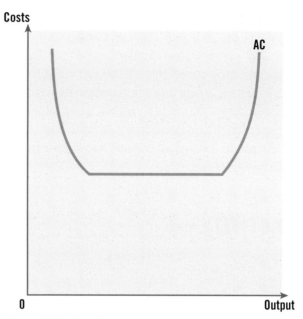

Figure 1.8 Modern costs curve

analysed. This is shown in Figure 1.8. There is no short-run average cost or long-run average cost, just an average cost 'curve' that might be 'trench' shaped.

COST-PLUS THEORIES

The use of the trench-shaped diagram and its accompanied rationale has led some economists to develop an alternative approach to analysing decision

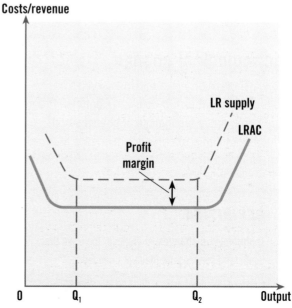

Figure 1.9 Cost-plus theories

making within large businesses. It is suggested that firms may calculate their long-run average costs and then add a profit margin in order to determine their long-run supply curve. This is illustrated in Figure 1.9 It is important to note that any change in demand between output OQ_1 and OQ_2 will not lead to a change in price. The firm in question will prefer to alter production to ensure that demand and supply are kept in equilibrium.

ACTIVITY ····:·

Draw a long-run average cost curve diagram that shows gradual economies of scale followed by both internal and external diseconomies of scale.

learning tip

The last two sections have presented two different ways of treating costs faced by firms. Traditional economic analysis is based on a rigid distinction between the short and the long term. This provides a rationale for the existence of the U-shaped average cost curve and the concept of returns to scale. Alternative treatments regard the distinction between short and long run as artificial, and consider that firms can be much more flexible and responsive in their reactions to changing market conditions.

Technological change

The ways in which products and services are produced are subject to constant changes. Progress means that these **technological changes** both reduce potential costs of production and also reduce

DEFINITION

Technological changes: changes in the ways that goods and services are made or provided

the competitive advantages which larger firms have tended to have in comparison to smaller businesses.

Reduction in costs of production

The development and application of Information and Communications Technology (ICT) can reduce the costs of production to both large and small businesses. Operations which would have previously meant the employment of specialists or the outsourcing of business functions can now be undertaken more cheaply. This applies to many administrative functions such as stock control, payroll, and financial management.

As will be discussed in greater detail in Chapter 6, improvements in communications have contributed to the globalisation of both production and marketing, allowing companies both large and small to take advantage of lower production costs in different parts of the world.

Moreover, the use of the Internet to link producers and consumers, at a much lower cost than previously, allows small businesses to sell to millions of customers.

Making markets more competitive

The earlier section on economies and diseconomies of scale illustrated the considerable competitive advantage which larger businesses may have traditionally enjoyed over smaller rivals.

This is illustrated in Figure 1.10 on page 20, which shows why smaller firms often find it difficult to survive when in competition with larger, already established rivals. The average costs of a firm operating to the left of *OX* will be much higher, while a larger rival operating to the right of *OX* clearly has a competitive advantage. It could undercut the price charged by the new entrant and still make a profit. *OX* is referred to as the level of output associated with the **minimum efficient scale of production**.

ECONOMICS IN CONTEXT

TECHNOLOGICAL CHANGE: WHERE NEXT?

Over the last 40 years, computing developments have had a profound effect on the productive process. Some estimates indicate that in this period global computing power has increased a billion-fold. Today's fusion cars have more computing power than the main-frame computers used in the Apollo space programme. Computers and the Internet dominate our lives and have made globalisation possible.

But which technologies will dominate the future – artificial intelligence, genetic engineering, nuclear fusion or nanotechnology? Forty years ago no one predicted our world. Why should we be any more prescient?

And which side are you on? Will these technological changes save the planet or hasten its destruction? Will

they increase inequalities or reduce them? Will they give power to the people or further strengthen the control of governments? Will technological advances and greater efficiencies compensate for shortages of energy, food and clean water?

DEFINITION

Minimum efficient scale of production: the lowest amount of production consistent with earning significant *economies of scale*

The positive effects of technological change are illustrated by the addition of a new long-run average cost curve showing both lower costs of production and a lower minimum efficient scale of production.

Revenue

'**Revenue**' is the term used by economists to describe those flows of money that are received by a firm. This is distinct from 'costs', which refers to those payments made by firms.

Different firms earn revenue in different ways. For example, private-sector business revenues will be largely determined by the value of sales of goods and/or services. Charities largely depend on donations made by the public. Schools and colleges rely on

funding provided by government agencies according to formulas based on student numbers. In short, all firms need revenue from somewhere.

The analysis in this section is based on an example of a firm operating in the private sector, but it can also be applied to public and voluntary sector organisations.

Calculating average revenue and total revenue

Average revenue (AR) is the name given to the amount of revenue gained from selling a product

DEFINITIONS

Revenue: flows of money that are received by a firm

Average revenue (AR): price per unit of sales – usually abbreviated to price

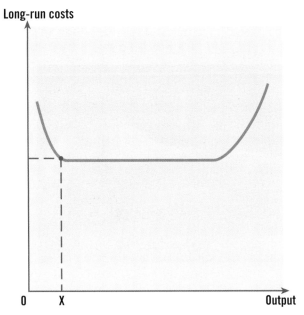

Figure 1.10 Minimum efficient scale of production

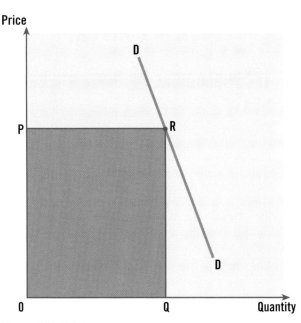

Figure 1.11 Total revenue

divided by its sales. This is more usually referred to as the price of a good or service. *Total revenue* (TR) refers to the total amount of revenue gained from selling a particular quantity of a good or service. Calculating the values of these two concepts is straightforward for those businesses that rely on the sales of a good or service as the demand curve shows the relationship between sales and different prices. In Figure 1.11 *OP* is the price that will be paid if *OQ* is sold. In other words, *OP* is the average revenue. Total revenue is simply price multiplied by the number of items sold: *OP × OQ*. Therefore, the shaded area *PRQO* represents the total sales revenue earned.

Marginal revenue

Marginal revenue (MR) is defined as the change to revenue that occurs if sales are changed by one unit. In Figure 1.12, if sales are increased from 10 units to 11 units, revenue will rise by £28. (Ten units are sold for £50 each, giving a total revenue of £500, but to sell 11 units the firm has to accept a lower price of £48 per unit, giving a new total revenue of £48 × 11 = £528.)

> ### DEFINITION
>
> **Marginal revenue (MR):** the change in revenue brought about by changing sales of a given number of units

If sales are further increased, the marginal revenue will continue to decline. In other words, if the demand curve is sloping downward to the right, more goods can only be sold at a lower price, which means that MR will always be less than AR. Thus, if the demand curve for a product or service is represented by a straight line, the marginal revenue curve will bisect the angle formed by the average revenue (or demand) curve and the vertical axis as shown in Figure 1.12. Note that the marginal revenue is plotted against the mid points of sales represented on the horizontal axis.

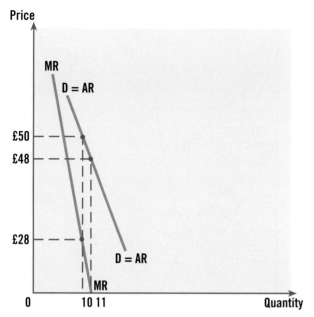

Figure 1.12 Derivation of marginal revenue

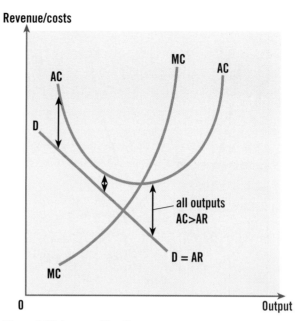

Figure 1.13 Loss-making firm

Putting costs and revenue together

The graph on page 8, showing short-run costs can be superimposed on top of the average and marginal revenue graph in Figure 1.13. It should be clear that this illustrates a business that would not be likely to survive. At any point on the diagram, average costs are above average revenue or price. This firm is clearly making a loss in the short run.

On the other hand, Figure 1.14 shows a range of outputs at which average cost is both above and below average reserve. Between OQ and OQ_2, the business would be making some level of profit.

Profits

At this stage in the analysis of a firm's behaviour, it is important to clarify how economists define the term 'profit'. They use the term *normal profit* to define the amount of additional return, once all costs have been met, that is just sufficient to keep a business working at its current level of production. Anything above this is called '**supernormal**' or

'**abnormal profit**'. If a firm is making less than normal profits, it is making a loss.

> ### DEFINITIONS
>
> **Supernormal (or abnormal) profit:** anything in excess of *normal profit*

Business objectives

The work that you did on pages 2–7 on business objectives needs to be brought into the analysis, because understanding these is helpful in determining the level of output chosen by an individual firm. Three scenarios will be considered:

● survival

● sales maximisation

● profit maximisation.'

To survive, a business must choose an output between OQ and OQ_2 (see Figure 1.14). If a business

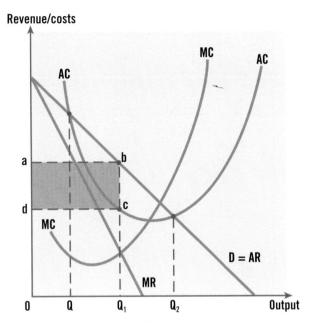

Figure 1.14 Supernormal profit-maker

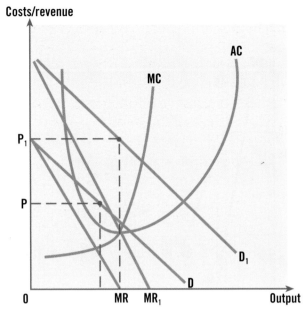

Figure 1.15 Traditional cost theory

wanted to maximise on sales, it would produce OQ_2. It is slightly more complicated using graphical analysis to identify the profit-maximising output. Profit maximisation quite simply means producing the largest profit possible. This output is found by applying what is known as the profit-maximising rule. This means choosing the output OQ_1 at which marginal costs (MC) and marginal (MR) revenue are equal. At this output, the gap between average revenue and average costs is maximised. If a firm chooses this output, total profits equal to the shaded area *abcd* would be earned. As AR is greater than AC (average cost), these would be called supernormal or abnormal profits.

If the firm decided on an output to the right of OQ_1, marginal costs would exceed marginal revenue – in other words, expanding production beyond OQ_1 would raise costs by a larger amount than any increase in revenue, reducing total profits. On the other hand, any point to the left of OQ_1 would mean that marginal costs were less than marginal revenue, meaning that if output were expanded, revenue would grow by more than costs. Only at the point at which MR equals MC will profits be maximised.

> **learning tip** The revenue earned by a firm will be determined by the interaction of price and the demand for its good or service. Data on revenue and costs can be put onto the same graph, and this can be used to predict the levels of output chosen by different types of firms, according to their business objectives.

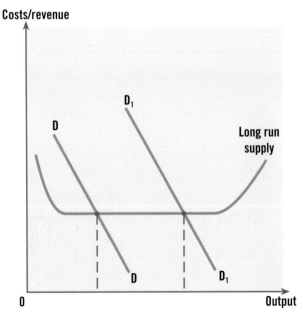

Figure 1.16 Alternative cost theory

If modern approaches to long-run costs are adopted, the application of this model to predicting the likely behaviour of firms will lead to very different outcomes compared to the use of more traditional models. The use of these two models to predict the response of a firm to an increase in demand is shown in Figures 1.15 and 1.16. Figure 1.15 shows that any change in demand will result in a change in output and price, whereas Figure 1.16 shows that an increase in demand from D to D_1 leads to a change in output but not in price.

ACTIVITY ⋯⋮

Suppose a business seeks to maximise profits. How will it change production in response to increases in:

a demand

b variable costs

c fixed costs?

2 Competitive markets

On completion of this chapter you should be able to:

- use diagrams to illustrate the short- and long-run equilibrium of the perfectly competitive firm
- understand how a perfectly competitive firm might be expected to behave in response to changes in market conditions
- critically assess the proposition that perfect competition should result in an efficient allocation of resources
- evaluate the short- and long-run benefits of competitive markets.

This section of the AQA specification consists of three parts and this is reflected in the structure of this chapter, which consists of sections on:

- The model of perfect competition
- Competition and the efficient allocation of resources
- Competitive market processes.

long-run equilibriums of both the individual firm and a perfectly competitive market. This requires you to develop the concepts learned in Chapter 1 about revenue and costs. You are also expected to critically assess the validity of the model, and the proposition that its application should result in an efficient allocation of resources.

BUILDING ON AS

The AS course required you to have an overall understanding of what economists mean when they use the term 'competition'. The main focus was on learning how competitive markets might work and how they might fail. You need to be sure that you retain this overall understanding, as it will help you when it comes to knowing more about the theoretical model of perfect competition.

The model of perfect competition

Perfect competition is the name given to a theoretical construct useful in understanding the behaviour of small firms operating in highly competitive markets. Understanding the mechanics of competitive behaviour enables economists to analyse those

STEPPING UP TO A2

Perfect competition is a neat model which is easy to understand and very useful in helping you analyse how actual markets work. You need to learn the assumptions that are used to develop this model and how to draw diagrams to illustrate both short-run and

DEFINITION

Perfect competition: a market consisting of a very large number of small firms

Price taker: a perfectly competitive firm has to accept the price set by market forces – hence the phrase price taker

factors which are likely to contribute to both allocative and productive efficiency. The model of perfect competition has been developed on the basis of a series of simplifying assumptions. Thus, a perfectly competitive market consists of a large number of small firms, in which each firm:

● produces an identical or homogenous product – in other words, the output of one firm within an industry is perfectly substitutable with the output of another

● contributes only a tiny proportion of the final output of the industry

● sells to customers who also have a perfect knowledge of the behaviour of all the firms operating in the industry

● has perfect knowledge of the behaviour of other firms in the industry

● has absolute freedom to enter or leave the industry.

The combined effect of these assumptions is very important. It means that an individual firm operating in a perfectly competitive market will not be able to set or influence the price of the product or service it produces. Each perfectly competitive firm produces such a small proportion of the total output of an industry that it is obliged to accept the price that is set by the market as a whole. For example, it is very unlikely that an individual producer of wheat can influence the price of such a globally traded commodity. Economists describe this kind of firm as a **price taker**.

If an individual firm were to set a price above that set by the market, customers, because they have perfect knowledge, would know that cheaper substitutes are being supplied by all the other firms in the industry. Each producer or service is assumed to be identical and consumers would simply switch demand from the high-priced good to a cheaper substitute. Demand for the more expensive product would be zero.

Conversely, there is no advantage to an individual firm in trying to set a price below that set by the market price; this would merely reduce profits or

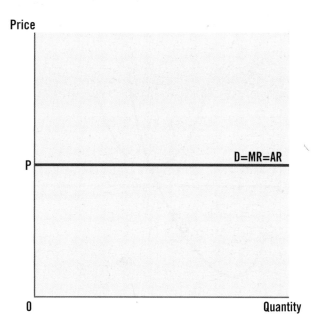

Figure 2.1 Demand facing the perfectly competitive firm

create losses. As will be explained on page 27, a firm setting a price below that determined by the market will in the long run go out of business.

Finally, because each firm produces so little in relation to the total size of the market, each can sell its entire output as long as it accepts the market price. This means that the demand curve facing an individual perfectly competitive firm is perfectly elastic – as shown in Figure 2.1, where the market set price is *OP*. This perfectly elastic demand curve means that any extra output will be sold for *OP*. This means that the marginal revenue (MR) curve will be identical to the demand or average revenue (AR) curve.

> **learning tip**
> The preceding explanation is short but crucial to your understanding of how a perfectly competitive market might work. Go through it slowly and make sure you understand the relationship between the assumptions of the perfectly competitive model and how they give rise to the unique situation where price = average revenue (AR) = marginal revenue (MR).

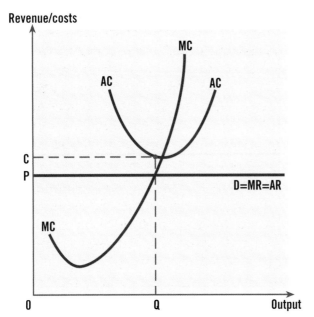

Figure 2.2 Loss-making pc firm

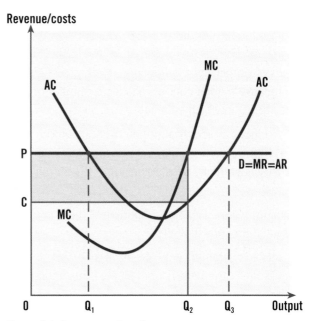

Figure 2.3 Supernormal profits

Short-run equilibrium of the perfectly competitive firm

Whereas the application of the perfectly competitive model leads to a 'special case' in terms of the perfectly elastic demand curve at the market price, the costs faced by a perfectly competitive firm will be characterised by the same features as faced by any other firm. As explained on pages 8 and 13 in Chapter 1, the short-run average cost curve is U-shaped and the marginal cost curve cuts the average cost curve at its lowest point. These two curves can be superimposed on top of the demand curve, which for the perfectly competitive firm will also be the marginal revenue and average revenue curve. In the short run, there are three possibilities in terms of the relationship between costs and revenue. The perfectly competitive firm could be making:

● normal profits

● a loss

● supernormal (or abnormal) profits.

The last two scenarios are illustrated below.

MAKING A LOSS

In Figure 2.2, average costs are greater than price, at all levels of output. Irrespective of the chosen output of this perfectly competitive firm, it will always make

a loss. The loss will be minimised if the firm chooses output OQ, where marginal cost is equal to marginal revenue.

SUPERNORMAL (ABNORMAL) PROFITS

In Figure 2.3, the demand for the product is such that between outputs OQ_1 and OQ_3 average revenue exceeds average costs – in other words, *supernormal profits* can be earned. If the firm wishes to maximise profits, it should follow the rule of equating marginal cost with marginal revenue, which would lead to output OQ_2. The shaded area shows the level of supernormal profits.

Long-run equilibrium of the perfectly competitive firm

In the long run, as long as the industry itself is in equilibrium, there is only one possible equilibrium for the perfectly competitive firm. This is the situation of normal profits (see Chapter 1) illustrated in Figure 2.4. The reasoning for this is simple and follows on from the assumptions outlined at the beginning of this section.

In Figure 2.4, the average cost curve is at a tangent to the demand curve. This shows that at output OQ_2, average costs are equal to price. In this situation,

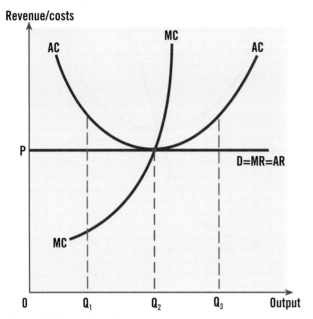

Figure 2.4 Normal profits

a perfectly competitive firm will be earning normal profits, that level of profit which is sufficient to stop the firm from exiting the industry, but insufficient to attract new entrants to the industry. Choosing an output other than where marginal cost equals marginal revenue would result in making a loss, for example outputs OQ_1 or OQ_3.

In the short run, a firm could be earning supernormal profits, as illustrated in Figure 2.3. The assumption of

perfect knowledge between producers in a perfectly competitive industry means that rival businesses will find out and be attracted by the prospect of making greater profits. Moreover, in the long run there is nothing to stop other firms from entering the industry (freedom of entry). The effects of this on the industry as a whole are illustrated in Figure 2.5(a), where the supply of the good or service will be increased as shown by a shift to the right from S to S_1.

It follows that the equilibrium price will fall and, as far as the individual firm is concerned, this will be represented by a downward shift in the perfectly elastic demand curve from D to D_1. This downward movement facing the individual firm is shown in 2.5(b).

The falling price will eventually eliminate the supernormal profits, leading to the proposition that, in the long run, the perfectly competitive firm can only make normal profits. This is confirmed when short-term losses within the perfectly competitive model are analysed.

In Figure 2.2, D is below average costs at all levels of output. The profit-maximising firm will minimise its losses if it chooses the output of OQ at which MC = MR. Some individual businesses will not be able to sustain losses over a period of time and they will go out of business or switch to the production of more profitable alternatives. If this happens on an industry-

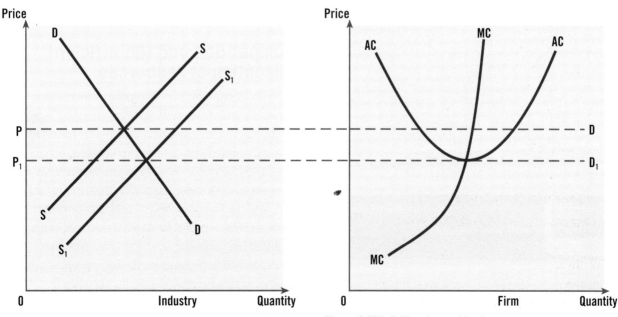

Figure 2.5(a) Increasing supply curve for industry   **Figure 2.5(b) Falling demand for firm**

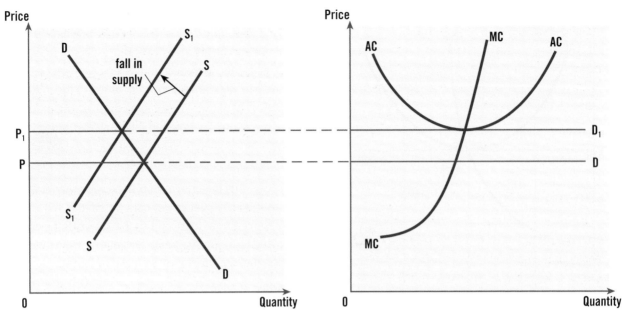

Figure 2.6(a) Losses/to normal profits – industry

Figure 2.6(b)   Increasing demand for firm

wide basis, some firms will leave the industry and total output will fall.

This reduction in supply in the industry is shown in Figure 2.6(a), where supply shifts from S to S_1 leading to an increase in market price from OP to OP_1.

ACTIVITY ⋯⋮

Use diagrams to show why it is not possible for an individual firm operating under conditions of perfect competition to make supernormal profits in the long run.

This increase in market price will feed back to the individual firm as shown in Figure 2.6(b) by the upward shift in the demand curve from D to D_1, resulting in a return to normal profits.

 learning tip See if you can do the above task with your text shut.

ACTIVITY ⋯⋮

Which of the following comes closest to conforming to the characteristics of a perfectly competitive market? Justify your choice by reference to the assumptions made in building up the model of perfect competition:

a   retail groceries

b   pork production

c   the stock market.

Competition and the efficient allocation of resources

The model of perfect competition outlined in the previous section provides a very compelling argument to support those economists and governments who argue that more competitive markets are more desirable than those which are less competitive. The analysis leading to the prediction that, in the long run, a perfectly competitive firm can only expect to make sufficient profits to stop it leaving an industry, and that the existence of short-run supernormal profits will attract new entrants that will ensure that normal profits become the norm, suggests that competition is likely to prevent firms from exploiting consumers and making excessive profits.

The model can also be used to predict that competitive markets are characterised by other attractive features. The application of this model produces a set of important predictions. Perfectly competitive markets should produce an optimum allocation of resources which will be efficient:

● productively

● allocatively.

Productive efficiency

The concept of **productive efficiency** can best be understood by reference to the equilibrium of the perfectly competitive firm and industry. This is illustrated in Figure 2.7, and it is important to note that, given the assumptions of perfect competition, the individual firm will be obliged to produce the output at which average costs are minimised. The profit-maximising rule of equating MC with MR has to be applied if the firm is to avoid making a loss, and that coincides with the lowest, or optimum, point on the average cost curve.

Suppose that the owner of one firm operating in this industry has a 'eureka' moment and discovers a new, quicker, cheaper way of making the product. If the new production technique is quicker and cheaper, the average cost curve will shift downwards to the right, dragging the marginal cost curve with it. The

profit-maximising firm will expand production to OQ_1 and will now be making supernormal profits, shown by the shaded area in Figure 2.8.

This situation will only persist in the short run, as all competitors have perfect knowledge of what is going on within the industry. They will find out how the innovating firm has been able to cut production costs and copy the more efficient means of production. New firms might enter the industry.

This long-run change will involve an increase in the industry-wide supply of the product. This rise in supply will force prices down and the firm that began the process with its 'eureka' moment will be back to earning normal profits.

An added twist to this argument is that, if particular firms are slow in copying the more efficient means of production, they will find themselves making losses as output in the industry increases. Loss-making firms will be forced out of the industry.

The logic of this analysis is that, if the assumptions underpinning the perfectly competitive model were to be met, competition between large numbers of firms producing identical goods would ensure that there would be a continuous incentive to develop cheaper, more efficient ways of producing goods and providing services.

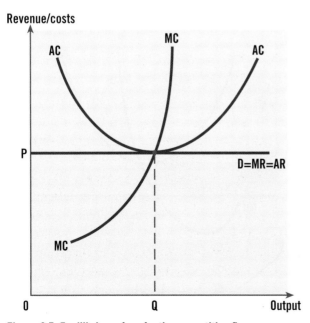

Figure 2.7 Equilibrium of perfectly competitive firm

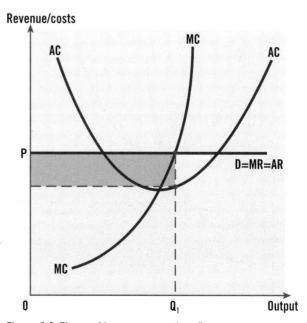

Figure 2.8 Firm making supernormal profits

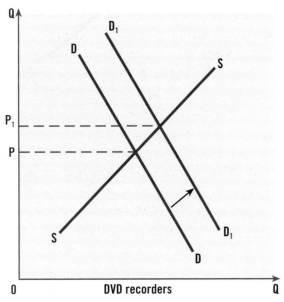

Figure 2.9 Changing DVD market

The reward for this would be short-term supernormal profits. The sanction for not keeping up with competitors would be losses and business failure. In theory this should ensure that the real beneficiaries would be the public, who would be assured of a constant stream to newer, better, more cost-effective products and services.

Allocative efficiency

Allocative efficiency refers to consumer sovereignty and is achieved when firms produce where $P = MC$. In a perfectly competitive market, it is consumers who ultimately determine which of the world's resources are used to produce what products and services. This can be analysed diagrammatically by considering what happens if consumers' tastes change for some reason.

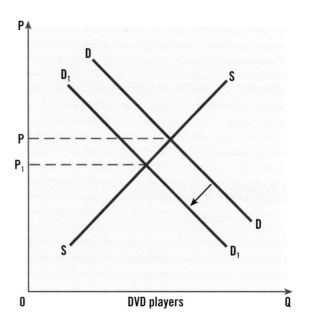

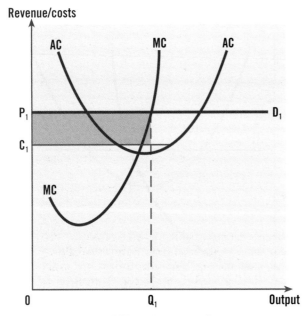

Figure 2.10 Long-run DVD market – recorders

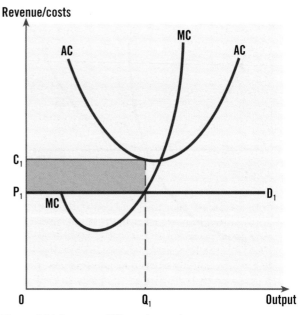

Figure 2.11 Long-run DVD market – players

Assume there is an increase in demand for DVD recorders at the expense of DVD players. Two changes will take place: there will be a shift to the right in the demand curve for recorders; there will be a shift to the left in the demand for players. This will lead to a rise in price to OP_1 for recorders and a fall in price to OP_1 for players – as shown in Figure 2.9.

When translated into changes in demand facing the perfectly competitive producers of recorders and players, the latter will be faced with potential losses and the former supernormal profits. This is shown in Figures 2.10 and 2.11.

The long-run response to this situation is that losses will force some firms to drop out of the player market, while new firms will be attracted into the recorder markets. New long-term equilibriums will be reached in which both sets of firms earn normal profits but the industry output of recorders will have increased, while the production of players will have been reduced.

The essence of the analysis is that, if the assumptions are true, perfect competition will force businesses to change production in line with customer demands. If they fail to respond, they are likely to go out of business.

However, the analysis does not stop here. More successful companies will make larger short-run profits. They will be able to pay more to attract scarce factors of production. Owners of these factors will sell their capital, land, labour or enterprise to the highest bidder and resources will be diverted to the production of goods that are most in demand. Therefore, if all industries were perfectly competitive, there would be

ECONOMICS IN CONTEXT

HOW GREEN ARE OUR APPLES – AND DOES IT MATTER?

Seventy-six per cent of apples consumed in the UK are imported from overseas. In the last 30 years 60 per cent of apple orchards in the UK have disappeared. Of the 2,300 different known varieties of apples only two are commonly stocked in supermarkets. Even in September and October, the majority of apples sold in UK supermarkets are imported.

These changes can be seen as the outcome of competition. Logic indicates that we now buy most of our apples from abroad because imports are cheaper. UK producers can't compete with low-cost imports and so turn their orchards into something else for which there is a demand. Some argue that this is a good example of the price mechanism at work. But there are costs that arise from these changes – costs which could be presented as negative externalities:

- air miles – the more of these we clock up the more the earth warms up
- bio diversity – genetic variations are being rapidly eroded, undoing nature's protective systems
- destruction of wildlife habitats – orchards are homes to delicate biosystems
- healthy eating – transport and preservation of apples and pears requires extra pesticides and waxing.

Other economic agents have their role to play – the European Union's Common Agricultural Policy (CAP) and the big UK supermarkets are major players in this market, but is the destruction of orchards a price worth paying?

an optimum allocation of resources. Consumers would determine what is produced, and these goods and services would be produced at the lowest possible cost.

> ### DEFINITIONS
>
> **Dynamic efficiency:** long-run increases in efficiency

STRETCH AND CHALLENGE

Investigate this or other examples of disappearing UK production. Analyse the causes and suggest possible outcomes.

Competitive market processes

Whereas allocative and productive efficiency are static measures – they refer to efficiency at a given point of time – economists are also interested in **dynamic efficiency,** efficiency over a period of time, and this is associated with the ability of an economy to develop new technologies and new processes over time.

It can be argued that the closer markets come to being perfectly competitive the greater will be the incentive for firms to be productively efficient. There are lots of ways in which competitive firms can gain greater market share by trying to make their product or service better in some way than those of competitors. These include:

● improving the quality of their products

● reducing costs of production

● meeting customer needs more quickly

● leaving markets in which demand is likely to fall

● entering markets in which demand is likely to rise.

The crucial question is whether or not there is sufficient incentive for firms to be dynamic in response to market changes if any competitive advantage is likely to occur only in the short run. Innovation and improvement should lead to short-run supernormal profits, but in the long term innovations will be copied. Hence some economists argue that

more competitive markets are not necessarily those that are dynamically efficient.

Dynamically efficient economics

It is not easy to find examples of economies that appear to be dynamically efficient and highly competitive.

For example, in the 1980s, the Japanese economy was seen to be dynamically efficient because new approaches to business organisation emphasised the importance of total quality management, in which all employees were expected to be involved in quality improvement, and there was zero tolerance for any errors in manufacture and supply. Supply-chain improvements meant that smaller stocks were carried and many businesses adopted 'just in time' approaches to the supply of stocks. Such approaches made the Japanese economy very dynamic but it was also characterised by the very strong influence of large businesses with varying degrees of monopoly power.

More recently, dynamic efficiencies in the Chinese economy have contributed to very significant rates of economic growth. They appear to have been driven by a combination of entrepreneurship from small businesses and ruthless intervention by central government to bring about major infrastructure changes in terms of internal communications networks and energy supplies.

ACTIVITY ····

Use diagrams to predict what will happen to short-run supernormal profits of an individual firm if:

a new entrants are attracted to the industry

b demand for the product increases

c customer ignorance is reduced.

Critically assessing the perfectly competitive model

However, these predictions apply only if the assumptions required to build up the perfectly competitive model are actually satisfied in the real world.

The validity of the model can be tested by asking two sets of related questions:

● Are the assumptions valid?

● What is the effect on the model if any of the following assumptions are relaxed?

○ homogenous outputs

○ many firms

○ perfect consumer knowledge

○ perfect producer knowledge

○ freedom of entry and exit.

HOMOGENOUS OUTPUTS

One way of testing this assumption is to ask whether a particular product or service can be identified with an individual producer. Clearly, branding is designed to ensure that we differentiate most consumer products from each other.

Companies use branding to build up brand loyalty, which ultimately means that customers are prepared to pay more for one brand than another. Take away the packaging or label, and goods become much more homogenous – one computer is much like another. Moreover, the closer we get to raw materials, the harder it is to distinguish between the outputs of one producer from those of another.

You need to ask: 'If the assumption of absolute homogeneity is relaxed, and the other assumptions are held in place, will the perfectly competitive model result in productive, allocative and dynamic efficiency?'

MANY FIRMS

It is not hard to think of industries that are made up of many individual producers who are forced to accept the price set by the market. Most producers of agricultural products and those that can be simply produced using little capital or expertise probably fall into this category.

However, as shown in later chapters, production in some industries is increasingly controlled by fewer producers. The crucial question you must try to answer is: 'If the assumption of many firms is relaxed, and the other assumptions are held in place, will the perfectly competitive model result in productive, allocative and dynamic efficiency?'

PERFECT CONSUMER KNOWLEDGE

This is not a very realistic assumption. It has been said that the average consumer knows only the likely price of fewer than twenty different items in a supermarket stocking 15,000 different products. Individually, we may be expert about some products and services. But collectively, the evidence is that we might be nearer to perfect consumer ignorance than we are to perfect knowledge.

PERFECT PRODUCER KNOWLEDGE

This is harder to assess. Successful businesses need to have a good knowledge of developments within their industry. By the same token, it is in the interest of firms to keep things secret. Sometimes this is protected by law, as with patents. Although there are exceptions – such as the formula for making Coca-Cola – it is reasonably safe to assume that over a long period of time, producers have relatively good knowledge of their industry.

FREEDOM OF ENTRY AND EXIT

Some economists argue that this is the crucial assumption and that there is no clear 'yes' or 'no' answer as to its validity. Three factors are likely to be important:

● What are the costs of entry or exit?

● What are the objectives of businesses within a given industry?

● The legislative framework – are there legal barriers to entry and exit?

The cost of entering many modern industries, such as telecommunications, electronics or vehicle production, are likely to provide an enormous barrier to entry, and existing businesses will tend to be hostile to incomers. On the other hand, barriers will be fewer in industries where smaller-scale production is the norm.

ACTIVITY ···⫶

Assess the extent to which the Internet can be argued to have boosted competition and improved allocative, productive and dynamic efficiency.

3 Concentrated markets

On completion of this chapter you should be able to:

- know what economists mean when they use the terms monopoly and oligopoly
- understand the factors which affect the ability of a firm to set prices
- understand how and why firms grow
- assess degrees of monopoly power
- use diagrams to analyse the monopoly model
- distinguish between collusive and non-collusive oligopoly
- use different models to analyse interdependence on oligopolistic markets
- understand price discrimination
- use the concepts of consumer and producer surplus to assess the possible impacts of monopoly
- discuss the significance of market contestability
- compare different measures of efficiency in concentrated and competitive markets.

This chapter is based on the AQA specification and is divided into six sections:

- Concentrated markets
- The growth of firms
- Monopoly
- Oligopoly
- Market power
- Economic efficiency.

BUILDING ON AS

For your AS you will have learned that monopoly can be seen as an example of market failure. Monopolists exist when there are barriers of entry and exit from particular markets and they can charge higher prices, and impose more restriction on choice, than would be the case in more competitive markets. However, it is possible for monopolies to enjoy economies of scale that could potentially be passed on to customers in terms of lower prices and greater choice.

STEPPING UP TO A2

For A2 you are required to learn how to use diagrams to model the possible behaviour of monopolistic firms. You will also be expected to have a good understanding of oligopoly and different types of behaviour associated with this kind of market structure. You are required to assess the impact of monopolistic and oligopolist firms on consumers, assess the validity of the concept of market contestability, and compare the outcomes of firms operating in concentrated markets with those of firms operating in competitive markets.

34

Concentrated markets

Industries in which production is in the hands of one or a relatively small number of firms are called **concentrated markets**. Economists use two concepts to help understand the behaviour of firms in such markets.

A **monopoly** in theory is an industry in which there is only one firm. The demand facing the firm is the same as that facing the industry as a whole. In UK competition law, any firm with a 25 per cent or more share of the market can be said to be a monopoly.

Oligopoly is much more common and applies to industries dominated by a small number of businesses.

Concentrated markets tend to occur when:

● **barriers to entry** limit the entrance and exit of firms

● market shares become concentrated in a small number of firms

● customers can easily differentiate between products.

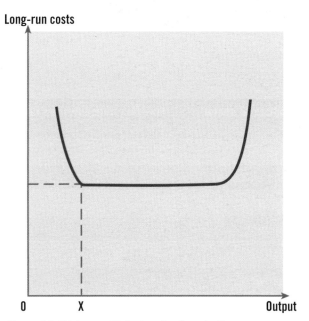

Figure 3.1 Minimum efficient scale of production

the model of perfect competition. The existence of barriers to entry often accounts for the development of concentrated markets. Such barriers take many different forms but the most common is the high capital costs facing any potential entrant, associated with relatively high minimum efficient scales of production. This is illustrated in Figure 3.1, where existing large-scale producers are able to undercut prices charged by any new entrant producing less than *OX*.

Barriers to entry can also be the result of government intervention, such as the granting of patents, licensing the production of a good or service to a small number of firms, or difficulties in recruiting employees with the required mix of skills and expertise.

Concentration ratios

Economists use **concentration ratios** to illustrate whether or not production in a given market is in

> **DEFINITIONS**
>
> **Concentrated market:** a non-competitive market dominated by a small number of firms
>
> **Monopoly:** technically speaking, when one firm has a 100 per cent market share
>
> **Oligopoly:** a market dominated by a small number of firms
>
> **Barrier to entry:** factor limiting ability of new firms to enter a market

> **DEFINITION**
>
> **Concentration ratio:** the market share in the hands of a given number of producers – usually 3 or 5

Barriers to entry

You will have noted in the previous chapter that the absence of barriers to entry is a characteristic of

the hands of a few or many firms. These involve the calculation of the share of output of the leading firms in a given market.

Industrial sector	Five-firm concentration ratio (%)
Tobacco	99.5
Iron and steel	95.3
Motor vehicles	82.9
Cement	77.7
Water supply	49.7
Footwear	48.2
Bread and biscuits	47.0
Carpets	21.8
Clothing	20.7
Plastics processing	8.8

Table 3.1 Market share of five largest firms in different sectors

Table 3.1 is based on the total proportion of market share of the five largest firms in a given market. As its name implies, a three-firm concentration ratio would involve adding together the market shares of the three largest firms. The present government uses a five-firm ratio to produce a measure of competitiveness in key economic sectors.

These ratios suggest that two interrelated factors can create concentrated markets:

● differing levels of economies of scale – for example, in steel and cement

● the extent of barriers to entry – for example, in clothing and water supply

Product differentiation

Another technique that is used to give firms a degree of monopoly power is **product differentiation**. Some products are very similar, if not identical, but producers use advertising and marketing to create separate and distinct markets for products which might in reality be very similar to others on the

market, for example those companies that supply petrol and diesel. Some customers exhibit brand loyalty and this gives the supplier extra power in that market.

DEFINITION

Product differentiation: the ability of producers to make similar products appear different to consumers

Price makers and price takers

These three factors, differentiation, concentration and barriers to entry, all contribute to creating a demand curve in concentrated markets that is different from those found in perfectly competitive markets. A very small element of any of these three factors will change the shape of the demand curve and it will no longer be perfectly elastic. The more significant differentiation, concentration and barriers to entry become, the less elastic the demand curve will become.

Once the demand curve loses its perfect elasticity, it becomes potentially possible for a firm to reduce output and sales in an effort to boost the price of the good or service in question. Alternatively, the firm can choose to cut its price in an effort to gain more customers. The success of these strategies will depend upon the elasticity of demand for the product or service, but the crucial point is that the firm is now a potential **price maker** rather than being a *price taker*, which is the case within the model of perfect competition.

DEFINITIONS

Price maker: a firm with sufficient market power to have some influence in determining the price of its products or services

This places the firm operating in a concentrated market in a totally different position from that of a firm operating within a perfectly competitive market. In the latter, the individual firm has no influence over price – if it were to raise prices above market levels, it would lose all sales; if it were to cut its price below market prices, it would, in the long run, make a loss.

Firms in concentrated markets, with high barriers to entry producing highly differentiated products, will face less elastic demand curves. Should the price elasticity of demand be relatively inelastic, raising prices will boost total revenue, leading to greater potential profits. The actual behaviour of firms with this degree of market power is analysed in more detail in the sections which follow on pages 46–50.

The growth of firms

It is helpful to understand how firms might grow to become monopolists or oligopolists. Firms can get bigger in two different ways. They can grow by:

- internal expansion
- external growth (mergers and takeovers).

Internal expansion

Firms grow in size by increasing total sales or turnover. This can be achieved by either:

- out-competing rivals and gaining greater market share, or
- being part of an expanding market.

Both approaches require development of greater productive capacity. To some degree, these growth strategies can become self financing, because retained profits can be used to provide the finance for expansion. Internal growth can lead to economies of scale and lower long-term costs of production, which can provide greater competitive advantage and therefore help further growth.

Firms that successfully pursue such policies will also usually find it easier to raise additional funds, either from banks or from the stock market. Most oligopolistic firms are plcs, and this gives them much greater access to finance for expansion but, at the same time, this makes expanding companies vulnerable to takeover. Once shares are freely traded on the stock market there is nothing to stop other businesses, individuals or controllers of equity capital from taking over a plc – especially if they are competing in the same market as larger, better-resourced firms.

External growth (mergers and takeovers)

Firms can also grow in size and economic power by **merger** when two businesses agree to collaborate to form one. More commonly, one business takes over another, either by outright purchase or by the accumulation of a controlling interest of shares. Both external forms of growth are usually referred to as mergers. These take three forms:

- vertical – by which one firm merges with another involved in different stages of the production chain (for example, electricity supply companies buying into electricity generation)

- horizontal – when mergers take place between companies at the same stage of the production chain (for example, Wal-Mart and Asda)

- conglomerate merger – where firms from different industries merge (for example, a tobacco company taking over an estate agency chain).

Merger activity provides a rapid means of building up market share. It helps to protect firms from competition and to ensure greater control over the productive process. However, as will be outlined in the section on page 39, it can also reduce customer choice and increase monopoly power.

Merger activity tends to be greatest towards the peak of the economic cycle. Successful companies generate profits, which can then be used to part-finance further acquisitions.

> ### DEFINITION
>
> **Merger:** two or more firms joining together to form one larger firm

ECONOMICS IN CONTEXT

ENERGY GROUPS FEAR MONOPOLY

By Rebecca Bream in London

Energy companies yesterday expressed concern about the prospect of a takeover of British Energy, fearing it could lead to one company having a monopoly over the best UK sites for new nuclear reactors.

After a report in the *Financial Times* that UBS had contacted energy companies to gauge interest in buying the UK government's 35.2 per cent stake in British Energy, the nuclear group yesterday confirmed it was in talks with 'interested parties'.

Source: Financial Times

ACTIVITY ···

What are the implications of a monopoly in the UK for the production of nuclear energy?

Demergers

Over the last decade, there has been an increase in **demergers**. Increasing competition and globalisation can leave large conglomerates at a disadvantage compared to firms more clearly focused on a particular economic activity .

Improvements in technology (especially ICT), the further development of subcontracting, multi-skilling of workers and the development of flatter, less hierarchical, and more customer-focused organisations are combining to reduce the cost advantages enjoyed by conglomerates.

DEFINITION

Demerger: the splitting up of a large firm into two or more separate entities

The fashion in business is increasingly to 'concentrate' on core activities. Selling off non-core activities is another way of financing further focused growth and development. An example is the restructuring of GEC. Its defence-related business was sold off to British Aerospace, and the company has been renamed Marconi to concentrate on growth in the ICT sector.

Monopoly

In order to understand the behaviour of both monopolists and oligopolists, it is useful to understand how economists have built up a theoretical model of monopoly in a similar way to that used for the model of perfect competition. This model is based on two related simplifying assumptions:

● Production of a whole industry is in the hands of one firm.

● Complete barriers prevent the entry and exits of firms.

These assumptions mean that the demand curve for the individual firm will be the same as that for the industry as a whole. Moreover, there is no distinction – as there is with perfect competition – between the short- and the long-run equilibrium of the firm. If a

Soviet supermarkets offered little customer choice

monopoly is total, barriers to entry are absolute and this prevents other firms competing away excess profits. The monopolist will be able to set the price or quantity sold, and therefore has considerable freedom to pursue particular economic and social objectives.

Possible price, sales and output levels can be analysed graphically – as shown in Figure 3.2, where demand and average revenue are above average costs at outputs between OQ and OQ_2. This means that a monopolistic firm could set a price anywhere between OP and OP_2, and make more than normal profits.

In this case, a profit-maximising monopolist would produce at OQ_1 and a sales maximiser at OQ_2. Barriers to entry would ensure that this short-run situation was also the long-run position.

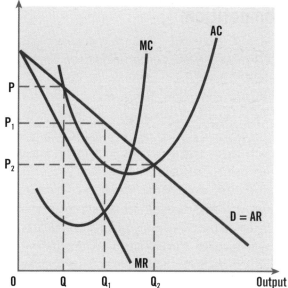

Prices/costs

Figure 3.2 Demand and cost conditions facing a monopolistic firm

> **learning tip**
> This is one of the diagrams that you should be able to draw in your sleep – practise, practise and practise again, making sure that you label everything, that the MC cuts the AC at its lowest point, and that usually AC < AR.

If monopolies existed that conformed to this model:

● average costs of production would not necessarily be minimised as shown in Figure 3.2, where both sales and profit maximisers produce at points above the lowest possible average cost

● excessive profits could be earned in the long run – barriers to entry prevent new firms entering the industry in pursuit of greater profits

● firms would not have to attempt to maximise profits – average costs are covered by any output between OQ and OQ_2

● firms would not necessarily have to respond to changes in demand – in a competitive market firms have an incentive to respond to changes in demand, but this disappears if there is no threat from new entrants

● there would be little incentive to innovate – what's the point, if the monopoly already earns supernormal profits and has no fears of competition?

● customer choice could be restricted – one of the reasons for the collapse of the old USSR was the inability of state-run monopolies to respond to customer choice – customers had to accept what was on offer or go without.

ACTIVITY ⋯⋗

Use diagrams to show how a profit-maximising monopolist might react to:

a an increase in demand

b an increase in variable costs

c an increase in fixed costs.

> **learning tip**
> Don't jump to conclusions and don't be dogmatic in answering questions in the examination – the paragraph above starts with the important preposition 'if' – there are lots of ifs and buts in making comparisons between perfect competition and monopoly, the main one being that there are few industries that conform to the assumptions of either model. The models are still useful, however, as they indicate the features of two possible extremes.

Comparisons with perfect competition

The possible outcomes in terms of price and output under monopoly and perfect competition can be compared using the diagram already developed to analyse monopolies. This is reproduced again below in Figure 3.3, which indicates that, if both the monopolist and the industry as a whole were faced with the same cost conditions, in the short run, prices under monopoly would be higher than prices under perfect competition. It also shows that the monopoly output would be lower. Under perfect competition, competitive pressures are such that individual firms have to produce where MC equals price. If this applied to a whole industry, perfectly competitive output would be at OQ and price at OP, whereas a profit-maximising monopolist would charge OP_1 for a smaller output OQ_1.

This conclusion depends on two major assumptions:

● The monopolist's objective is to maximise profits – a monopolist could choose the same output and price combination that would apply to perfect competition, just as it could sell more at a lower price.

● Both monopolist and perfectly competitive firms would be faced with the same average and marginal cost conditions.

The second assumption is not very realistic, as it implies that economies of scale do not exist. One argument used to justify the existence of monopolies is that they are able to enjoy the benefits of economies of scale that may arise in increasing size, which then leads to falling long-run average costs. The effects of this possibility are illustrated in Figure 3.4, where MC_2 represents lower long-run costs that might be generated by economies of scale enjoyed by the monopolist. In this case, the profit-maximising monopolist will charge OP_1 for output OQ_1, compared to OP and OQ for the perfectly competitive industry.

Of course, it could be argued that monopolies are inherently bureaucratic and that this could generate diseconomies of scale and force up long-term costs – the only way that this conjecture can be resolved is by examining the cost structures within particular industries to establish the minimum efficient scale of production.

ACTIVITY ⋯⟩

How close are the following to being monopolies as defined in this chapter? Justify your answer.

a Microsoft

b Network Rail

c the only store in a village.

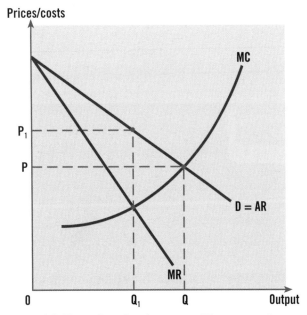

Figure 3.3 Monopoly and perfect competition compared

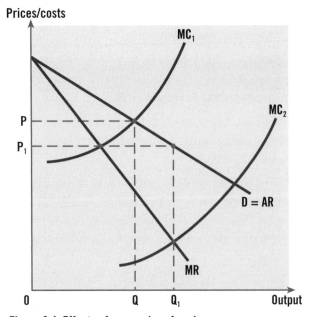

Figure 3.4 Effects of economies of scale

Are village shops examples of monopolies?

> **learning tip**
>
> Just remember that graphical analysis has been used to compare output, prices and profits under the two extremes of perfect competition and monopoly. The use of this analysis indicates that prices might be lower and outputs higher under conditions of perfect competition than under monopoly. However, this simple comparison ignores the existence of economies of scale and the greater freedom that a monopolistic firm has to pursue differing objectives.

Oligopoly

Oligopoly literally means competition among the few, and this appears to be a much more realistic model to apply to most markets that exist in the United Kingdom. The model was first developed in the 1930s, when economists realised that traditional ways of analysing the behaviour of firms failed to take account of the growing tendency for many industries to be dominated by a small number of large firms. There are two principal assumptions that underpin this model.

First is the existence of barriers of entry to and from the industry. These will vary from industry to industry, but their existence makes the analysis of oligopoly closer to that of monopoly.

The second assumption is the interdependence of decision making. The assumption is unique to this model and means that individual firms make decisions about prices, marketing, product design and so on with reference to how they perceive their competitors will respond. Each firm is affected by the actions of others.

Barriers to entry

Oligopolists are protected by barriers to entry and are likely constantly to erect new barriers in order to maintain long-term market share and profits. Barriers to entry which apply to oligopoly are likely to include the following:

● capital costs – especially in capital- and technology-intensive firms such as Sony Music

● high levels of **sunk costs**

● national and global branding Nike, Adidas and other leisurewear firms have spent billions of pounds on promoting a global image that would be both costly and difficult for a newcomer to match

● patent and copyright – especially important in pharmaceuticals (for example, GlaxoSmithKline)

● technological expertise – especially when backed up by large research and development expenditures (for example, Nokia)

● takeover – dominant firms often respond to the threat of new entrants by taking them over (for example, Microsoft).

> **DEFINITION**
>
> **Sunk costs:** non-recoverable fixed costs

Interdependence

The second assumption, the **interdependence** of decision making, is very significant, because it makes it much more difficult for economists to model the behaviour of an oligopolistic firm. The behaviour of one firm will depend on its perceptions of how other firms will react to changes. The responses of other firms will depend on their perceptions of the responses of others. It is harder, therefore, to predict how oligopolistic firms are likely to behave.

> ### DEFINITIONS
>
> **Interdependence:** how decision making between oligopolistic firms can be affected by the decisions of other oligopolistic firms
>
> **Non-price competition:** when firms use advertising, branding and other techniques in preference to cutting prices to attract more customers

As has been noted earlier (page 25), if a firm is operating under conditions of perfect competition it has no market power, in the sense that it cannot influence the price for which its output is sold. Such a firm is a *price taker*. Similarly it was shown that a monopolist is a *price maker* having the power to set the price charged for its output. The issue of interdependent decision making places the oligopolist in a very different position. An oligopolist firm can be a price maker. It could cut its price in an attempt to attract a bigger market share. This will only work if competitors do not follow suit. If they all copied the decision of the oligopolist price maker, all are likely to be left with the same market share but reduced profits. Worse still, from the oligopolist's position, is that price cuts could trigger others to cut prices even further, leading to a price war – in which all would be potential losers.

Economists have noted the increased risks faced by oligopolists, especially the threat of price wars, and have suggested that oligopolists have an incentive to keep prices stable and indulge more in **non-price competition**. This could take the form of spending more on:

ECONOMICS IN CONTEXT

NTT DOCOMO SIGNALS FIERCE MOBILE PRICE WAR

By Mariko Sanchanta in Tokyo

NTT DoCoMo on Wednesday reacted to the arrival of the first new entrant in the Japanese mobile market in 13 years by introducing lower-cost pricing plans.

The move by Japan's leading mobile phone operator is the latest salvo in the intensifying pricing war among Japan's mobile operators after EMobile announced plans with an end-of-March launch offering a service without the traditional monthly subscription fee.

DoCoMo said on Wednesday that the changes to its pricing plans would cut revenues by Y80bn ($752m) in its next financial year from April 1. This loss would be partly offset by increases to its

monthly charges for its mobile Internet service, i-mode, which was expected to add Y50bn to revenues.

DoCoMo, which still has a 53 per cent market share, is frantically trying to shore up its subscriber base amid a wave of defections following the introduction of a regulatory change in 2006 that enabled consumers to keep their phone numbers when moving accounts between providers.

In the nine months to December, DoCoMo added only 529,400 subscribers against KDDI's 1.4m gain and 1.7m additions by Softbank, which took over Vodafone's local operations in

2006. DoCoMo reported an 8 per cent fall in operating profit for the period.

DoCoMo said it would start offering 24-hour free calls between family members who subscribe to its discount plan, beginning on April 1.

The move mimics that of rival KDDI, which last week unveiled a package waiving charges for calls between family members. KDDI's shares subsequently sank to a 20-month low after analysts said the new plan would erode its revenues by Y25bn in the fiscal year starting April 1.

Source: Financial Times

- advertising
- after-sales service
- promotional offers
- product differentiation.

These are just some of the techniques designed to make a product or service more attractive without having to resort to cutting prices. This provides an explanation for the large amounts of resources that are devoted to marketing and advertising – both functions would not be required by perfectly competitive or monopolistic firms.

ACTIVITY ⋯⋰

Why has this price war occurred?

Assess the extent to which mobile phone subscribers in Japan are likely to benefit from the price war described in the article above.

Collusive and non-collusive oligopoly

The concept of interdependence in decision making is particularly important when trying to make sense of the behaviour of oligopolists. Economists make a clear distinction between two different types of oligopolists:

- **non-collusive oligopolists**, who will embrace the risks of competition in order to compete with their rivals to gain greater market share
- **collusive oligopolists**, who will seek to avoid the risks associated with competition by co-operating with other businesses. Colluding firms may seek to set common prices or levels of output for each.

The new Volkswagen Polo is unveiled

NON-COLLUSIVE OLIGOPOLISTS

Predicting the outcomes of decision making by oligopolists is difficult. To take an example: Volkswagen needs to decide on the recommended selling price for its new Polo. It is currently selling a basic version of the Polo for £8,999. However, some competitors, such as the Nissan Micra, are available more cheaply, while others, such as the Vauxhall Corsa, are more expensive.

There are fears in the automobile industry that car prices are likely to fall. So what should Volkswagen do? If it cuts its price and competitors follow suit, it will end up with the same market share. If it cuts its prices and competitors fail to respond, its market share may increase. What if Vauxhall or Nissan make larger price cuts?

One approach used by economists to try to make sense of such competitive behaviour is by use of **game theory**, first developed by psychologists when trying to predict human responses in a similarly

DEFINITIONS

Non-collusive oligopolists: oligopolists who compete with each other

Collusive oligopolists: oligopolists who try to co-operate with each other

DEFINITION

Game theory: a theory developed by psychologists to model interdependent behaviour and applied to oligopolists

unpredictable situation. At a simple level, this can be restricted to looking at the behaviour of one firm and the possible responses of another. This is illustrated in Figure 3.5.

To begin with, assume that the market for small cars is shared equally between Volkswagen and Nissan. They charge the same price of £8,999 for cars with similar specifications, and they both receive total profit of £200 million. This is depicted in box A of the matrix.

The outcomes of Volkswagen cutting £1,000 from its recommended price will depend upon the responses of Nissan. If it keeps its original price, Volkswagen will gain a bigger market share and a larger proportion of the industry profit. This is illustrated in box C. Alternatively, Nissan could copy Volkswagen, leaving both with an equal market share but reduced profits because of the price cut. This is shown in box D.

A fourth option is that Volkswagen maintains its price at £8,999, but Nissan cuts its price to, say, £7,999. In this case, both Volkswagen's market share and profits will be cut, as shown in box B.

This approach to the analysis of the behaviour of oligopolists yields an important prediction. For Volkswagen, option C would give the best possible return, but it is also the most risky. It depends on Nissan ignoring an aggressive price cut. Option B is the worst outcome, while options D and A are the least risky. Logic dictates that Volkswagen ought to collude with Nissan.

The essence of game theory is that there is a range of possible outcomes in response to market changes or changes in the behaviour of firms. Game theory focuses on alternative strategies that firms may pursue. Cautious firms will elect a strategy that is least risky. This is called a **maximin strategy**, whereas an approach that involves taking greater risks to gain higher levels of profit is called a **maximax strategy**. If both approaches lead to the same outcome, firms are said to be playing a dominant strategy game.

DEFINITIONS

Maximin strategy: taking less risks and accepting lower potential profits

Maximax strategy: taking greater risks to obtain higher potential profits

COLLUSIVE OLIGOPOLISTS

Game theory can be used to demonstrate that it is in the interests of oligopolistic firms to collude – that is, form agreements to reduce the risks attached to competition (especially price competition). Collusion can take three forms:

● *open*, in which firms make a formal collective agreement. This is called a cartel and will usually bind its signatories to agreed price levels and/or production quotas. With some exceptions, cartels are illegal in the UK and in most other Western countries.

● *informal,* in which firms find ways of evading legal restrictions in order to maintain common prices. It is thought that informal agreements are common in the UK, especially in the markets for electrical goods, cars and perfume. However, as this form of activity might be the target of government investigation and intervention, it is hard to find evidence of secret agreements.

● *tacit* behaviour, in which individual oligopolists arrive at common policies without formal or informal agreements. Some industries are dominated by a particular firm and others will follow its pricing

	£8999	Nissan	£7999
	A Each shares market, earning £200m profit		**B** Nissan takes larger market share + £350m profit
Volkswagen			
	C VW captures larger market share + £350m profit		**D** Equal market shares, each with profit of £100m

(£8999 and £7999 label the Volkswagen rows on the left side of the matrix)

Figure 3.5 Game theory matrix

STRETCH AND CHALLENGE

KINKED DEMAND CURVES

An alternative theoretical treatment of the behaviour of oligopolists is that associated with the American economist Paul Sweezy. He observed that even if oligopolists were in competition with each other, prices in such markets tended to be stable. He used a simplified form of game theory, reasoning that, as pricing decisions by oligopolists were interdependent, an individual firm would be very reluctant to raise its prices because it would fear that none of its competitors would follow suit.

On the other hand, he argued, an individual firm would be reluctant to cut its prices because this decision would be copied by competitors. In other words, the oligopolist would be faced with an elastic demand curve in terms of price rises and an inelastic curve for price cuts. This is illustrated graphically in Figure 3.6.

This theory has been attacked by a number of economists as lacking in any empirical validity. Figure 3.7 illustrates a different explanation of price stability under oligopoly. This is derived from the modern theory of the firm outlined on page 17. In this case, the demand for the product or service in question could fluctuate quite widely and the business would be able to operate to the same profit margins on individual sales without having to suffer the additional costs which might be associated with changing prices in response to changes in demand.

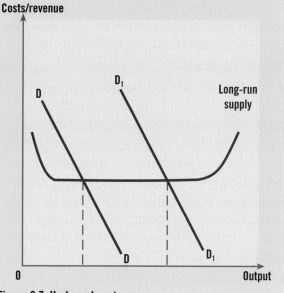

Figure 3.6 Kinked demand curve

Figure 3.7 U-shaped cost curve

decisions. This is called **price leadership** and in the UK, ESSO is seen as a leader in terms of petrol prices, Kellogg for breakfast cereals and Nike for trainers. Common prices and other apparent collusion can arise when firms in industries follow

Pubs and restaurants put a substantial mark-up on food and drink

DEFINITION

Price leadership: influential firms whose pricing decisions are copied by others

common pricing formulas and pay similar amounts for factor inputs. Most pubs mark up the price of beers and lager by 100 per cent; local stores add 40 per cent to the cost price of confectionery and similar products; and restaurants add 500 per cent to the cost of ingredients to price their menus. This can lead to competitive firms charging similar prices for the same meals.

Collusion, though attractive to oligopolists as a means of reducing risks and safeguarding profits, has particular dangers, especially as both formal and informal agreements break the law.

NON-COLLUSIVE BEHAVIOUR

Although there must be a strong temptation for oligopolists to avoid unnecessary risks by colluding with each other, some businesses are likely to be more aggressive and confrontational. Stable relationships between oligopolist firms can be upset by:

● *new technologies.* The ways in which goods and services are produced is constantly changing. As this process is likely to occur unevenly across the firms making up an industry, some firms are likely to find themselves producing goods more cheaply than their competitors. For example, digital technologies are revolutionising the printing and media industries. Those businesses in the forefront of this change are likely to try to use their lower production costs to drive competitors out of the industry.

● *changes in ownership.* As with technology, the ownership of plcs in the UK is not always static. Changes at the top can lead to changes in business strategy, especially if the goal is to drive up shareholder value. The hostile acquisition of rivals and aggressive behaviour in building up market share are non-collusive strategies. In particular, some firms may start price wars by deliberately selling close to, or below, costs of production, with a view to driving out competitors.

STRETCH AND CHALLENGE

Construct a matrix to predict possible outcomes of interdependent decision making in an industry of your choice.

<table><tr><td>**learning tip**</td><td>Analysing the behaviour of oligopolists is far more complex than analysing firms operating in other market structures. Graphical</td></tr></table>

analysis is less helpful, as outcomes in terms of pricing, output and profits are less predictable.

Particular industries may be characterised by high levels of competition, while in others tacit agreements result in high levels of price stability and little or no competition.

ACTIVITY ····⦂

Which of the following industries comes closest to satisfying the assumptions of oligopolistic competition? Justify your choice.

a brewing

b airlines

c electricity generation.

Market power

Economic theory demonstrates that firms that are monopolies or oligopolies have considerable market power to set prices, determine customer choice, limit competition and keep out new market entrants. These firms are also often very large, commanding turnovers greater than most countries in the world, and able to use this economic power to influence the behaviour of governments. Economists differ in their assessments of the impact of such large firms, but have developed further theories and techniques to help measure market power and advise governments of possible intervention strategies. This section is devoted to:

● price discrimination

● consumer and producer surplus

● contestable markets.

Price discrimination

One method of measuring the degree of power that any firm has in a given marketplace is to establish the degree to which it is able to charge different customers different prices for the same product or service. This is called **price discrimination** and is an aspect of market power used by firms to boost revenue and profits.

> ### DEFINITION
>
> **Price discrimination:** charging different customers different prices for the same good or service

Most of us are used to being charged a range of different prices for particular goods or services. Air fares are a good example. Customers flying from London to New York can pay anywhere between £200 and £1,800 for the same seat in the same aircraft. In order to benefit from price discrimination, airlines need to ensure that the following conditions must be fulfilled:

● The firm must have some degree of market dominance and be a price maker.

● Demand for the good or service will be spread between different customers, each with differing price elasticities of demand for the product or service.

● These different market segments have to be separated from each other.

● The proportion of fixed to total costs is likely to be high.

MARKET DOMINANCE
Only those firms that are facing a downward-sloping overall demand curve for their products or services will be able to charge different prices to different customers. The more monopoly power a firm enjoys, the more it can price discriminate. On the other hand, those firms that are closer to being perfectly competitive will have only a limited opportunity to charge different prices to different customers. Clearly, there is a limited number of airlines flying between London and New York. Those that offer the most flights will be able to set prices rather than having to accept the 'market' price.

DIFFERING PRICE ELASTICITIES OF DEMAND
A discriminating monopolist will wish to charge higher prices to some of its customers and will be prepared to sell the same product or service to others at a lower price, as long as this boosts overall revenue.

Airlines exploit this by charging much higher fares to those who have to fly at particular times or whose air fare is likely to be part of an expense account. Other market segments, such as young people travelling around the world, are likely to be much more price sensitive and will only be attracted by lower fares. Another important segment for some airlines is the holiday market. Holiday companies may make block bookings of seats but will expect significant discounts. Finally, seats that are hard to sell can be sold through 'bucket shops' (travel agencies specialising in cheap tickets) and through travel agencies dealing in last-minute bookings.

SEPARATION OF MARKETS
Elaborate strategies such as those outlined above will only work if it is impossible for one set of airline customers to sell on its cheaper tickets to passengers who would otherwise be prepared to pay higher fares. This is relatively easy for the airlines, because tickets can only be used by a named person. Other price discriminators use time to separate markets. Train tickets bought at different times of the day cost different amounts and can be used only on specified trains.

RELATIVELY HIGH FIXED COSTS
The bulk of the costs of flying from London to New York are fuel, maintenance and debt repayment. Once committed to the flight, the airline has low levels of variable costs. Put another way, marginal costs of carrying additional passengers are low. It costs little more to carry 350 passengers than it does to carry 349. Hence, the airline will add to its profits once it has covered the costs of extra meals, ticketing and costs associated with the 350th passenger.

If variable costs are relatively more significant, marginal costs will be higher and a profit-seeking company would be less likely to use discounts to gain additional customers.

Consumer and producer surplus

Another way in which economists attempt to assess the impact of non-competitive behaviour by firms is by the use of two concepts:

● consumer surplus

● producer surplus.

CONSUMER SURPLUS

This concept uses graphical analysis to illustrate the benefits that customers gain from consuming a particular product or service. Figure 3.8 illustrates consumer surplus and OP represents an equilibrium price with the level of sales at OQ.

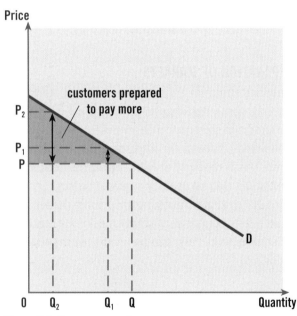

Figure 3.8 Consumer surplus

The last customer is prepared to pay the market price for the product, but all earlier customers would have been prepared to pay more. For instance, OQ_1 customers would have been prepared to pay more than OP, and OQ_2 customers would have been prepared to pay still more. The vertical distances indicate how much more some customers would have been prepared to pay. Taken together, the shaded area represents an additional benefit enjoyed by consumers of this product. This is referred to as consumer surplus.

PRODUCER SURPLUS

A similar analytical approach can be made to gains made by producers of a good or service. In Figure 3.9, OQ producers receive OP for their total output, but some producers would have been prepared to supply the good or service for less. OQ_1 producers were prepared to supply for OP_1, whereas OQ_2 producers were prepared to accept even less at OP_2. The shaded area, therefore, represents producers' surplus.

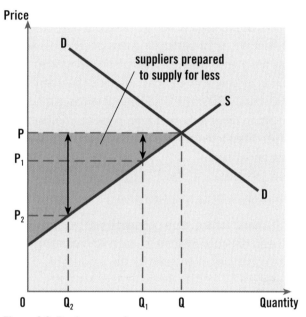

Figure 3.9 Producer surplus

This concept is applied to understanding the impact of monopoly power. Figure 3.10 shows that a profit-maximising oligopolist or monopolist will produce at OQ and charge OP for its output, whereas a perfectly competitive industry facing the same cost structure will produce at OQ_1 and charge OP_1 for its output.

Consumer surplus under monopolistic conditions will be the equivalent of area a, but under perfect competition it would be larger and equal to $a + b + c$.

Producer surplus, on the other hand, is bigger under monopoly, consisting of $d + b$, compared with a perfectly competitive producer surplus of $d + e$. In other words, this graphical analysis shows that producers gain while consumers lose.

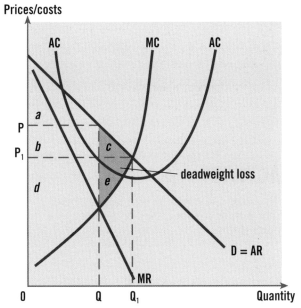

Prices/costs

Figure 3.10 Deadweight welfare loss

Overall, *c + e* represents losses under monopoly of both producer and consumer surpluses. This area is known as **deadweight welfare loss** of monopoly.

ACTIVITY ···:·

How might consumer and producer surplus be affected by the following?

a reduction of barriers of entry in an industry

b the establishment of a cartel in an industry.

Contestable markets

This is an alternative approach, which involves the adaptation of traditional theory to account for a different type of competition that may occur within concentrated markets. The theory of **contestable markets** is based on the premise that firms will operate competitively if they fear competition in some way. There are a number of variants of this theory, and it is argued that a monopolist will behave like a competitive firm if:

- there is a fear of takeover
- barriers to entry and exit are minimised.

DEFINITION

Contestable markets: markets in which the fear of competition or takeover forces firms with market power to behave competitively

FEAR OF TAKEOVER

No plc is free from the fear of takeover, and senior managers of such firms have to compete with other businesses on the stock market. Rising share prices are associated with business success and will be fed by stock market perceptions of potential profits, levels of customer service, responsiveness to changes in demand, and so on.

Monopolistic and oligopolistic firms that fail to pursue those and other objectives associated with competitive behaviour will, the theorists argue, be punished by the stock market and share prices will fall, making such firms more liable to takeover.

It could be argued that this describes the position of Marks & Spencer. The fear of takeover has galvanised the board of directors to look critically at all aspects of the performance of this market leader in fashion retailing.

MINIMISATION OF BARRIERS TO ENTRY AND EXIT

A market is said to be perfectly contestable if there are no barriers to entry. If this were the case, other firms would be attracted to those industries in which supernormal profits are being made.

In order to prevent increased competition, firms operating in a contestable market will keep prices down, and ensure that profits are kept to normal levels. Exit barriers need also to be minimised. If sunk costs are significant, firms already in an industry will be deterred from leaving, as they cannot transfer such resources to other uses. Moreover, new entrants will be deterred if they are unable to transfer capital elsewhere.

Government intervention

One of the main policies pursued by many governments to promote greater competition is the attempt to turn non-contestable markets into those that are contestable. This is usually achieved by intervention to reduce barriers to entry. Examples of such policies in the United Kingdom include the auctioning of bandwidth to competing companies, giving access to the BBC to independent production companies, and the establishment of privately funded academies to replace schools in areas of high deprivation. Further consideration of possible government intervention is developed in Chapter 4.

ACTIVITY ····⋗

Why does the author of this article argue that Korean markets should become more contestable?

ECONOMICS IN CONTEXT

KOREA'S EARLY AGEING

Anyone blinded by east Asia's dazzling rise into thinking that the entire region is one unending economic success story should ponder the case of South Korea. Once held up as a model of precocious development, which rapidly transformed itself from an agricultural into an industrialised society, east Asia's third largest economy is sinking into premature middle age.

After bouncing back from the 1997 economic crisis, growth has dwindled to an average of 4.2 per cent in the past four years, well below potential. Competitors in China and other lower-cost countries are fast eroding Korea's industrial base. Its companies are moving plants offshore as fast as they can, while a wave of increasingly strident xenophobia at home risks diminishing still further the country's modest foreign direct investment inflows.

This faltering performance is all the more surprising because Korea still possesses enviable assets. It has a well-educated population, modern infrastructure, a high level of Internet penetration and an industrious, if militant, workforce. Its companies are leaders in industries including electronics, cars, steel and shipbuilding, and some are household names worldwide.

What went wrong? Korea has long aspired to Japan's traditional industrial model. Unfortunately, it has succeeded in copying too many of its weaknesses and not enough of its strengths. Its growth depends heavily on exports, concentrated in a relatively narrow range of manufacturing industries. Much of its domestic economy lacks dynamism and is hobbled by restrictive practices. With the arguable exception of television soap operas, it has failed in recent years to develop thrusting new businesses. Korea's economy is also dominated even more heavily than Japan's by large incumbent producers, the chaebol, which stifle emerging rivals at home while increasingly placing their own investments abroad.

The growing challenge from China is fast making this situation untenable. If Korea is to continue to prosper, it must wean itself off its dependence on volume manufacturing and rapidly generate profitable new activities in which China does not compete head-on. That calls for radical action to stimulate diversification, innovation and enterprise by opening its economy to competition from new entrants. The country needs to make its market contestable by international as well as domestic producers, particularly in sectors such as financial services, where it is unlikely to succeed without foreign expertise.

Regrettably, President Roh Moo-hyun's administration has lacked both the vision and political courage to pursue vigorous reforms. However, the inauguration of Mr Roh's successor and parliamentary elections next year offer an opportunity for a fresh start. History suggests that, with the right political leadership, Korea is quite capable of seizing it. But the time left to do so is starting to run out.

Source: Financial Times

Economic efficiency

Chapter 2 included an assessment of the extent to which competitive markets are likely to contribute to:

- allocative efficiency
- productive efficiency
- dynamic efficiency.

In this chapter you have been shown that concentrated markets in which there are degrees of monopolistic or oligopolist power can produce theoretical outcomes which are less efficient against all three criteria listed above.

In short, it is possible to argue that a profit-maximising firm with monopolistic or oligopolist power has less incentive:

- to respond to changes in customer demand, especially if there are few substitutes available; this could result in allocative inefficiency

- to produce at minimum average cost, resulting in productive inefficiency

- to innovate and undertake technological changes contributing to dynamic inefficiencies.

However, this comparison assumes that firms operating in concentrated markets will be faced with cost structures similar to those operating in competitive markets, will not enjoy economies of scale and will not be motivated by the fear of takeover to innovate and invest in research and development.

It can be argued that the combination of technological advance, globalisation, and the very high cost of investments to remain competitive mean that a dynamically efficient economy requires large companies with monopolistic or oligopolistic power. Only firms of this size can afford to undertake the

- research and development
- training and development of staff skills
- investment in non-human capital

that are required for dynamic efficiency.

However, economists can only try to resolve the strengths and weakness of large and small firms of concentrated, contestable and competitive markets by empirical research.

4 The labour market

On completion of this chapter you should be able to:

- understand and use marginal productivity theory
- analyse the different factors which affect the supply of labour
- assess the role of market forces in determining wage rates and theoretical levels of employment in perfectly competitive markets
- evaluate the impact of imperfections in labour markets
- assess the ability of trade unions to influence wage rates and employment levels
- understand the effect of minimum wage legislation
- consider the impact of wage discrimination based on gender, ethnicity and other factors in labour markets
- understand why income and wealth are unequally distributed in the UK
- evaluate government policies to alleviate poverty.

This chapter is divided into eight sections based on the AQA A2 specification:

- The demand for labour
- The supply of labour
- Wage determination
- Imperfections in the labour market
- Government intervention in labour markets
- Wage discrimination
- Inequalities in wealth and income
- Poverty and government policy.

STEPPING UP TO A2

A2 requires a much more detailed understanding of labour markets, and the theories that economists use to analyse their workings. You also need to know about different labour market imperfections and the effects of both minimum wage legislation and wage discrimination. Finally, it is expected that you will have a general understanding of income and wealth inequalities and their impact on the economy.

The demand for labour: marginal revenue productivity theory

The demand for any factor of production is a **derived demand**. Factors are not demanded in their own right; they are demanded because they can be combined to produce goods and services that, under competitive conditions, can be sold for a profit. It follows that entrepreneurs will be primarily interested in the contribution that the use of a factor is likely to make to profitability. This will, in turn, be dependent on two linked factors:

BUILDING ON AS

In AS you will have learned that the demand for labour is a demand derived from the final demand for the good or service produced using that labour. You will also appreciate that the labour market is a factor market connected to other markets in the economy, and you should have considered the impact of minimum wage legislation.

- the amount each factor contributes to overall production

- the price that can be gained from selling the product or service.

The demand for labour that is particularly productive in producing outputs which command a high price is likely to be much higher than the demand for less productive labour producing goods or services which sell cheaply. On page 12 in Chapter 1, the law of diminishing marginal returns was outlined. To recap, in the short run, output can only be increased by using more of a variable factor. Average costs of production will drop as output is expanded, an optimum where average costs are minimised will be reached and, thereafter, average costs of production will rise, showing increasing inefficiency. This provides a rationale for the U-shaped average cost curve.

If this 'law' is applied to labour productivity, output per worker will rise, reach a peak and then fall. The application of the law of diminishing marginal returns can also be interpreted as meaning that the output per worker will increase until an optimum is reached. After this, growing inefficiency in the short run will result in lower output per worker. This produces a hump-shaped marginal physical product curve, as shown in Figure 4.1.

Output per worker

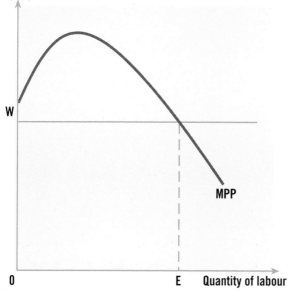

Figure 4.1 Marginal physical productivity curve

> **learning tip**
>
> Read through the explanation above again. The average cost curve is 'U' shaped because average costs of production are being measured on the vertical axis, while the marginal physical product curve is hump-shaped as the physical amount of extra production is being measured on the vertical axis.

As has already been noted, the bottom line for most producers of goods and services is the amount of profit they are likely to make. Therefore, they are not only interested in what every worker can produce in physical terms but, most importantly, the value of that output of each worker. It follows that the value of any worker's output will be determined by the revenue that can be gained for what has been produced. Thus, multiplying the additional output produced by each worker by the price that can be gained from selling that output gives the **marginal revenue product** of that worker. The additional revenue gained will ultimately be determined by the demand for that output.

DEFINITIONS

Derived demand: when the demand for one good, service or factor depends on the demand for another good, service or factor

Marginal revenue product: the change in revenue caused by changing a given number of workers employed

The shape of this demand curve will depend on the degree of competition in that particular market. If the market is perfectly competitive, any additional output will be sold for the same price as the proceeding unit. This means that the marginal revenue product curve will have the same shape as the marginal product curve.

However, if the market is less than perfectly competitive, additional output will only be sold at a

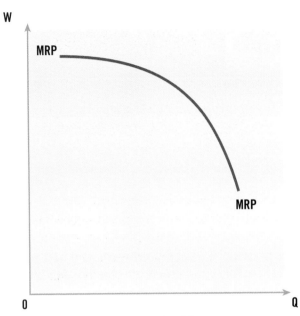

Figure 4.2 Marginal revenue productivity curve

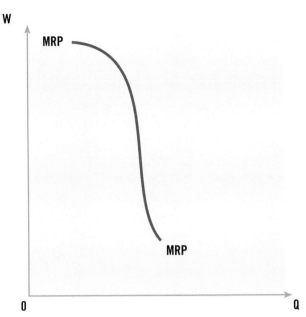

Figure 4.3 Marginal revenue productivity curve in a less competitive market

lower price. This will have the effect of increasing the gradient of the marginal revenue product curve. These two possibilities are illustrated in Figures 4.2 and 4.3.

Thus, if a kitchen fitter employs an additional joiner who can assemble two kitchens per week, and each kitchen earns the company an additional £1,000 net of other expenses, the weekly marginal revenue product of this worker would be £2,000. It follows that any change in either the demand for the product or

the productivity of any individual worker will have an effect on the MRP curve. This increasing demand for the final product will increase the revenue received for each unit, shifting the marginal revenue product curve upwards to the right as shown in Figure 4.4.

Falling labour productivity would have the opposite effect, leading to a downward and leftward shift of the marginal revenue product curve, as shown in Figure 4.5.

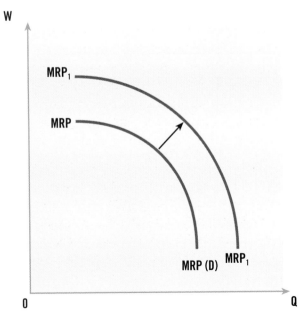

Figure 4.4 Increasing marginal revenue productivity curve

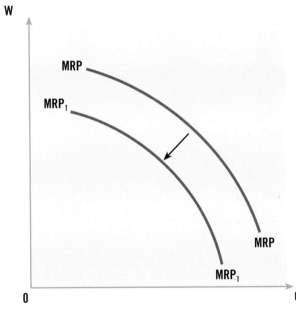

Figure 4.5 Decreasing marginal revenue productivity curve

Wages

Figure 4.6 Demand curve for labour

The marginal revenue product curve determines the shape of the demand curve for labour and it is drawn in a similar way to demand curves for final goods and services – if plotted against wage rates, it falls downwards from left to right, showing that the demand for workers will increase if wage rates decrease and that rising wage rates would lead to falling demand. This is illustrated in Figure 4.6.

Elasticity of demand for labour

There will be variations in the elasticity of demand for different types of labour, which will be a function of three linked factors:

- the elasticity of demand for the final product or service – the more inelastic demand for the final product or service
- the proportion of labour costs in the total cost of production – if this is relatively insignificant, the elasticity of demand for labour will be less
- the ease with which one factor can be substituted for another – if it is easy to replace labour with machines, the demand for labour in respect to changes in the wage rate will be more elastic.

STRETCH AND CHALLENGE
There are quite a lot of 'ifs' used in building up the marginal revenue product theory of the demand for labour. Identify at least three, and critically evaluate their significance.

The supply of labour

Learning about the supply of labour is more straightforward than understanding the demand for labour. The supply of labour is determined by the willingness of workers to undertake a particular job. There are two factors identified by economists which are likely to affect the supply of labour to a given occupation:

- monetary rewards
- non-monetary returns.

Monetary rewards

For most of us, the wage or salary offered by an employer will have a major influence on whether or not we are prepared to do a particular job. It follows that higher wage rates provide an incentive for workers to undertake particular jobs. As far as you and I are concerned, higher wages enable us to enjoy a higher standard of living and lower wage rates have the opposite effect. Employers use a whole range of financial incentives to attract workers and to get us to work harder. Thus, the use of commission payments, bonuses and overtime payments provide evidence that many workers are motivated by thoughts of financial return. Moreover, it is not uncommon for those taking on dangerous or unpleasant jobs to be offered higher wages to compensate them.

It has been argued by some economists that there could be an inverse relationship between wage rates and the willingness to work. Higher hourly rates of pay provide workers with the opportunity to work less and enjoy more leisure time. However, as noted on page 58, there is little empirical evidence to support this contention.

Non-monetary factors

Wage rates and salaries are not the only influence on the supply of labour. Human behaviour is complex and many other factors affect the willingness of workers to undertake particular jobs. These include:

- terms and conditions of service
- the status and power attached to a particular job
- job satisfaction
- perks and extra benefits
- social attachments.

Although it is possible to put a price on some of these factors, some people are more highly motivated by non-monetary factors than by the attraction of making loads of money.

High status is as powerful an incentive as monetary reward

The supply of labour is affected by other non-monetary factors, as not all workers are capable of undertaking all jobs. These include:

- skills which can be both innate and learned
- educational and training factors
- qualifications and the time that it takes to achieve them
- social mobility
- migration.

However, in much the same way that we modelled final product markets it is reasonable to assume that, other things being equal, the supply of labour for a particular job is likely to be higher if wage rates rise and lower if they fall. This is illustrated in Figure 4.7.

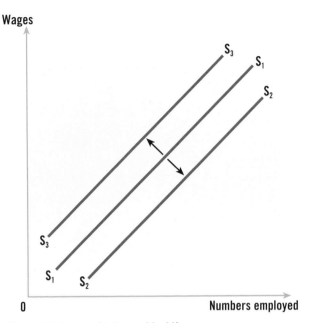

Figure 4.7 Supply of labour with shifts

Any change in any of the non-monetary factors listed above is likely to lead to a shift in supply. Thus, the provision of private medical insurance or a bigger car is likely to lead to a shift from S_1 to S_2 to the right in the supply of labour, whereas worsening terms and conditions of service is likely to reduce the supply of potential workers at each possible wage rate, as shown by the shift from S_1 to S_3.

ACTIVITY ⋯⋗

Rank in order of importance the ten factors that have been identified as non-monetary factors affecting the supply of labour. Justify your choice of the most important and least important factor.

The elasticity of supply of labour

The elasticity of supply of a particular kind of labour will be primarily influenced by the availability of the particular skill needed for a particular job and/or length of training required. It can be argued that some people are born with particular skills which cannot be easily replicated. This would make the supply of this type of labour relatively inelastic. Similarly, if it takes a long time to train a person for a particular job, the supply of that kind of labour will be less responsive to a change in wage rates.

Wage determination in perfectly competitive markets

It is now possible to put the demand and supply analysis together, as shown in Figure 4.8, which indicates that the demand for a particular form of labour will be equal to its supply at a wage rate of *OW*, and that *OE* workers will be employed. If the market were perfectly competitive and the wage rate was above this equilibrium, for example at OW_1, it would cost more to employ some workers than they would be contributing to the revenue of the business. If the business wanted to remain as profitable as possible, it would pay to cut the number of workers employed from *OF* to *OE* until the last worker adds as much to revenue as she or he adds to costs.

Conversely, if wage rates were at W_2, it would pay employers to employ more workers (from *OD* to *OE*),

who would contribute more to revenue than they would to costs.

This analysis indicates that, if firms seek profits in markets that are competitive, and if workers are primarily influenced by what they earn, employers will go on employing more and more workers until the last worker adds as much to revenue as he or she does to costs.

The application of the marginal revenue product (MRP) theory to wage determination is another example of the use of modelling by economists. In this case, any change in factors affecting demand or supply of labour will be followed by changes in the wage rate and numbers employed. Thus, if there is an increase in demand for the final product or service for which labour is required, the MRP and hence the demand curve for labour will shift to the right, throwing this labour market into a short-term disequilibrium. This is illustrated in Figure 4.9 by the shift in demand for labour from D_1 to D_2. If the wage rate remained at *OW*, the demand for labour would exceed the supply and employers of this type of labour would find it difficult to recruit. One way of attracting more workers would be to increase rates of pay. This increase in the wage rate to OW_1 would ensure that this labour market returned to equilibrium and that the numbers employed would increase from *ON* to *OM*.

> **learning tip**
>
> Note the application of a marginal rule – carry on taking on more and more workers until the last worker adds as much to revenue as they do to costs as represented by their wages. An employer who ignores this and employs more workers will add more to costs than to revenue, therefore reducing potential profits.

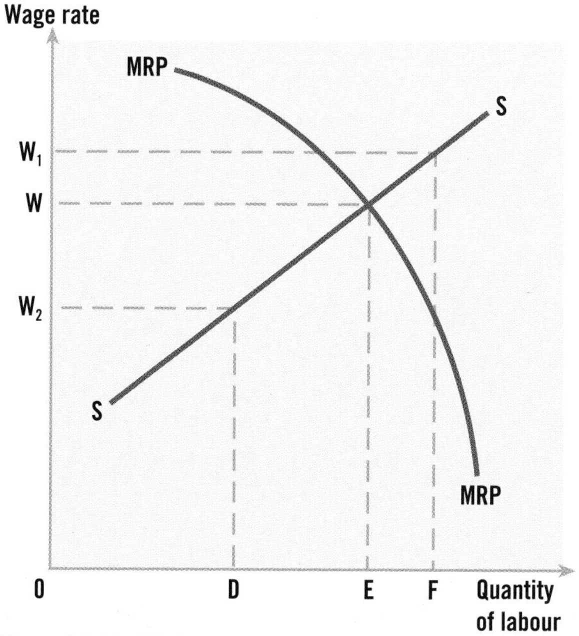

Wage rate

Figure 4.8 Equilibrium wage rate

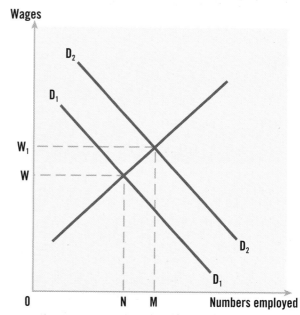

Figure 4.9 Effects of increase in demand for labour

ACTIVITY ····⋮⋮

Use graphs to predict what happens to wage rates and the number of bricklayers employed if the market for their labour were perfectly competitive, when:

a   an improved frost inhibitor for mortar is developed

b   there is trade union action that limits overtime

c   interest rates rise

d   green-belt land is released for building.

learning tip This may sound repetitive, but the AQA specification is clear that you need to understand the likely outcomes in terms of wages and levels of employment if labour markets were perfectly competitive. Just as with the final goods market, it is highly unlikely that all the assumptions underpinning perfect competition are likely to be met. All markets are likely to contain some imperfections, but the perfectly competitive model provides a yardstick by which the efficiency of real-world markets might be judged.

Assessing the role of markets in determining wage rates

The model outlined above is often called a classical or neoclassical theory of wage rates. It is largely derived from the model of perfect competition explained in Chapter 2. The validity of this model can be challenged, especially in respect of its two

principal sets of assumptions, which are that:

● employers seek to maximise profits and are able to calculate the marginal revenue product of each employee and use this information to determine how many workers will be employed

● workers are primarily motivated by monetary considerations and will move from job to job in response to changes in relative wage levels.

The validity of both these sets of assumptions can only be confirmed by empirical study – that is, research into the behaviour of both employers and workers. However, it is possible to explore the appropriateness of these assumptions in greater detail.

STRETCH AND CHALLENGE

How far is it possible to use classical theories of wage determination to account for the differences in earnings between doctors and nurses?

Employer behaviour

Unless they have an A-level or degree in economics, it is unlikely employers would understand you if you asked them, 'What is your marginal revenue product or marginal productivity?' However, ignorance of formal economic concepts does not mean to say that such relationships do not exist. It makes sense from a business point of view not to pay workers more than they bring to a company, and it makes sense to employ more workers if their productivity contributes to greater profits. Thus, while it is unlikely that Tesco, for instance, has calculated the contribution that each shelf-stacker makes to its overall profitability, effective store managers will have some working knowledge of how much work can be expected of each employee on a given shift. It is likely that slow workers will be replaced, and those who work quickly and show initiative be promoted.

Similarly, employers such as Tesco give their store managers large bonuses if profit targets are met or exceeded. In this case, it is possible to see that, although the language of economics might not be used, the principles underlying the theory are broadly applied.

Not all jobs are the same. In some occupations, it is much harder to measure the output of individual workers. If teamwork is important, it is harder to quantify the contribution of each individual, while in other jobs it is difficult to identify the output measures that would be used to measure the productivity of individual workers. How, for example, would you assess the productivity of your teachers and lecturers? Would it be in terms of exam passes, the support given to slow learners, or the intellectual challenge of lessons? Even if it were possible to agree on suitable measures, what would be the best way of relating salaries and numbers employed to outputs? It would be very disruptive to hire and fire teachers at short notice.

Finally, even where employers have found it possible to carefully measure the outputs of individual workers, using these to devise pay and incentive schemes, and to hire and fire at will, can create undesirable side effects. In the 1970s, complicated payment systems in some UK industries such as motor vehicle manufacture, led to industrial conflict and low levels of productivity.

One of a number of causes of this industrial conflict was the existence of very complicated piece-rate payment systems, which were meant to link productivity and pay but had the effect of creating hundreds of different pay scales and thereby creating more problems for managers than the schemes were worth.

This analysis needs testing against the actual behaviour of employers, but it is probably reasonable to conclude that:

● employers who pay workers with no regard to their productivity and contribution to profitability are unlikely to be successful in the long term

● the development of rigid and complicated payment systems and constant hiring and firing of workers can cause lasting damage to worker/employee relationships and thereby damage profitability.

For these reasons, it might be helpful to consider a different kind of demand curve for labour – one that

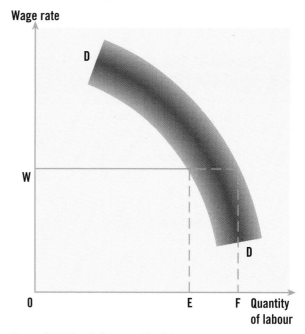

Figure 4.10 Banded demand for labour

is broader and less well defined at the edges, as shown in Figure 4.10 above.

This acknowledges that it is hard to measure the output of each worker. Not only that, it is disruptive to constantly change pay or levels of numbers of workers employed. It also shows that at a given wage rate, *OW* employers would be prepared to employ between *OE* and *OF* workers, only changing the numbers employed if wages or the marginal revenue product were to change significantly.

Worker behaviour

As far as workers are concerned, the response to the simple question 'Does money matter?' is likely to be 'Of course it does, but…'. Most of you reading this book would be better off financially if you were doing something else – for example, stacking shelves at Tesco. You might make the perfectly reasonable economic argument that studying economics is a means to boosting your long-term earnings because it will help you (we hope) to get a better-paid job in the future. But any job? Are you prepared to:

● do something boring for the rest of your life

● move away from family and friends

● work unsocial hours

● do a job that you regarded as unethical

59

- be treated badly by an employer
- work in dangerous conditions?

Clearly, these considerations will have different effects on different individuals. But for some, these non-monetary factors will be important, and for this reason it is perhaps a mistake to represent the supply of labour as a single upward-sloping demand curve from left to right showing a very precise relationship between pay levels and the willingness of particular workers to do a given job.

Habit, social obligation and inertia are all factors that will have the effect of limiting the mobility of labour between different occupations. However, as with employers and the profit motive, it would be foolish of economists to ignore the significance of pay rates and their influence on the supply of labour. You will know by now that economists like symmetrical arguments. It will therefore come as little surprise that it might be more helpful to represent the supply of labour as a band rather than a curve. This is illustrated in Figure 4.11, which shows that a given number of workers will be prepared to work at a particular job for between OW and OW_1. Some of these workers will seek work elsewhere if the wage rate falls below OW. The supply of workers will only increase at wage rates above OW_1. This revised application of the demand and supply model may be more realistic and could

be added to the demand curve in Figure 4.10. This is illustrated in Figure 4.13.

If this is a more accurate representation of the labour market, there will not be a unique point of equilibrium between demand and supply of labour and this could lead to greater stability in wage rates and the numbers employed. However, should demand and supply conditions lead to a wage rate outside of the area *abcd*, wage rates and the numbers employed would change.

learning tip Remember that traditional (classical) theory of wage determination is based on the assumption that both workers and employers are primarily influenced by wage rates in deciding both the demand and supply of labour. This may be an over-simplification of behaviour and may limit the usefulness of this part of economic theory. On the other hand, wage rates clearly influence both the demand and supply of labour.

ECONOMICS IN CONTEXT

GROWING INCOME INEQUALITY IN THE UK

Over the last 20 years or so, there has been a great increase in wage inequalities which has been particularly marked in the USA and the UK. Three possible explanations have been offered to explain these trends.

One theory is that increased trade with developing countries has pushed down the prices of goods produced by less skilled workers.

Another suggestion is that technical change, especially the ongoing IT revolution, has increased demand for skilled workers, pushing up their wages relative to the wages of the unskilled.

Third, it has been argued that trade unions have been responsible for increasing inequalities by increasing the incomes of union members relative to non-unionised workers.

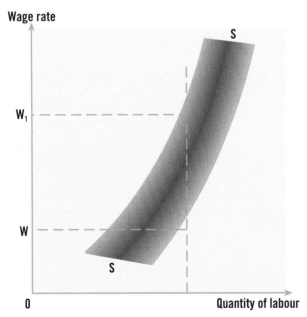

Figure 4.11 Banded supply added to demand

ACTIVITY ····⋮⋮⋮

How might wage rates for catering workers in the UK be affected by the following?

a increased barriers to those immigrating to the UK

b a cut in interest rates

c an increase in the value of the pound.

ACTIVITY ····⋮⋮⋮

Use demand and supply analysis to show how each of these possible explanations might account for growing inequalities in incomes in the UK.

STRETCH AND CHALLENGE

What evidence would you collect in attempting to evaluate the validity of these three possible explanations of income inequalities in the UK?

Imperfections in the labour market

Many factors affect how labour markets actually work in practice. Three important factors which may lead to imperfections in the labour market are:

● trade unions

● monopsonistic employers

● imperfect or asymmetric information.

Trade unions

Trade unions can have a direct impact on labour markets. This should come as little surprise, as they were set up to improve the pay and conditions of workers. Although their functions have become more diverse, it is argued that they exist to serve the best interests of their members, and protecting and improving on pay and conditions of those at work will always be important.

Trade unions and employers may engage in collective bargaining to agree pay and conditions. This can happen at national level, where employers and unions will come together to determine nationally agreed pay and conditions – for example, the fire brigade's union and local authority organisations representing their employers. The same process may take place at plant level. But in other cases, in which employers do not recognise trade unions, little may be achieved collectively.

Trade unions in the UK developed in the nineteenth century at a time when workers were often exploited. Pay rates were often low, workers' safety was ignored and employment was commonly very insecure. In these cases, the power relationship between individual workers and their employers was very one-sided. If an individual worker objected to some aspect of employment, he or she could be fired or sacked at will. Although not all workers were members, trade unions were able to counter this imbalance in power. The threat of strike or other industrial action posed a direct threat to the profitability of the business in question.

The membership card of the first national trade union in Britain

Economists have used the models of the labour market to try to assess the impact of trade unions. Neoclassical (right-wing) economists have tended to argue that anything that disturbs the free working of labour markets as outlined on pages 52–58 will have a negative effect on employment. Figure 4.12 can be used to illustrate that union efforts to push up wage rates from *OW* to, say, *OW₁* will result in falling levels of employment from *OE* to *OE₂*. In this model, trade union intervention may secure higher wages for some but only at the expense of an increase in unemployment.

In the UK, there is little direct empirical support for this argument. This is because historically, in the UK, increasing union activity has been associated with increasing prosperity. Similarly, trade unions appear to have less influence in times of recession. It is hard to pin down cause and effect. For example, greater trade union militancy in the UK motor industry in the 1970s, and in printing and mining in the 1980s, was associated with significant redundancy, which can also be explained by structural changes in those industries. Nonetheless, the role of trade unions and their possible impact on both wages and employment levels is hotly debated.

The argument that trade union activity directly pushes up unemployment is, perhaps, rather crude,

as shown by the application of the revised labour market model introduced in outline on page 57 earlier in this chapter.

In this case, the lozenge-shaped area *abcd* shown in Figure 4.13 contains a range of different combinations of wage and employment levels, which would all be acceptable to both workers and employers.

Should trade unions attempt to push wages up above *OW*, then it is likely that conflict between unions and employers would occur that could result in unemployment. This might provide a more convincing explanation of the possible impact of trade unions on competitive labour markets.

Monopsonistic employers

In some cases, there is only one employer of workers in a particular industry. They are called **monopsonists**. The analysis in the previous section was based on

> **DEFINITION**
>
> **Monopsonist:** a monopoly employer of a particular type of labour

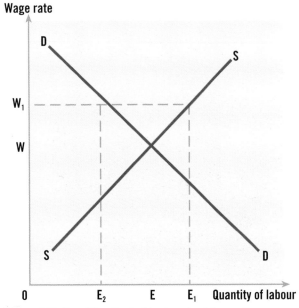

Figure 4.12 Possible effect of trade union intervention

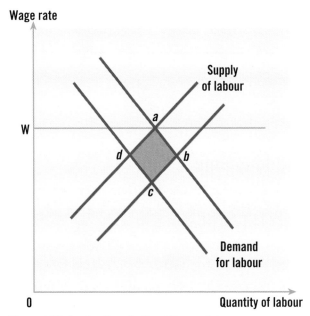

Figure 4.13 Application of alternative model

the assumption that there is competition between employers for particular types of workers. This might not always be the case. Many workers in Cornwall, for example, are dependent on a small number of large employers who are able to use their market power to pay lower wages than would be found in other parts of the country. In extreme circumstances, there may be only one employer of a particular type of labour – a monopsonist. Thus, the local police force is the only employer of policemen and women in a particular area.

In theory, a monopsonistic employer has market power in a similar way to a monopolist. They can, in theory, force down wage rates below the level that would be set in a more competitive market. This possibility is represented in Figure 4.14, in which *ACL* represents the supply of labour, showing the average wage rate that is paid to each worker.

If a monopsonist wanted to attract another worker, it would have to pay more than the average cost of the labour currently employed. Moreover, it would probably have to pay this higher rate to all those workers it already employs.

Conversely, employing fewer workers will cut the firm's wage bill. Thus, the marginal labour cost to a monopsonist will be higher than the average cost. If this firm wishes to maximise its profits, it will go on employing workers until the last person taken on adds as much to the firm's revenue as he or she adds to costs. This level of employment is represented by employment level *OE*, but the monopsonist will only have to pay out *OW* in wages. However, if this market were competitive, competition between rival employers would drive the wage rate up to *OW₁* and lead to the employment of *OE₁* workers.

BILATERAL MONOPOLY

What if a monopsonist is faced with a workforce that is 100 per cent unionised? This is called a **bilateral monopoly**. Both those demanding labour and those regulating its supply will have monopoly power.

> ### DEFINITION
>
> **Bilateral monopoly:** the combination of a *monopsonist* and a single supplier of labour – usually a trade union or professional association

Unfortunately, the graphical analysis used to model what happens in labour markets is of limited use. Wages and levels of employment will be influenced by demand and supply conditions, but they will be determined by the relative bargaining strengths of the two sides.

If the trade union is relatively strong, it will be able to push up wage levels and maintain levels of employment until that point at which the survival of the business is threatened.

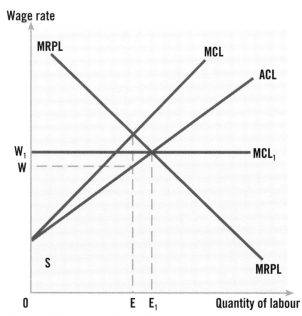

Wage rate

Figure 4.14 Monopsonistic labour market

Nike does not recognise trade unions in the Philippines

On the other hand, a relatively powerful employer will be able to push wages down to the level that it would pay if workers did not have a trade union to defend pay and conditions. In this case, wages will be forced down to subsistence levels – as is the case in the UK with some outworkers and in developing countries like Cambodia and the Philippines, where trade unions are not recognised by companies such as Nike and Gap.

ACTIVITY ·····⊱

Use graphical analysis to suggest how a monopsonistic employer might respond to:

a   an increase in demand for the product produced

b   the threat of a strike from a trade union representing the majority of the workforce

c   adverse publicity because of exploitation of workers in developing countries.

Imperfect information

One source of market failure identified in your AS course related to asymmetric information. This describes a situation in which buyers and sellers of a product or service have different levels of knowledge about the qualities and characteristics of what they might be buying or selling. An outcome of this could be that consumers undervalue or overvalue a particular product or service, resulting in an equilibrium that does not necessarily lead to an optimum allocation of resources. In the worst case scenario, this can lead to market failure. For example, if a company selling second-hand cars gets a bad reputation, it may fail to sell any cars.

The same reasoning can be applied to the labour market. In a simple form, employers might have little idea of the potential availability of workers with particular skills and this may lead them to offer more than would be needed to ensure the supply of particular kinds of workers. Similarly, employees may have imperfect knowledge of the different types of jobs and accompanying wage rates that might be available, leading them to accept jobs paying less than they may be able to receive from other employers.

Empirical research tends to indicate that asymmetric information applies to the labour market. Employers, especially those with specialist human resource functions, tend to have a better understanding of labour market information than those involved in job searching, whether they are already in employment or unemployed. Evidence indicates that time is a significant constraint on job searching and research in the early 1990s indicated that workers typically receive around 10 per cent less than they might reasonably be expected to earn if they had better labour market information.

ACTIVITY ·····⊱

Assess the contention that the Internet helps provide those searching for employment with more complete labour market information. You could do this by investigating possible wages/salaries in a career of your choice

---

Government intervention in labour markets

Governments intervene in labour markets, just as they do in other markets. Intervention takes many forms, including limiting the power of trade unions (see page 146 in Chapter 6), providing funding to increase training opportunities, passing health and safety legislation, regulating immigration, and imposing minimum wages. The introduction of the latter in the UK in 1998 was particularly controversial at the time, as it was argued by both employers and some economists that such intervention would result in business failure and increased unemployment. These fears were not realised.

Governments of different countries intervene in labour markets to try to ensure that workers receive what might be considered a socially acceptable level of pay. In the UK, since October 2007, workers aged 22 and over should receive at least £5.52 per hour.

Legal minimum wage rates were introduced by the Labour government in 1999. At the time it was argued that the effect of these might be to create unemployment in those industries in which prevailing

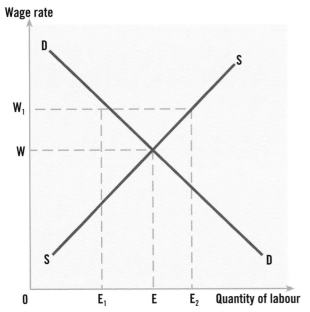

Figure 4.15 Possible impact of introduction of minimum wage

levels of pay were below what was to become the legal minimum. This argument is demonstrated in Figure 4.15. This shows the wage rate set at OW_1, above the market-determined equilibrium of OW, giving a demand for labour at OE_1, whereas the supply would be OE_2. In other words, fewer workers would be employed than would be the case if the wage rate were at the equilibrium of OW.

Although many argued that the result of the introduction of the minimum wage would be to push up unemployment, this does not appear to have happened. In the UK in 1998, the claimant count stood at 1.4 million and in January 2008 this had fallen to 0.8 million. This could be accounted for in many ways, not least government measures making it more difficult to claim benefit. However, the other measure of unemployment the labour force survey shows a fall (if a smaller one) in the same period from 1.8 million to 1.65 million.

The falling rate of unemployment since the introduction of the minimum wage could be explained in one of two ways:

- the introduction of the minimum wage coincided with an increase in demand for workers – this is illustrated in Figure 4.16 below

- the increase was not sufficiently large to change the behaviour of employers and workers, as shown in Figure 4.17.

Wage discrimination

This section takes account of a current trend in economics to focus on institutions, as much as on theory, in order to develop a more effective understanding of how economic institutions work.

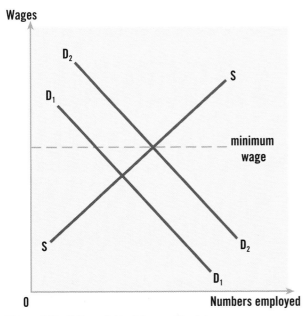

Figure 4.16 Shift to right of demand for labour

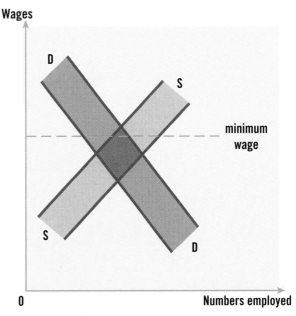

Figure 4.17 Bands

In some cases, it is hard to use traditional economic analysis to explain why particular groups of workers get paid different amounts from other groups of workers. There is evidence of different forms of discrimination in the job market relating to:

- gender
- ethnicity
- social class.

Gender discrimination

Although women in the UK are protected by legislation that makes it unlawful to pay them less than men if they do the same or similar work, there are persistent differences in the pay received by men compared to that received by women. This is illustrated in Figure 4.18.

The Labour government in power in 2008 uses the concept of the gender pay gap to measure progress made in narrowing the gap between the earnings of men and women. This indicates that the gap between the hourly earnings of men and women is narrowing. In 1974, women earned 30 per cent less per hour than men. In the last 27 years, this gap has dropped to 19 per cent. But, as with the other data, these statistics probably underestimate the gender gap, as men tend to work long hours.

The Labour government identified five key factors to explain the gender pay gap:

- human capital differences
- part-time working
- travel patterns
- occupational segregation
- workplace segregation.

HUMAN CAPITAL DIFFERENCES

These are differences in educational levels and work experience. Historically, differences in the levels of qualifications held by men and women have contributed to the pay gap. However, women are still more likely than men to have breaks from paid work to care for children and other dependants. It can be argued that these breaks have an effect on women's level of work experience, which in turn is argued to explain why women generally get paid less than men.

PART-TIME WORKING

The pay gap between women working part time and men working full time is particularly large and, as a large proportion of women work part time, this is a major contributor to the gender pay gap. Some of this gap is due to part-time workers having lower levels of

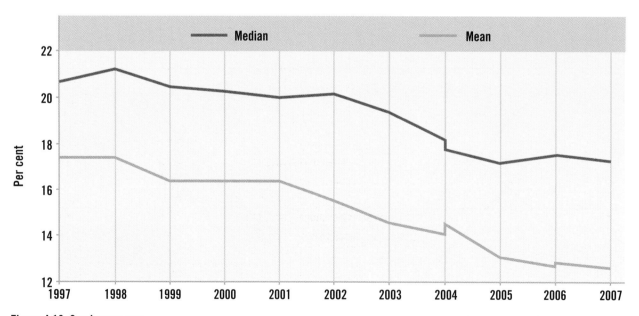

Figure 4.18 Gender pay gap
Source: Office of National Statistics. © Crown 2008

qualifications and less work experience. However, it is also due to part-time work being concentrated in less well-paid occupations.

TRAVEL PATTERNS

On average, women spend less time commuting than men. This may be because of time constraints due to balancing work and caring responsibilities. It can have an effect on women's pay in two ways. Women may have a smaller pool of jobs to choose from, and there may also be lots of women wanting work in the same location (that is, near to where they live), resulting in lower wages for those jobs.

OCCUPATIONAL SEGREGATION

As identified earlier, women's employment is highly concentrated in certain occupations – 60 per cent of working women work in just ten occupations, and

these are often the lowest paid occupations (see Tables 4.1 and 4.2). In addition, women are still under-represented in the higher-paid jobs within occupations – the 'glass ceiling' effect, which is used to describe the difficulties women have in gaining promotion to higher-paid jobs within organisations.

WORKPLACE SEGREGATION

At the level of individual workplaces, high concentrations of female employees are associated with relatively low rates of pay. And higher levels of part-time working are also associated with lower rates of pay, even after other factors have been taken into account.

Other factors that affect the gender pay gap include:

- job-grading practices
- appraisal systems

occupation	average gross weekly earnings	
	men	women
managers and senior officals	464.5	287.5
health professionals	1,059.0	725.0
teaching and research professionals	640.3	556.3
business and public service professionals	670.8	546.1
all technical occupations	537.2	421.6
health	473.8	427.8
public services	640.0	550.9
culture and media	451.5	364.1
business and public service	561.9	415.2
all administrative	358.4	284.2
secretarial	272.6	264.8
skilled agriculture	316.1	270.6
skilled metal and electrical	471.3	364.3
skilled construction	423.7	x
caring	289.2	213.9
sales and customer service	225.6	155.3
process plant and machinery operatives	402.4	262.0
transport drivers and operators	394.5	250.0
unskilled	292.5	126.9

Table 4.1 Gender differences in gross weekly pay
Source: Office of National Statistics. © Crown 2008

- reward systems and retention measures
- wage-setting practices
- discrimination.

In short, gender discrimination is deeply rooted within our society and is the result of social influences as much as it is of economic influences.

ACTIVITY ····⫶⫶

Assess the validity of the contention that women earn less than men because they have a lower marginal revenue productivity.

Ethnic and women workers tend to earn less than their white male counterparts

Ethnic discrimination

Although it is unlawful in the UK, workers from ethnic minority groups tend to be paid less than those who are white. This is illustrated in Figure 4.19. It appears that the factors resulting in discrimination against females in the workplace also apply to those from minority ethnic groups.

Racism can actually contribute to greater inequalities. If an employer believes that workers from minority ethnic backgrounds are somehow less productive than their white colleagues, the employer will perceive that their marginal revenue productivity is lower than it actually is. Economic analysis predicts

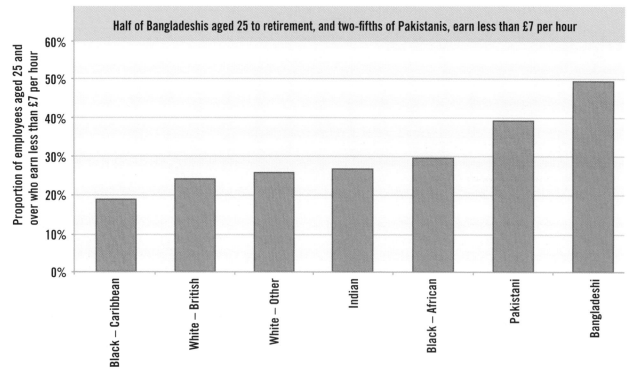

Figure 4.19 Data on ethic discrimination (average for 2005–2007; updated April 2008)
Source: Office of National Statistics. © Crown 2008

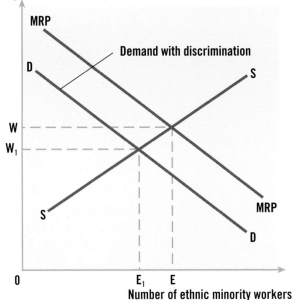

Figure 4.20 Effects of ethnic discrimination

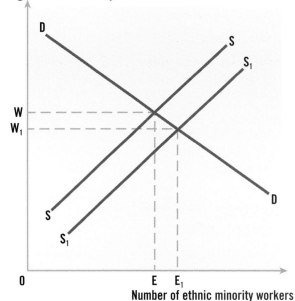

Figure 4.21 Effects of no ethnic discrimination

that the wage rate paid to workers from minority ethnic backgrounds will be below the allocatively efficient level, as Figure 4.20 shows.

This discrimination is likely to have a knock-on effect throughout the labour market. Those who cannot gain employment with the discriminating employer will seek employment with those employers who do not discriminate. This will increase the supply of

labour to the non-discriminating employers and lower the wage rate, as shown in Figure 4.21.

ACTIVITY ···❖

How far can differences in unemployment between different ethnic groups be explained using economic concepts?

ECONOMICS IN CONTEXT

ETHNIC GROUPS 'FACE JOB BATTLE'

Unemployment among ethnic minority communities is twice that of white workers, the TUC has said. It blames the employment gap on firms discriminating against candidates from ethnic minority communities.

Overall, 11 per cent of people from ethnic minorities are unemployed, compared with 5 per cent of white workers.

The TUC has warned that unless ethnic minority unemployment is tackled, then the government will fail to reach its target of eliminating child poverty by 2020.

'If one or both parents in a family are out of work, there is less money to go around, and as more black

and Asian adults are out of work, more ethnic minority children than white children are currently living in poverty,' said Brendan Barber, TUC general secretary.

He urged the government to start up job creation schemes and only to award public work contracts to firms that demonstrated a commitment to counter any form of discrimination.

'Active job creation schemes targeted on areas of high unemployment are a must if we are not to continue to see huge differences in the numbers of black and white people out of work,' Mr Barber added.

Discrimination by social class

It is, perhaps, less likely that employers actively discriminate according to the class that workers are perceived to have come from. However, the persistence of occupational immobility indicates that there are still strong social pressures limiting the access of children from working-class backgrounds to study at university and to work in some professions. Lack of appropriate qualifications can provide a significant barrier to occupational mobility.

The costs of negative discrimination

Negative discrimination can impose costs on a number of groups.

The group discriminated against clearly suffers. People within it are likely to be paid less than other workers doing the same job. They are also likely to find it harder to get jobs that fully utilise their abilities, or indeed any job. They may be overlooked for promotion and may not be selected to go on training courses. The existence of discrimination may discourage members from the discriminated group from applying for well-paid jobs and working for higher qualifications.

Producers who discriminate have a smaller pool of labour to select from. They may also not make the best use of any ethnic minority or female workers they employ. This will raise their costs of production and make them less competitive against rival firms at home and abroad.

Consumers will experience higher prices if producers discriminate.

The government may have to pay out more welfare benefits to groups that are discriminated against, and may have to spend time and money on legislation to end discrimination and tackle social tension.

The economy will lose out as a result of the misallocation of resources. Output will be below the potential output, which could be achieved if the group were not discriminated against in terms of employment, pay, promotion and training.

ACTIVITY ···⟡

In the UK in 2007, solicitors earned, on average, £900 a week, while secondary school teachers earned £610. As a class group, draw up a list of reasons why, in the light of this wage differential, most teachers did not become solicitors.

Inequalities in wealth and income

In all countries of the world, there are inequalities in the distribution of wealth and income. The existence of inequalities can provoke vigorous political and moral debate; extreme inequalities can lead to social unrest. Some economists and politicians would argue that inequalities in wealth and income are a necessary prerequisite for the effective working of economies, while others might contend that such arguments are merely a rationalisation for the existence of inequalities which are not morally justifiable.

> **learning tip**
>
> Watch out! This is potentially dangerous territory for a young economist, as the distinction between normative and positive economics can become very blurred.

Wealth is very unequally distributed among the UK population

Inequalities in wealth and income tend to go hand in hand. Wealthy people own more assets, such as property, stocks and shares, and the ownership of assets such as these generates income. Poorer people own fewer assets and therefore are less likely to generate income other than by selling their labour. The poorest are usually unable to sell their labour.

Throughout most of the twentieth century, income and wealth became more evenly distributed. However, the last two decades of the twentieth century saw a reversal of this trend and, now, at the start of the twenty-first century, a quarter of the UK population live in households with incomes below half the national average.

Wealth

Wealth is a stock of assets that have a financial value. The distribution of wealth can be considered in terms of how it is distributed between the population (size distribution), of the forms in which it is held, and according to the characteristics of

> **DEFINITION**
>
> **Wealth:** the value of assets at any point in time

those holding wealth. Table 4.2 shows the size distribution of marketable wealth between 1976 and 2003.

This table shows that, although there was a dip in 1986, the distribution of wealth in the UK has become more unequal. If the value of dwellings is excluded, half the population shares 1 per cent of the nation's wealth, while almost a third of wealth is owned by the wealthiest 1 per cent of the population.

WEALTH DISTRIBUTION BETWEEN DIFFERENT GROUPS

As would be expected, wealth is unevenly distributed between age categories. For example, people in their 40s and 50s have had more time to accumulate

United Kingdom Marketable wealth Percentage of wealth owned by:	Percentages							
Year	1976	1986	1996	1999	2000	2001	2002	2003
Most wealthy 1%	21	18	20	23	23	22	24	21
Most wealthy 5%	38	36	40	43	44	42	45	40
Most wealthy 10%	50	50	52	55	56	54	57	53
Most wealthy 25%	71	73	74	75	75	72	75	72
Most wealthy 50%	92	90	93	94	95	94	94	93
Total marketable wealth (£ billion)	280	955	2,092	2,861	3,131	3,477	3,588	3,783
Marketable wealth less value of dwellings Percentage of wealth owned by:	Percentages							
Most wealthy 1%	29	25	26	34	33	34	37	34
Most wealthy 5%	47	46	49	59	59	58	62	58
Most wealthy 10%	57	58	63	72	73	72	74	71
Most wealthy 25%	73	75	81	87	89	88	87	85
Most wealthy 50%	88	89	94	97	98	98	98	99

Table 4.2 Marketable wealth between 1976 and 2003

savings than people in their 20s and 30s, and do indeed have greater wealth.

However, the amount of wealth held also varies between ethnic groups and genders. White adults have more wealth than adults from ethnic minorities. The group that currently has the lowest holding of wealth per head is people with a Bangladeshi background. Men also have more wealth than women.

CAUSES OF THE INEQUALITY OF WEALTH

The causes of the inequality of wealth are obviously linked to the sources of wealth and include the following:

● *the pattern of inheritance.* In the UK, significant holdings of wealth have traditionally been passed on to the next generation on the basis of primogeniture (the right of the eldest son to inherit to the exclusion of others). Indeed, major estates and connected titles are still passed on to the eldest son. But in countries where property and other assets are distributed among the children on the death of their parents, wealth becomes more evenly distributed over time.

● *marriage patterns of the wealthy.* The wealthy tend to marry other wealthy people. This further concentrates wealth in the hands of the few.

● *inequality of income.* As already noted, people with high incomes are more able to save and earn interest.

● *different propensities to save.* Those who save a higher proportion of their income will accumulate more wealth than those who save a smaller proportion.

● *luck.* This plays a part in terms of the success of businesses that people start and in terms of who wins money.

> **DEFINITION**
>
> **Income:** earnings to the owners of factors of production over time

Distribution of income

Whereas wealth is a stock with a given value at a given point of time, **income**, in the form of wages, rents, profits and interest payments, is regarded as a flow earned over a given period of time. In the UK, as in most other countries, income is less unequally distributed than wealth. Within a country the distribution of income can be considered in terms of how income is shared out between the factors of production (functional distribution of income), between households (size distribution) and between geographical areas (geographical distribution of income). Table 4.3 shows that the richest 1 per cent of the population receives 8.6 per cent of the national income whereas the poorer 90 per cent share 59.5 per cent.

THE FUNCTIONAL DISTRIBUTION OF INCOME

Income is a flow of money over a period of time. It can be earned by labour in the form of wages, by capital in the form of interest, by land in the form of rent and by entrepreneurs in the form of profits. In the UK, wages still account for the largest percentage. However, this percentage is falling. In 1987, 61 per cent of household income came from wages, but by 1997 it was down to 56 per cent. By contrast, income from dividends, interest and rent (collectively known as investment income) has been rising.

In addition to earned income and investment income, households can receive income in the form of social security benefit. The relative shares of earned income, investment income and transfer payments depend on a variety of factors, but principally on the level of employment and the relative power of labour and capital.

SIZE DISTRIBUTION OF INCOME IN THE UK

In recent years, the distribution of income in the UK has become more unequal. The widening of the gap between those with high incomes and those with low incomes was particularly noticeable between 1980 and 1990, and again since 1997.

There were a number of reasons for this rise in income equality. One was the cut in the top tax rates, which benefited the rich. Another was the rise in top executive pay, which was sparked initially by privatisation. At the other end of the income range, there was a decrease in the real value of benefits – particularly Jobseeker's Allowance – and a rise in the number of lone parents.

The percentage of families with dependent children that are headed by lone parents more than doubled between 1971 and 1996. The lack of support in bringing up the children means lone parents are often not in work or only in part-time jobs.

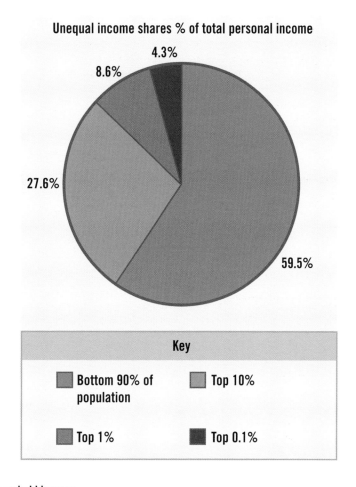

Unequal income shares % of total personal income

Key	
■ Bottom 90% of population	■ Top 10%
■ Top 1%	■ Top 0.1%

Table 4.3 Distribution of household income

Source: Institute for Fiscal Studies: SPI, 2004/5 figures

ECONOMICS IN CONTEXT

MEASURING THE SIZE DISTRIBUTION OF WEALTH AND INCOME

A common method of measuring the degree of inequality of income and wealth distribution between households is the **Lorenz curve.** This is named after the US statistician Max Otto Lorenz.

As well as measuring the extent of industrial concentration, a *Lorenz curve* can be used to compare the distribution of income and wealth over time and between countries.

As shown in Figure 4.22, the horizontal axis measures the percentage of the population, starting with the poorest. In the case of income distribution, the vertical axis measures the percentage of income earned. A 45 degree line is included. This is called the line of income equality, because it shows a situation in which, for example, 40 per cent of the population earns 40 per cent of the income and 80 per cent of the population earns 80 per cent of the income. The

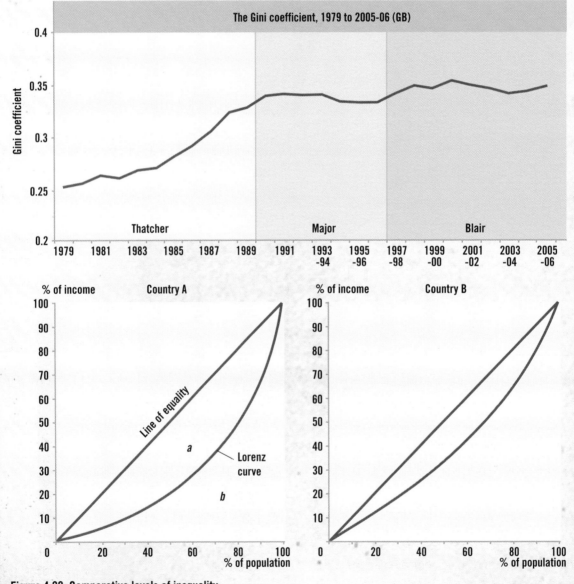

Figure 4.22 Comparative levels of inequality

actual cumulative percentage income shares are then included on the diagram.

In practice, this will form a curve that starts at the origin and ends with 100 per cent of the population earning 100 per cent of income, but this lies below the 45 degree line. The greater the degree of inequality, the greater the extent to which the curve will be below the 45 degree line. Figure 4.22 shows that income is more unevenly distributed in country A than in country B.

The **Gini coefficient** measures precisely the degree of inequality shown on a Lorenz curve. In Figure 4.22, this is the ratio of a/a + b. Complete equality would give a ratio of 0 and the bigger the difference the greater the value giving a theoretical possibility of complete inequality equalling 1. In practice, the ratio will lie between 0 and 1, and the nearer it is to 1, the more unequal the distribution of income.

DEFINITIONS

Lorenz curve: a graphs used to measure the extent of income inequality

Gini coefficient: a numerical value used to measure the extent of income inequality

CAUSES OF INCOME INEQUALITY BETWEEN HOUSEHOLDS

These include:

● *unequal holdings of wealth.* As wealth generates income in the form of profit, interest and dividends, differentials in wealth cause differences in income.

● *differences in the composition of households.* Some households may have, say, three adults working, whereas other households may have no one in employment. Indeed, low income is closely associated with a dependency on benefits.

● *differences in skills and qualifications.* Those with high skills and qualifications are likely to be in high demand and hence likely to be able to earn high incomes.

● *differences in educational opportunities.* Those who have the opportunity to stay in education for longer are likely to gain more qualifications and develop more skills and so, as indicated above, are likely to increase their earning potential. Indeed, lifetime earnings of graduates are noticeably higher than those of non-graduates.

● *discrimination.* The income of some groups is adversely affected by discrimination in terms of employment, pay and promotion opportunities.

● *differences in hours worked.* Most full-time workers earn more than part-time workers, and those who work overtime earn more than those who work the standard hours.

● *taxation policy.* Wealth is less heavily taxed than income and this along with regressive taxes redistributes income from the poor to the rich.

GEOGRAPHICAL DISTRIBUTION OF INCOME

Income is unevenly distributed between the regions of the UK. For example, in 1997 the average disposable

Region	Average gross weekly income
	(UK Index = 100)
North East	165
North West	183
Yorkshire & Humberside	182
East Midlands	191
West Midlands	189
East	218
London	264
South East	258
South West	194
England	212
Wales	158
Scotland	183
Northern Ireland	142

Table 4.4 Average gross weekly income

income per head was £11,084 in London, £8,661 in Scotland and only £8,464 in Northern Ireland. Table 4.4 shows average gross weekly income for the period 1998–2001 in the different regions of the UK.

However, there are variations within regions not illustrated in this data. Thus, London as a whole has a high income per head, but also includes some of the most deprived districts in the UK.

> **learning tip**
>
> For your exam, you need to remember that, for many people, the most important forms of wealth they hold are their homes and their pension rights. Wealth is very unevenly distributed in the UK. The wealthiest 10 per cent of the population own 50 per cent of the wealth. The main cause of this inequality is inheritance. Differences in holdings of wealth give rise to differences of income. Other causes of the inequality of income are differences in earnings ability (which, in turn, reflect differences in skills and qualifications) and differences in the composition of households. Income is more evenly distributed than wealth, although the last two decades have witnessed a rise in inequality.

ACTIVITY ····⟩

Using the information given in Table 4.4, plot Lorenz curves for the distribution of marketable wealth between 1976 and 2000.

Poverty and government policy

The meaning, measurement, causes and effects of poverty

One of the main outcomes of the unequal distribution of wealth and income in the UK economy is that it results in poverty. In the last two decades, the number of households with incomes below 60 per cent of average income has risen. It is estimated, for example, that in the UK a third of children (4.5 million) live in poverty. This section discusses the meaning, measurement and consequences of poverty.

ABSOLUTE POVERTY

Economists distinguish between **absolute poverty** and **relative poverty**. People are said to be in absolute poverty when their income is insufficient for them

ECONOMICS IN CONTEXT

BRITAIN SHAMED BY CHILD POVERTY

Even if all parents available for work managed to get jobs, child poverty in the UK would only fall by two-thirds, according to a Unicef report: Child Poverty in Rich Nations.

This is because about half of people living in poverty are in households where parents can't work – because of sickness, disability or the age of children – or because the minimum wage would still leave them earning too little.

Child poverty can only be addressed through a complex strategy aimed at reducing the number of children in workless households, reducing severe wage inequalities and cutting poverty among lone-parent families, the report concludes. Narrowing the gap between state benefits and the average wage will also be necessary.

The research, which examined data from the 23 OECD (Organisation for Economic Co-operation and Development) nations, found that Sweden, Norway, Finland, Belgium, Luxembourg and Denmark were the top six countries for having low levels of both relative and absolute child poverty.

The UK came a poor 20th for relative child poverty and 14th out of 16 countries for which absolute poverty figures were available.

Sweden and Norway had among the highest numbers of lone parent families and Finland and Belgium among the highest proportions of workless households. But these indicators were compensated for by reduced wage inequalities and state benefit payments near to the average wage, while the UK has wide income inequality.

to be able to afford basic shelter, food and clothing. Even in rich countries, there are some people who still do not have any housing. It has been estimated that in England in 2000 there were 1,600 people sleeping rough. Of course, the problem of absolute poverty is more extensive in poor countries.

DEFINITIONS

Absolute poverty: those living on incomes below a given threshold

Relative poverty: poverty in relationship to average levels of wealth and income in a given economy

RELATIVE POVERTY

While people in the UK may consider themselves poor if they are living in poor accommodation, have a television but no video recorder and can only afford to go out once a week, people in, say, Mali might regard themselves as well off if they had the same standard of living. This reflects the difference between absolute and relative poverty.

People are relatively poor when they are poor in comparison to other people. They are those who are unable to afford a certain standard of living at a particular time. As a result, they are unable to participate in the usual activities of the society in which they live.

Table 4.5 is based on three items that most people in the European Union (EU) might have expected to be able to afford in 1995, and gives some indication of differences in living standards across the EU. The UK does not compare well with the other countries. The UK, Portugal and Greece had a relatively high percentage of households who did not appear to be enjoying a high living standard. Of course, if the same items were considered for most developing countries, the figures would be much higher.

Relative poverty varies between countries and over time. Someone who is regarded as poor in the USA might be regarded as relatively rich in, for example,

Ethiopia. Fifteen years ago in the UK, a personal computer might have been regarded as something of a luxury for a household. However, these days it might be viewed as necessary to participate in the activities of society.

If a country experiences a rise in income, absolute poverty may fall. However, if those on high incomes benefit more than those on low incomes, relative poverty may rise.

	Eat meat every other day %	New clothes %	A week's holiday %
Portugal	6	47	59
Greece	35	32	51
Spain	2	9	49
United Kingdom	10	15	40
Irish Republic	4	7	38
Italy	6	15	38
France	5	10	34
Belgium	4	10	26
Austria	8	10	24
Denmark	2	5	16
Netherlands	2	13	15
Luxembourg	3	5	14
Germany	5	15	12

Source: Social Trends 29, 1999, Office for National Statistics

Table 4.5 Percentage of households that did not feel that they could afford certain items, 1995

MEASURING POVERTY

To assess the extent to which poverty is a problem, it has to be measured. Economists often define as poor those whose income is less than 60 per cent of the average income (adjusted to take account of family size).

The current Labour government (first elected in 1997) has set itself the task of eradicating child poverty within a generation and now publishes a poverty audit. This includes poverty statistics and assesses the government's performance against a set of indicators in the form of targets. The first poverty audit came out in September 1999. It found that:

● one-quarter of the population were living in households with incomes below the poverty line of £132 a week – half the national average income

● one-third of all children (4.5 million) lived in poverty – three times the number in 1979

● more than half of the 5.6 million people claiming income support, Jobseeker's Allowance and incapacity benefit had been on benefits for more than two years

● one-fifth of children lived in households where nobody worked – which was twice the 1979 level

● the proportion of families with dependent children that are headed by lone parents increased from 8 per cent to 21 per cent in 1996.

Among the government's targets are:

● an increase in the proportion of working-age people with a qualification

● improving literacy and numeracy at age 11

● reducing the proportion of older people unable to afford to heat their homes properly

● reducing the number of households with low incomes

● reducing homelessness

● reducing the number of children in workless households.

Particular groups are more prone to poverty than others. These include the old, the disabled, the sick, lone parents with children, the unemployed and those from ethnic minorities. For example, in 1995/96, 66 per cent of Pakistani/Bangladeshi households were in the bottom fifth, and in 1996/97, 42 per cent of lone parent families were in the bottom fifth of the income distribution.

CAUSES OF POVERTY

Essentially, the amount of poverty experienced depends on the level of income achieved and how it is distributed. The reasons why particular people are poor include the following:

● *unemployment.* This is a major cause of poverty, with some households having no one in employment.

● *low wages.* Some workers in unskilled, casual employment earn very low wages. For example, a significant proportion of workers in Northern Ireland and the north-east are on low wages. However, just because someone earns low wages does not necessarily mean he or she is poor. It is possible that this person could live in a household with a high-income earning partner or parents.

● *sickness and disability.* Most of the long-term sick and disabled are dependent on benefits and this takes them into the low-income category.

● *old age.* For pensioners, state benefits are the largest source of income. However, occupational pensions and investment income are forming an increasing proportion of the income of some of the old.

● *the poverty trap.* This arises when the poor find it difficult to raise their disposable income because any rise in gross income results in them having to pay more in taxes and receiving less in benefits.

● *being a lone parent.* Not having a partner to cope with the raising of a child may make it difficult for someone to obtain full-time employment.

● *reluctance to claim benefits.* A number of people do not claim benefits that could help to supplement their incomes. This is because either they are unaware of their entitlements or they fear social stigma.

The old are particularly vulnerable to poverty

THE EFFECTS OF POVERTY

Poverty, especially absolute poverty, has a number of serious adverse effects on those who experience it. The poor tend to suffer worse physical and mental health and indeed have a lower life expectancy.

The children of the poor suffer in terms of receiving less, and often a lower quality of, education. They are less likely to stay in full-time education after the age of 16, have few books at home and attend low-performing schools. They are also less likely to have a personal computer in the home and to travel abroad. All these factors tend to result in them gaining fewer qualifications and a vicious circle of poverty developing.

The poor can also feel cut off and even alienated from society, unable to live the type of life that the majority can experience.

Poverty places additional costs on the rest of society – the poor suffer greater ill health, commit more crime, and are less productive than the rest of society.

learning tip

Absolute poverty is experienced by those whose income is below that needed to achieve a minimum standard of living, whereas people experience relative poverty when they are poor relative to others. Most economists define as poor those whose income falls below half of the average income. Most of the poor are dependent on benefits and a major cause of poverty is that no one in the household is in employment. The poor are less healthy and their children's educational prospects are adversely affected.

ACTIVITY ····

1   Is poverty in the UK growing?
2   What are the main causes of poverty?
3   Will an increase in real GDP reduce poverty?
4   What is the connection between education and poverty?

learning tip

In preparation for your exam, make sure you can:

1   explain how the definition of relative poverty above differs from absolute poverty as it is usually defined.

2   evaluate the difficulties in measuring relative poverty and absolute poverty.

Government policies to alleviate poverty

The extent to which a government intervenes to affect the distribution of income and wealth depends on the extent to which it believes that the free market distribution is inequitable, the effects such inequality will have on society, and the effects it believes any intervention will have on incentives and efficiency.

Neoclassical economists do not favour significant intervention. This is because they believe that differences in income act as signals encouraging workers to move jobs, and differences in wealth promote saving and investment. They also argue that the provision of benefits above a minimum level for those who cannot work – for example, the disabled and sick – can encourage voluntary unemployment.

In contrast, Keynesians believe that intervention is justified because market forces will not ensure an efficient allocation of income and wealth, and that low levels of income and wealth can cause considerable problems for the households involved – including having a detrimental effect on the educational performance of the children. They also think that significant differences in income and wealth can cause social division, with the poor feeling socially excluded.

Conservatives and other right-wing parties tend to regard the existence of inequalities as a necessary characteristic of the free working of markets. Labour and the Liberal Democrats are more likely to favour redistributative policies. But even within these parties there is no clear consensus regarding the importance of such policies compared to other policy objectives.

Governments can influence the distribution of income and wealth in a number of ways, including:

- taxation
- cash benefits
- benefits in kind.

TAXATION

The UK government uses eight main sources of government tax revenue. Those such as income tax are relatively more progressive. They take a higher percentage of the income or wealth of the rich, which reduces inequalities in income and wealth. On the other hand, regressive taxes, such as VAT, take a higher percentage of the income of the poor, making the distribution more unequal.

The most effective means of redistributing wealth and therefore affecting the distribution of income is by the use of inheritance tax. However, this only applies to people leaving more than £250,000, and thereafter applies as a simple percentage of the value of the estate of someone who has died. There are also many ways in which the impact of inheritance tax is minimised, which means that this is a very under-used means of redistributing wealth.

The overall effects of taxation on the distribution of wealth can be assessed by comparing pre- and post-tax distribution. In the UK, because of the significance of income tax, the overall effect of the tax system is to reduce inequality.

CASH BENEFITS

There are two types of cash benefits – means tested and universal. Means-tested benefits – for example, family credit – are available to those who claim them and who can prove their income is below a certain level. Universal benefits are available to everyone in a particular group regardless of income – for example, families with young children receive child benefit.

There is great debate about the effectiveness of these two kinds of benefits. It has long been argued that child benefit, which is paid to all mothers at the same rate regardless of their income, should be replaced by benefits specifically targeting the poor. The problem is that not everyone who is entitled claims non-universal benefits. Old people, in particular, do not claim all those benefits to which they are entitled. It is also argued that means-tested benefits are actually more expensive to administer than universal benefits.

BENEFITS IN KIND

These include the provision of, for example, health care, education and school meals. The take-up of these benefits depends on the age composition of the household (for example, the elderly make the most use of the NHS) and attitudes and opportunities to access the provision (for example, more middle-class children stay in education after 16 than working-class children).

OTHER POLICES DESIGNED TO REDISTRIBUTE WEALTH AND INCOME

There are many other ways in which the government can use its spending to promote greater equality – including the following.

- labour market policy, the Minimum Wage Act of 1998, anti-discrimination acts, and government subsidising of training reducing income inequality

- macroeconomic policy influencing the distribution of income and wealth in a number of ways. For example, measures to reduce unemployment may benefit low-income households and regional policy reduces geographical inequalities of income and wealth.

- the amount spent on education and training to increase the skills of the least well-off

- similarly, the amount of spending targeted at the least healthy or the worst housed to promote greater equality – especially if it is financed by taxation of the better-off.

learning tip

There are fundamental differences of opinion between economists as to how governments should respond to inequalities in wealth and income. There are those who believe that inequalities provide incentives for us all to work harder and that, in the long run, everyone benefits from this 'trickle-down' effect. On the other hand, some economists argue that governments should intervene more directly to create more equality.

ACTIVITY ····▷

What would be the effects of increasing inheritance taxes in the UK?

ACTIVITY ····▷

Assess the validity of the suggestion that the government would achieve more to alleviate poverty if it abolished all forms of intervention, leading to a cut in government spending which would allow a reduction in rates of income tax.

5 Government intervention in markets

On completion of this chapter you should be able to:

- distinguish clearly between pure public goods and quasi public goods
- evaluate the extent to which inequalities of income and wealth are a result of market failure
- discuss the causes of environmental market failure
- evaluate the sources of government failure
- understand how cost-benefit analysis might be used to assess the social costs and benefits of economic decisions
- evaluate the costs and benefits of UK and EU competition policy
- have a deeper understanding of market-oriented supply-side policies, including the creation of internal markets and public–private partnerships
- distinguish between equity and equality.

This chapter is divided into five sections:

- Market and government failure
- Cost-benefit analysis
- Competition policy
- Public ownership, privatisation and deregulation
- Equality and equity.

STEPPING UP TO A2

In some ways, you do not have to learn a great deal more in terms of content. You will be expected to have a greater technical expertise when it comes to public and private goods, market-oriented supply-side policies, cost-benefit analysis and issues relating to inequalities in income and wealth.

You will be expected to 'evaluate' more, and deal with more complex stimulus material and, as you should have already learned, write a good 'two part' essay.

BUILDING ON AS

Different aspects of market failure, government intervention and government failure were a significant part of your AS course and all that you learned last year needs to be brought forward to help you do as well as you can in answering the questions in a potentially difficult exam.

This section helps you to understand the broader context in which economists consider market failure and government intervention (social efficiency). It also explains the significance of property rights and gives further consideration to the possibility of government failure.

Market and government failure

Chapter 4 dealt with assessing the effectiveness of the price mechanism as a means of allocating resources. You will have also learned that if markets are perfectly competitive and if there are no externalities, the price mechanism will achieve an allocation of resources that is productively and allocatively efficient and it can be argued that such an economy will also be dynamically efficient. In other words, the world's resources will be used as effectively as possible to meet the demands of customers in the marketplace.

You will have learned for AS that the existence of positive and negative externalities provides a rationale for government intervention to improve the other inefficient allocation of resources. The theoretical effects of government intervention can be illustrated graphically, as shown by Figure 5.1. This shows the marginal social cost (MSC) curve to represent a negative externality and indicates that if the government were to introduce a tax equivalent to the vertical distance *ab* it would be able to ensure an optimum allocation of resources because at OP_1 and

OQ_1 an equilibrium is reached at which customers are paying the total cost to society of what they are consuming.

For A2 you are expected to have a deeper understanding of the following concepts associated with market and government failure.

- public, private and quasi goods
- imperfect information
- income inequalities
- environmental market failure
- property rights.

Public, private and quasi goods

You should be familiar from your AS work with the characteristics of *public* and *private goods*. The consumption of public goods are said to be:

- *non rivalrous,* in the sense that the additional consumption of that good adds nothing to the costs of production, for example, street lighting

- *non excludable* – that is, it is not practical to exclude consumers of a good or service they do not pay for – again street lighting is an example.

The opposite applies to private goods. Additional consumption results in an increase in the costs of provision and, once consumed, that good or service is not available for someone else to enjoy, for example, a bag of crisps. It is argued that there is a clear relationship between the price of a private good and its demand and that this ensures that the market mechanism is the most effective way of ensuring that these demands are met.

If, however, there is not a clear relationship between demand and price, as is the case with public goods, then the price mechanism cannot be relied on to supply such goods or services and this provides a rationale for the state provision of, for example, defence, law and order, street lighting and national parks.

There is a third category known as **quasi goods** or non-pure public goods, goods and services for which there might be difficulties in excluding those who fail to pay, and which could be provided to others without a proportionate increase in the costs of production.

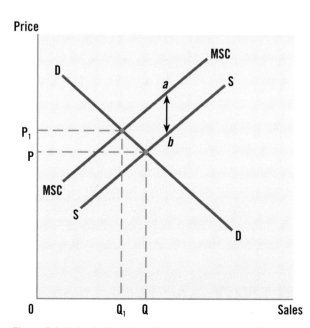

Figure 5.1 Using indirect taxation to remove a negative externality

STRETCH AND CHALLENGE

PARETO OPTIMALITY

Vilfredo Pareto (1848–1923) was an Italian economist who argued in favour of positive economics. He contended that social efficiency was reached in an economy when it was not an improvement to make an individual better off at the expense of making someone else worse off. Conversely, if it was possible to make someone better off without making someone worse off, an economy would be described as operating sub-optimally – that is, it would be socially inefficient.

This analysis depends on consumers and producers behaving in a rational way, which means that consumers will go on consuming, say, cola, as long as the marginal benefit (the satisfaction gained from the last mouthful) is greater than the marginal cost (the cost of that last mouthful). If, on the other hand, the additional cost is greater than the additional pleasure, the rational consumer will cut down the consumption of cola. Thus, the rational consumer will stop consuming cola when its marginal cost is equal to its marginal benefit.

You will also be familiar with the behaviour of a competitive firm wishing to maximise profits. It will go on producing until the marginal cost of production is the same as the marginal revenue gained from sales. If marginal cost is less than marginal revenue, then production will be expanded, whereas the profit-maximising firm will cut output if marginal costs exceed marginal revenue.

Finally, in Chapter 4 on the labour market, page 57, you learned that in a competitive labour market, a profit-maximising employer will go on employing more of an individual factor of production until the last unit adds as much to marginal revenue product as it does to costs.

If all economic agents are rational, and all attempt to equate marginal benefits with marginal costs, private efficiency will be maximised – that is, it would not be possible to make someone better off without making someone else worse off.

This analysis can be extended to considering social efficiency – that is, if the marginal social benefit of any activity is equal to the marginal social cost, then society as a whole is achieving Pareto optimality.

DEFINITION

Quasi goods: goods and services that can be viewed as private goods but can be supplied to others without a significant increase in costs

Other examples of quasi public goods are provision of education, health care, refuse collection and public transport. It would be possible to charge for these services, and exclude those who did not pay, but each produces significant positive externalities and this can be used as a justification for government provision, financed through taxation.

What is interesting is that categories of private, public and quasi public goods do not necessarily remain fixed. It is now feasible to regard road use as a private good. Similarly, modern technology could be used to turn lighthouses from being public to private goods.

ACTIVITY ···⫶

Assess the role of the Internet in transforming private goods into public goods.

Imperfect information

You will have learned that, in the model of perfect competition, both buyers and sellers have perfect knowledge of what is going on in their industry and marketplace. Although unrealistic, this assumption highlights the importance of both buyers and sellers having good information if markets are going to work effectively. Conversely, imperfect information can be a source of market failure.

Economists use the following concepts to analyse why some markets work better than others.

● **symmetric information** – which indicates that both buyers and sellers are both reasonably well informed about the products or services in a particular market – in this case both parties can make rational decisions as to whether or not they should buy or supply the product in question

● **asymmetric information** – this describes a situation in which either the buyer or the seller knows more than the other about the product or service.

DEFINITIONS

Symmetric information: when buyers and sellers are both reasonably well informed of factors affecting the sales of a good or service

Asymmetric information: when either buyers or sellers know much more than the other party about the factors affecting the sale of a good or service

The issue of asymmetric information is usually presented as one in which the producers and sellers of goods know more about their products than their buyers. If consumers are to make informed and effective choices of those products and services they may wish to purchase, they need knowledge and understanding of the prices and qualities of potential purchases. In theory, they need perfect knowledge, which is the term used by economists to describe a total and all-encompassing knowledge.

However, numerous studies indicate that consumer knowledge is far from perfect.

Customers perceive differences between products when there are none, and keeping track of the prices of competing products is too demanding for all but the most expert buyers.

Similarly, it is assumed that customers base purchases on rational decisions, that they are consistent and not swayed by irrational considerations. But customer choices are often unpredictable. Fashions and tastes change, as do perceptions as to what is good quality.

Customers might be unaware of the long-term costs of consuming particular products or services. Thus, there is a whole range of products and services that economists describe as **demerit goods**. The most obvious examples are tobacco, alcohol and illegal drugs. Customers are not aware or not willing to take into account the potential dangers of consuming these products, which means that a free market system is likely to over-produce them.

Customers might also be unaware of the long-term *benefits* of consuming particular goods and services. We, theoretically, all benefit from having a better trained and educated work force, as we do if more people chose healthier lifestyles. These types of goods are called **merit goods** and a free market system is unlikely to produce enough of them.

DEFINITIONS

Demerit goods: goods producing significant negative externalities and which are likely to be over-produced by the market system

Merit goods: goods producing significant positive externalities which are likely to be under-produced by the market system

The existence of asymmetric information does not necessarily stop markets working, but it does mean that the price mechanism might produce outcomes which:

- favour producers over consumers
- result in the over-production of demerit goods
- lead to the under-production of merit goods.

These shortcomings of the price mechanism may provide a rationale for intervention. Thus, governments may consider that, if consumers were left to themselves, they might make poor economic decisions, especially in relation to health and old age. Individuals have no way of knowing if they are likely to need health care in the future and because their information is imperfect they may make inadequate provision. This argument can be extended to justify government spending on measures to promote healthier lifestyles such as subsidies made to sports.

The encouragement of a healthier, fitter workforce also has third-party effects in terms of increasing productivity and decreasing the demands on health services. The existence of positive externalities provides governments with another reason for the provision of merit goods.

ACTIVITY ····⫶

How far does the article below provide evidence of asymmetric information? Should governments intervene to prevent rip-offs?

Income inequalities

You should remember from AS that freely operating markets create winners and losers. If you happen to have the skills that are required in an expanding market, you are likely to earn more than if your skills are no longer in demand.

The emphasis in the UK on market-oriented policies over the last 30 years has tended, according to a number of studies in growing inequalities, to favour middle- and higher-earning groups.

The extent to which inequalities in income and wealth can be described as an example of market failure is debatable. It can be argued that extremes of both poverty and wealth create negative externalities and result in the over-production of demerit goods.

ECONOMICS IN CONTEXT

RIP-OFF BRITAIN – WHO DOES IT MOST?

Ask this question, and the usual answer is: mobile phone companies, garages and energy suppliers. But what about banks? Recent disclosures that they routinely overcharge customers are just the tip of the iceberg. It is now emerging that students and young adults routinely end up paying more for loans than they need.

In some ways it's all their fault – the potential borrowers', that is. Too many young people think that the nice person on the end of the telephone line working for their friendly helpful bank is there to give impartial advice. Wrong. Wrong. Wrong.

Call centre customer advisers work to a script and, as they deal with requests for loans and overdrafts, have detailed access to customer profiles. They know if applicants have been overdrawn, have maxed out on their student loan, been declined a credit card. They also get bonuses according to the financial processes they sell, so the seemingly innocent – 'And is there anything else I can help you with?' is really a potential come-on.

Always ask what's the APR (annual percentage rate) and how much you will eventually pay back.

Environmental market failure

The main examples of potential environmental failure include:

- the exploitation and depletion of non renewable resources
- global warming
- extinction of floral and fauna.

ACTIVITY ⋯⦂

Use marginal analysis to illustrate the following:

a   a rise in temperatures associated with global warming

b   successful introduction of a 'carbon' tax

c   failure of a carbon-trading programme.

Property rights

You will have learned for the AS part of your A-level that one way of dealing with negative externalities is by introducing tradeable permits, whereby governments can encourage individual firms to reduce pollution by creating a market in which those firms that cut pollution the most have the most to gain.

This is an extension of one approach to dealing with externalities without the necessity of government intervention. This approach is associated with an American economist, Ronald Coase. In 1960, Coase argued that government intervention was not required to deal with negative externalities as long as **property rights** are well defined and transaction costs are relatively low.

DEFINITION

Property rights: the clear identification of who owns what

Coase argued that, if it is possible to extend rights to define who owns what property, to what uses it

can be put and what rights others have over it, then the owners would have an incentive to ensure that the value of their property was protected. Thus, if something that I own is damaged, it would be logical for me to sue the person who caused the damage. Clearly, if the legal or transaction costs to this action were relatively large, I might be dissuaded from seeking compensation.

The difficulty of applying this approach to internalising external costs is that it is hard to establish property rights in relation to many environmental resources. Who owns the air above my house and the water that flows from mountains to the sea? And what happens when it is difficult to identify the perpetrator of some perceived negative externality?

It is clear that the development of legal systems that include establishing the terms and conditions associated with contract law, the rights of buyers and sellers, the liability of particular types of businesses and the importance of insurance have all contributed to the development of economic systems that at least go some way to try to ensure that resources are used effectively. Indeed, great damage has been done to less developed and formally communist countries in applying market-led solutions in contexts where property rights were both ill-defined and ill-protected.

Government failure

The concept of government failure, included in your AS course, recognises that government intervention in markets may lead to unintended outcomes. Misplaced price intervention may create surpluses or shortages. Direct government controls can lead to the creation of new unregulated markets. Taxes and subsidies may distort the signals given by the price mechanism. Such arguments are often used by economists who favour the working of free market forces, who sometimes suggest that there is a straight choice to be made between free market or capitalist solutions and interventionist or socialist solutions.

The winner of the Nobel Prize for economics in 2001, Joseph Stiglitz, has suggested that much of this debate is misplaced. He has argued that free market ideology is fundamentally flawed, as 'whenever information is imperfect and markets incomplete, which is to say always, then the invisible hand works most imperfectly'.

Stiglitz goes on to argue that government interventions 'can improve upon the efficiency of the market' and that if information were perfect there would be little role for financial market regulation. He suggests that the failings of the market system – 'from massive inequity to unliveable cities marred by pollution and decay' – have led to the rejection of free market policies by all advanced industrialised countries. He suggests that it is more useful to discuss the appropriate balance between governments and markets.

ACTIVITY ····:

What assumptions have to be made for the free market system to ensure the optimum allocation of resources?

Cost-benefit analysis

Cost-benefit analysis is one of the statistical techniques developed by government economists to try to quantify both negative and positive externalities, determine possible levels of government subsidy, establish levels of taxation and help to reconcile the interests of different stakeholders. It is a technique that is used to help estimate the actual value of potential positive and negative externalities to establish the 'true' cost of different types of economic activity. This can aid the process of trying to estimate subsidies to encourage activity that has clear positive externalities and in so doing prevent or minimise scope for government failure.

DEFINITION

Cost-benefit analysis: a technique used to assess the relative significance of the social costs and social benefits of different forms of economic activity

Cost-benefit analysis can be applied to new investments and also to existing markets. For example, there was been a long-running enquiry into the building of the new terminal at Heathrow Airport. Supporters claimed that it would aid economic growth, not just of those directly concerned but also for firms and employees dependent on the continued growth and expansion of Heathrow. On the other hand, a range of interests opposed to the development argued that noise pollution, congestion and so on would impose additional costs on the local community.

As part of the process to decide whether or not permission was given for this new development, cost-benefit analysis was undertaken. In this case, the purpose was to identify both the positive and negative externalities. A public inquiry was set up to reveal the full costs to society (that is, the **social cost** of the new development) and the full benefits (that is, the **social benefit**).

DEFINITIONS

Social cost: the full cost to society of the provision of a good or service

Social benefit: the full benefits to society of the provision of a good or service

The government eventually decided that the social advantages outweighed the social disadvantages, and gave the go-ahead to one of the largest civil engineering projects ever undertaken.

The cost benefit process

Undertaking cost-benefit analysis usually involves the following.

- *identification and quantification of all private costs.* These are the fixed and variable costs the company or organisation undertaking the project would normally be expected to pay. In the case of the Heathrow terminal, this would have involved the cost of land, design, building, labour costs and many others.

● *identification and quantification of all external costs* – in other words, putting a monetary value to all the negative externalities. It is relatively straightforward to estimate the additional costs to those living in the vicinity to improve soundproofing. However, it is much more difficult to find monetary values for matters relating to environmental damage and degradation.

● *calculation of social cost.* This simply involves adding the private and external costs together to estimate the full cost to society of the project in question.

● *identification and quantification of all private benefits.* These are all the benefits that customers are prepared to pay for. Sometimes such calculations are straightforward, if the people who benefit actually have to pay for a new service.

● *identification and quantification of all external benefits.* As with negative externalities, this is more tricky because it involves identifying all those who are likely to benefit in some way, and putting a monetary value on their benefit. What is the benefit of a business person arriving at a foreign appointment on time? How do you assess the positive effects on the local economy?

● *calculation of social benefit.* These are the private and external benefits added together.

When all this has been undertaken, it is possible to make a direct comparison between the social costs of a project and the social benefits. In theory, if the social benefit exceeds the social cost, society as a whole would benefit from the development. If this relationship were reversed, society would be economically worse off.

Problems with cost-benefit analysis

The big challenge to those undertaking cost-benefit analysis is to put a financial valuation on external costs and benefits, and this requires a mixture of approximations, forecasts and guesswork.

Calculation problems are especially difficult when it comes to dealing with the costs faced by people. For example, what would be the value of building a road that cuts five minutes off the typical journey time of *n* thousand road users per week? If improvements to road safety demonstrate that fewer accidents will occur, it is reasonably easy to put a value to the lower demand for hospital and medical care, but what value should be given to a saved limb or even a saved life?

These practical difficulties are made harder as cost-benefit analysis is often used to assess the economic impact of controversial proposals. This was the case with the Heathrow extension mentioned earlier, in which rival stakeholders challenged the data that each side and the inspector were using.

Using cost-benefit analysis

Cost-benefit analysis is used in a number of ways, including in:

● public subsidy

● regulation

● planning.

PUBLIC SUBSIDY

If cost-benefit analysis demonstrates that there will be greater social benefit than social cost – that is, there is a net social benefit – then this analysis might be used to justify government subsidy to ensure that resources are used in such a way as to maximise public welfare.

REGULATION

Similarly, if cost-benefit shows that negative externalities outweigh positive, a rationale is provided for government intervention to limit or control such outputs. This could involve direct controls, pollution taxes or the introduction of tradeable permits.

PLANNING

As in the case of the expansion at Heathrow, cost-benefit analysis can be used to try to resolve the competing claims of different stakeholders. It can provide a more rational way of resolving controversial issues. It also provides government bodies such as the NHS and the Department of Environment with a means of deciding which investments in the public sector should be selected and which rejected.

> ## ACTIVITY ⋯⋗
>
> List three advantages and three problems associated with cost-benefit analysis.

> ## ACTIVITY ⋯⋗
>
> 1 Assess the contribution that cost-benefit analysis can make to rationing scarce resources in the public sector.
> 2 How would you go about undertaking a cost-benefit analysis on the hosting of the 2012 Olympics in London?
>
>
>
> **The site of the 2012 Olympic stadium**

Competition policy

The more detailed theoretical treatment of the significance of market structures tends to indicate that, subject to crucial assumptions, customers and societies will be better off if markets are competitive rather than monopolistic. However, there is growing evidence that concentration ratios in key industries tend to be increasing and that many firms develop strategies to avoid competitive pressures. This divergence between what might be seen as socially desirable and the actual behaviour of an increasing number of larger firms provides a challenge both to economists and to governments.

This section explores how governments have attempted to promote competition and limit the adverse effects of firms able to exercise monopoly power. The case against monopolies is summarised below. This is followed by consideration of anti-monopoly policies, those to promote competition, and a review of policies towards public ownership and privatisation.

The case against monopoly

Economic theorists have argued that monopoly power can result in:

● higher prices

● lower outputs

● less customer choice

● fewer innovations

● less efficient production – allocatively, productively and dynamically.

On the other hand, it can be argued that firms with monopolistic power:

● are large enough to compete successfully with other large companies for global markets

● have the resources to devote to research and development

● can be more socially responsible, for example, in public service broadcasting

● in the case of 'natural monopolies' such as transport networks and health care, avoid wasteful competition and duplication of services

● are justified in strategic and military terms, for example, in telecoms and nuclear power.

The economic arguments against monopolistic power are not conclusive. Governments are faced with the challenge of developing policies that guard against the potential excesses of monopolistic power while at the same time trying to ensure that possible benefits are not lost.

UK government policies on monopolies

The UK government has not always been suspicious of the motives and behaviour of firms perceived to have monopoly power. In the 1930s, the government promoted development of larger and more powerful companies, because it was considered that they would provide a more secure business environment. However, since the Monopolies and Restrictive Practices Act was passed in 1948, successive governments have looked more critically at the activities of large firms.

Control of monopolies in the UK is ultimately the responsibility of the government. Possible abuses of monopoly power are investigated by the Competition Commission (formally known as the Monopolies and Mergers Commission). This is a quasi-legal body that hears evidence prior to coming to a judgement about suspected abuses of monopoly power. Its findings are reported to the government, which has the final say about whether or not to take action.

The law defines a monopoly as being any firm that has a 25 per cent or greater share in a local or national market, or two or more firms supplying 25 per cent of the total market if it is suspected they are colluding informally. The 1980 Competition Act strengthened anti-monopoly legislation by identifying various types of uncompetitive behaviour, including:

● price discrimination

● selective distribution, where a firm refuses to supply particular companies

● predatory pricing, when firms deliberately cut prices below costs in an attempt to force competitors from a market.

The job of the Competition Commission is to establish whether or not uncompetitive behaviour is taking place and to balance this against possible benefits in order to make a judgement as to whether or not the firm in question is acting in the public interest.

The Commission and its predecessor have investigated many different possible instances of the abuse of monopoly power. These include the control of public houses by major breweries, high profit levels earned by the major supermarkets, selective distribution by Bird's Eye Walls and retail-only agreements by Rank Xerox. Various recommendations have been made, which have included price cuts, reduced expenditure on advertising and reducing barriers of entry.

The government also has the power to prevent the creation of monopolies by the merger of one or more

companies. The Competition Commission can be asked to investigate the likely outcomes of a merger and report their findings to the government, but government action to prevent mergers is very rare. Responsibility for action now lies with the Office of Fair Trading rather than the government minister in making the final decision as to whether or not a proposed merger should take place.

The legal framework used to curb the abuse powers of monopolists and oligopolists is tougher than that relating to their existence and creation. Restrictive trade practices is the legal terminology used to describe various forms of collusion. All such agreements have to be registered with the Office of Fair Trading and are banned unless participants can prove that they are in the public interest. The law recognises that collusion can bring benefits, such as protecting employment, promoting exports and ensuring safety standards are met.

But even if it is possible to prove the existence of such benefits before the Restrictive Practices Court, firms still have to demonstrate that possible benefits outweigh any harmful effects.

Similarly, a tough stance is taken towards limiting the power of manufacturers to set and enforce minimum retail prices for their products. Over the years, formal price-fixing agreements have been ended and they only currently exist for some medical products.

European Union legislation

The development of the single European market has meant that member states have been forced to adopt a common approach to competition policy, especially in respect of those firms that have monopoly power within the EU. There is no minimum market share that triggers investigation. Firms that behave unfairly towards consumers by their pricing policies or other activities can be referred to the European Court of Justice. If found 'guilty', they can be fined as well as being debarred from acting uncompetitively.

EU policies towards mergers and collusive behaviour are similar. The focus is on investigation of uncompetitive behaviour rather than market share.

ACTIVITY ····⟫

1 What is meant by the abuse of market power?

2 Will consumers suffer if a market is supplied by a monopolist?

3 What are the roles of the Competition Commission and the Office of Fair Trading?

Public ownership, privatisation and deregulation

Public ownership

As noted earlier, **public ownership** refers to those organisations owned collectively by all of us. This form of ownership is also referred to as **nationalisation**, and a number of economic arguments have been made to justify this extreme form of government intervention. These include:

● preventing the owners of 'natural monopolies', such as water supplies and the national grid,

DEFINITIONS

Nationalisation: transfer of ownership from the private to the public sector

Public ownership: collective ownership of resources

ECONOMICS IN CONTEXT

NORTHERN ROCK NATIONALISATION BILL PASSED

Friday, 22 February 2008

Emergency legislation allowing the government to nationalise troubled mortgage lender Northern Rock was passed late last night in Parliament.

The Banking (Special Provisions) Bill hit some last-minute hiccoughs as the Lords demanded Northern Rock should be subject to the Freedom of Information Act, as with other public bodies, and that an independent audit of the lender should be carried out to see what exactly the taxpayers were buying.

The government claimed Northern Rock should not be open to freedom of information requests as it would hit the bank commercially.

Yvette Cooper, chief secretary to the Treasury, told parliament:'Ron Sandler [the new government-appointed head of Northern Rock] will publish his strategic business plan, which will include the overarching strategic aims for Northern Rock. The house will recognise it would not be appropriate to publish detailed commercially sensitive information.'

Conservative MP Philip Hammond blasts Ms Cooper for wasting debate time with 'rubbish and waffle' and went on to question the position of the Jersey-based investment arm of Northern Rock.

He said:'There is a clear need for an audit of the situation in Northern Rock, including an analysis of the quality of the loan book.'

There are concerns that some of the best Northern Rock mortgage assets are held by Granite, which will not be nationalised.

However, Ms Cooper accused the opposition of wanting to 'play games with what we should all recognise is an extremely serious issue concerning the future stability of the banking system and the future of Northern Rock'.

Speaking last night, Tory shadow chancellor George Osborne said: 'We will continue to press for Freedom of Information so the public know what they are buying.

'It's a case strengthened by the view expressed in the City that the lack of Freedom of Information may undermine bondholder confidence.'

He added: 'Nationalisation is the worst option for Northern Rock, but at least our vigorous scrutiny in parliament has forced important concessions that make a bad bill slightly better.'

At 23:06 last night, the speaker of the House of Commons announced Royal Assent was given to the Banking (Special Provisions) Act 2008.

Source: myfinances

exploiting customers who cannot easily purchase substitutes

● ensuring the provision of unbiased information, as is meant to be the case with the BBC

● undertaking major infrastructure changes which would not be undertaken by the private sector, for example in road building

● guaranteeing vital supplies in times of war, such as coal, iron and steel

● ensuring equality, such as NHS provision of universal health care.

Over the last 30 years, many businesses formerly in public ownership have been transferred to private ownership and the advantages and disadvantages of such policies are analysed below.

STRETCH AND CHALLENGE

Why did the government nationalise Northern Rock?

Privatisation

The Conservative government under Margaret Thatcher, elected in 1979, favoured market-based strategies in an effort to improve the performance of the UK economy. It believed that the efficiency of the UK economy would be improved if nationalised industries were sold off to the public sector. Two aspects of their polices related to the control and influence of monopolistic and oligopolistic power:

● **privatisation**

● the introduction of competitive forces into those organisations that remained in the public sector.

DEFINITION

Privatisation: transfer of ownership from the public to the private sector

First, businesses such as BP, ICL (Computers) and British Sugar operating in competitive markets were transferred from public to private ownership. In the mid-1980s, Sealink, Jaguar, British Telecom and British Gas were sold. At the end of the decade and in the early 1990s, more complicated sell-offs, such as the water, electricity and rail industries, were undertaken. The Labour government elected in 1997 indicated that it would continue these Conservative policies by privatising air traffic control. However, it has now backed away from selling off the Royal Mail.

In addition to fitting in with the overall policy of promoting the private sector at the expense of the public sector, privatisation created additional government revenue estimated to have exceeded £60 billion.

ARGUMENTS IN FAVOUR OF PRIVATISATION

It can be argued that:

● firms in the private sector have more incentive to increase efficiency and meet the needs of customers

● government interference in nationalised industries increased their inefficiencies

● privatisation enables firms to access investment funds not available when in public ownership

● government revenue is increased, allowing the possibility of tax cuts and/or increases in government expenditure.

ARGUMENTS AGAINST PRIVATISATION

Arguments against privatisation include:

● transferring firms with monopoly power from the public to private sectors increases the chances of consumers being exploited by higher prices and poorer services

● public-owned assets are sold for less then they are worth, leading to windfall gains for the new owners

● fragmentation of natural monopolies leads to wasteful duplication of services.

learning tip

You need to remember that public policy associated with trying to prevent the abuses of monopolistic and oligopolist power has traditionally been based on a legal framework that has focused attention on ownership and structural aspects of large companies. Merger and monopoly policy has not been strictly or consistently applied in the UK, and few sanctions have been used against firms whose actions have been judged to be against the public interest. More recent developments in European law, and the developing role of regulatory bodies, place greater emphasis on examining unacceptable behaviour by large firms, backed up by the use of fines and direct controls.

In recent years, governments in the UK have also attempted to encourage the development of more competitive markets through privatisation and the introduction of internal markets and other structures within the public sector. Some of these policies appear to have been more successful than others, but it is too early to assess the long-term impact of these changes on society as a whole.

Increasing competition within the public sector

The previous section examined government policies designed to limit the abuses of market power by monopolists and oligopolists. Using privatisation to transfer economic functions from the public to the private sectors has also been described. Governments have realised that, for political and social reasons, it may be inappropriate to privatise some functions. An alternative policy is to try to create more competitive structures within the public sector. This has involved:

- the creation of internal markets
- compulsory competitive tendering
- league tables
- private finance initiatives (PFIs).

EVALUATING THE PERFORMANCE OF THE PUBLIC SECTOR

It was, and still is, hard to assess the performance of the public sector. Some elements, such as public libraries, have always been run as 'public services'; others, such as British Rail, were expected to 'break even' (that is, make neither a profit nor a loss). Yet others – for example, the NHS – were expected to meet any demands. Some, like the Coal Board, found it difficult to make a profit, whereas British Gas was highly efficient. It is clear, however, that firms operating in the public sector:

- were insulated from market pressures
- suffered varying degrees of political interference.

MARKET PRESSURES

Managers of firms operating in the private sector need a high regard for the profitability of their businesses. Those who ignore the bottom line are unlikely to keep their jobs, and privately owned businesses that consistently make losses will go out of business, be taken over or reorganised.

Those working in the public sector have traditionally been insulated from concerns about profitability. They have been able to take decisions without reference to revenue, costs and profit. In the past, schools, hospitals and other public services were run with little control over expenditure. Instead, local authorities and central government provided funding to ensure that each covered its costs.

Employees in the public sector considered that their jobs were secure and there was, therefore, less incentive for them to be productive and cost efficient. These factors have been called 'x inefficiencies' and could be represented by the higher average costs of production that can occur if firms are insulated from competitive or market pressures.

POLITICAL INTERFERENCE

Although firms in the public sector were theoretically given varying degrees of independence from government interference, it was inevitable that politicians had some say in key decisions:

● Major spending decisions had a direct effect on jobs and the popularity of both MPs and the government. Many firms in the public sector found government finance more generous immediately before elections than after.

● Some MPs were more effective than others in lobbying for government support for particular industries – for example, major steelworks were built at Newport and Port Talbot.

● Profits from the public sector were taken by the Treasury to boost government revenues.

All the above could have contributed to government failure in the sense that government intervention might make a bad problem worse.

INTERNAL MARKETS

In the 1980s, the Conservative government realised that the total privatisation of the public sector would be both politically unacceptable and very difficult to implement. One way of trying to introduce competition was by the creation of internal markets, involving the creation of individual cost centres and greater independence in financial decision making.

Thus, in the NHS, budget-holding doctors were given the freedom to purchase medical care from those hospitals providing the most attractive service. Hospitals were expected to compete for business from GPs. This represented a radical change in established procedures, which could have had devastating political effects had the government been prepared to allow failing hospitals to go 'bust' and close. The incoming Labour government abandoned these policies in 1997 but later reintroduced a version of them by devolving budgets to and increasing the power of primary care trusts (groups of local medical practices) at the expense of hospitals.

A version of an internal market exists within the BBC, in which independent programme makers have the freedom to employ camera operators, directors, costume designers and so on from within the BBC or from outside contractors.

COMPULSORY COMPETITIVE TENDERING

Local and central government departments were compelled by legal changes to put the provision of services out to tender. This meant that, rather than a council employing refuse collectors, it was required to invite private companies to bid for contracts to collect domestic and commercial refuse. The rules relating to tendering have now been relaxed to permit councils to tender for the provision of their own services.

The impact of these policies is difficult to measure. Who supplies food and drink in your school/college? Have prices changed? Is there more choice? Has the quality of service increased?

There is some evidence to suggest that the use of outside contractors in the health service has contributed to a decline in hygiene standards, while in other services greater competition has had the effect of driving down the relative wages of the less skilled and worsening working conditions. On the other hand, some local government functions have been characterised by very poor levels of service. It might be fair to say that more competition creates more efficient outcomes, but these greater efficiencies might carry additional costs or externalities with them.

LEAGUE TABLES

Conservative governments in the 1980s also tried to apply market disciplines to education. This has been continued by successive Labour governments. One aspect of this policy has been to publish league tables to compare the performance of different schools, hospitals and local councils. Those scoring well could be rewarded with additional resources or greater freedom from central government control.

Again, it is hard to assess the impact of these reforms. Competition implies winners and losers, and thus we might expect to see improvements in some schools, colleges and hospitals – but possibly only at the expense of failure and closure of others. The Labour government elected in 1997 has tried hard to improve education and health standards by applying these principles of greater competition, but it may have created government failure – for example, the short-term switching of resources in hospitals away from general patient care to dealing with accident and emergencies to meet government-imposed targets. Similarly, there has been greater pressure on some schools to exclude difficult students, thus boosting league table performance.

PRIVATE FINANCE INITIATIVES

Finally, the Labour government has placed considerable priority on PFIs to provide much needed new capital spending. Although the detail of such schemes to build hospitals, schools, roads and even to renew London's underground are complicated, the key concept is simple. The government reaches agreements for capital spending projects to be completed for agreed amounts, to a required standard and by a given deadline. It is argued that private sector entrepreneurial skills are better than those of managers in the public sector, and that this strategy should ensure projects are completed on time and to budget.

As discussed previously, evaluation of the success of these policies is difficult. The National Audit Office has indicated that PFIs can be less efficient and more costly. Much depends on the ability of public sector organisations like health trusts and local education authorities (LEAs) to manage and oversee the running of such projects.

PUBLIC–PRIVATE PARTNERSHIPS

The present government, though committed to the benefits of more competitive markets, has also attempted to promote greater partnership and collaboration between the private and public sectors and other stakeholders.

For example, regional policies are now meant to be driven by a series of Regional Development Agencies made up of representation from different stakeholders. Their role is to develop economic and social policies which will take account of the specific needs of different regions in England. At a country level, other partnerships are meant to contribute to economic planning and development at a sub-

regional level. These agencies are used to channel development funds from the EU Social Fund to meet local priorities.

learning tip
Try to remember that in recent years, governments in the UK have attempted to encourage the development of more competitive markets through privatisation and the introduction of internal markets and other structures within the public sector. Some of these policies appear to have been more successful than others, but it is too early to assess the long-term impact of these changes.

ACTIVITY ·····⫶

Select an area of the public sector, such as the health service, waste collection, or education that has been opened up to competitive forces; evaluate the effectiveness of these changes.

Equality and equity

The concepts are important in understanding why governments might intervene if it is considered that inequalities and unfairness generated by market-based solutions are not socially acceptable.

learning tip
Be careful – when we get into discussion of equality and fairness it is easy to make normative judgements – there is nothing wrong in that but you need to make it clear to your examiner that you understand the difference between making a positive statement and one that is normative.

Equality

A market economy creates inequalities in income and wealth. This was explored on pages 70–76 of Chapter 4. At a very simple level, those who own factors of production, including their own labour, that are in high demand are likely to earn more than those who own factors of production for which there is relatively less demand. If you are particularly impoverished, your income will be low or non-existent. As noted in Chapter 4, Lorenz curves and Gini coefficients are measures of the inequality of incomes within an economy and studies across the world indicate that there are widespread variations in how incomes are distributed. Statements about inequalities can be expressed positively without any judgements as to the desirability or otherwise of inequalities.

Equity

Equity, on the other hand, is much more likely to involve normative judgements, as it depends upon notions of fairness. Economists refer to two types of equity:

> **DEFINITION**
>
> **Equity:** social or judicial 'fairness'; also the value of the shares issued by a company

- *horizontal* – the identical treatment of individuals in the same situations, for example, the equal payment of men and women doing the same job

- *vertical* – this recognises that everyone has different characteristics but that all are entitled to the same treatment, for example, treating those from different ethic groups equally when it comes to the provision of health care or education.

It should be clear, from learning about differences in wages and incomes in Chapter 4, that we live in a society that, according to these definitions, is neither equal nor fair. How far such differences are attributable to market-based systems or to cultural and social factors is a far harder question to answer, as is the extent to which the government should intervene in an attempt to remove or minimise inequalities and unfairness.

ACTIVITY ····⁞

How far is it possible to provide economic justifications for government intervention in markets? Assess the likely impact of government intervention in a market of your choice.

Exam Café

Relax, refresh, result!

Relax and prepare

How do you revise?

Lin

Something I remember from lower down the school is the use of MIND MAPS. These can be very helpful in economics, because lots of topics are linked to each other in lots of ways. For example, get an empty page and write the words 'MARKET PRICE' in a 'balloon' in the centre. Then draw an arrow labelled 'DEMAND' and make a list of things other than price that can influence consumers (incomes, tastes, etc.). Draw another arrow labelled 'SUPPLY' and make a list of things other than price that can influence producers (raw materials, costs, etc.). Then show the effects on price if supply increases or decreases and demand increases or decreases. Then you need to show the effects of a price change, with arrows labelled 'elasticity'. Draw one 'branch' showing what happens to total revenue when price changes and demand is price-elastic, another for when demand is price-inelastic. Then you could make a list of influences that affect the price elasticity of demand of a product.

The more you add to your mind map, the more you'll think of further things to add, and you'll end up with a page that summarises a huge amount of the economics, and which reminds you that the topics do not exist in separate compartments, they are all inter-linked. Mind maps help you take an *overview* of a new topic, and review topics that you already know about.

When I was doing subjects like physics and geography lower down the school, some teachers helped us remember important facts using MNEMONICS. For example:

Many Volcanoes Emit Mulberry Jam Sandwiches Under Normal Pressure

This was a way of remembering the planets in our solar system in order of their distance from the sun: *Mercury, Venus, Earth, Mars, Jupiter, Saturn, Uranus, Neptune, Pluto.*

Some experts are saying that Pluto is not big enough to be a true 'planet', so I suppose they have a new eight-planet mnemonic. I also remember that when I learned to drive, my instructor was always repeating the initials 'MSM' for mirror, signal, manoeuvre, which is a similar type of memory aid. I've heard that doctors, nurses and paramedics use a lot of memory aids to help with the long lists of things that they often have to recall quickly. My A-level teachers don't seem so fond of mnemonics, so I have made up a few of my own for Economics. Here's one:

Start Playing Conkers Now
for
Substitutes Positive, Complements Negative

This helps me to remember whether to put a 'plus' or 'minus' sign in front of the cross elasticity of demand coefficient. Before I made up this mnemonic I could never remember whether the CED for substitutes or complements was positive or negative. I could sit down with a diagram and work it out, but under exam conditions this lost valuable time.

Shelpa

I agree that mnemonics and mind maps are two great ways of brain-training. My elder sister works in a bank, and she reckons that learning a subject is a bit like building up a bank account. You should invest regularly, and the little bits you add will soon mount up to a good sized balance. When she was doing her banking exams, she said that every day she would put some time aside for READING, THINKING and WRITING.

Economics is a subject that needs all three of these. It's not a subject that makes you remember a whole string of facts. Instead there is quite a small number of *key ideas* that you must *understand* thoroughly. By reading, thinking and writing every day, you build up a stock of understanding. During those times when you need to do something else, or you just want to relax, this balance is something you can draw on for a while until you need to resume your studies.

Refresh your memory

Revision checklist

Can you …?	Turn to page …
Define profit and explain why maximum profit occurs when MC = MR	4, 22
Explain the difference between the short run and long run in economics and distinguish between short-run diminishing returns, and long-run returns to scale	8
Draw graphs and explain how different types of cost (fixed, variable, total, average, marginal) behave as output increases	9–13
Draw graphs and explain how different types of revenue (average, marginal, total) behave as sales increase	19–20
Explain what is meant by market structure, and describe how market structure can change, e.g. through technical progress	1, 18–19
Using diagrams to help you, show how price and output are determined under perfect competition	25–28
Explain why competition is thought to increase efficiency	28–32
Using diagrams to help you, show how price and output are determined under monopoly and oligopoly	39–40, 45
Explain how and why firms grow	37
Define and explain the terms: collusion, interdependence, price discrimination, consumer and producer surplus, contestable markets, static and dynamic efficiency	32, 42–49
Use the concept of marginal product to explain the demand for labour	53–55
Explain the major influences on the supply of labour, including monetary and non-monetary considerations	55–56
Use supply and demand analysis to explain why wage rates differ between different occupational groups	57
Discuss the effects on labour markets of factors such as trade unions and minimum wage legislation	61, 64–65
Identify factors that affect the distribution of income and wealth; explain how government policy can change these distributions and evaluate anti-poverty policy; distinguish between equity and equality	72–80 96–97
Evaluate the costs and benefits of government competition policy	94–96
Give arguments for and against public ownership and privatisation	92–93
Explain the main principles of cost-benefit analysis	88–90

Key word quiz

Define:

1 Normal profit
2 Perfect competition
3 Monopoly
4 Oligopoly
5 Allocative efficiency
6 Labour market

Get the result!

Student answers

These are answers to the following part (c) of a data-response question:

'Discuss whether it is possible for governments to reduce poverty by redistributing income and wealth.' (25 marks)

Helen's answer

Examiner comments:
Helen describes a Lorenz curve, but could have drawn a simple version in order to illustrate her description.

In spite of the lack of a diagram, this is a good introduction, with Helen showing good economic awareness. She has clearly read widely.

Examiner comments:
Good 'application' here, with clear logic applied to economic concepts.

A Lorenz curve can be used to show that the distribution of income and wealth in the UK is far from equal. If the graph were a straight line, then the bottom 20% of households would receive 20% of the income and so on. In reality, the bottom 20% receive only about 4% of the income while the top 20% receive about 65% of income, and this percentage has been increasing steadily since the 1980s. The government could help to reduce this inequality in various ways.

For example, there could be a more progressive tax system, with a tax band for high-income earners greater than the current higher rate of 40%. It would be reasonable to charge, say, a marginal rate of 50% on that part of an income that exceeds £100,000 per year. This could be coupled with an increase in direct benefits to the lower paid, so that the government acts like Robin Hood, taking from the 'rich' to give to the 'poor'. However, an important point is that even without an increase in so-called 'transfer payments', a progressive tax still has a redistributive effect. This is because whether you are rich or poor, you receive a 'social wage' through the provision of public services such as the NHS which are available to all regardless of income. Taxes based on the ability to pay, together with a universal social wage, reduce inequality whether or not benefits are increased, but obviously higher benefits will increase the effect.

This addresses income, but wealth is largely untaxed in this country. For example, there is no such thing as a 'land tax', and inheritance tax has proved very unpopular now that more families, not just the aristocracy, are finding that the value of their houses might make them liable. Extract C shows that many more people than ever before are being caught in the inheritance tax net. One of the easiest ways to be wealthy is to be born with wealthy parents, so a government that seriously wants to tackle inequalities in wealth has to use some form of tax on inheritance. It is also true to say that there are links between wealth and income. For example, wealthier families are more likely to be able to afford to increase the life chances of their children by paying for a better education, which will increase their earning power in the future. And high-income earners can, in turn, better afford to save, and therefore increase their stock of wealth for the future.

Indirect taxes, such as VAT, tend to be regressive, since they are collected on spending rather than on income. For this reason, some basic items such as fresh food are not taxed in this country. But when things that we cannot do without, such as petrol, are taxed, less well-off families are hit harder than wealthier families. A reduction in indirect taxes and a shift towards direct taxes would therefore also help redistribute income, but this fact is not well understood by the media or the general public and politicians are scared of such a policy.

The government might choose to attempt to reduce inequality not through re-distributing money, but through benefits in kind. Investment in education, for instance, in order to boost qualifications and skills for a larger proportion of the population, would increase people's earning power. Also, social housing and increased NHS spending will improve health and therefore make people more fit for work. These may be more effective ways of reducing poverty in the long run. One thing we can be sure of is that some form of government intervention is necessary if society really wishes for more equality. The market system, if left to work by itself, is sure to lead to unequal shares of income and wealth.

Absolute poverty exists when the population cannot get access to the necessities of life. Most economists would agree that this is not a problem in the UK, and there is no need for anyone here to be homeless or starving. However, there is a problem of relative poverty and government policies over the last few years have actually resulted in the widening of inequalities in income and wealth rather than their narrowing.

Examiner comments:
Good knowledge, together with further evaluation. While it is difficult to argue with this statement, Helen could have said something about *why* the market system, left to itself, is 'sure to lead' to inequality, e.g. by arguing that without government action, profits will automatically flow towards the owners of productive resources. Or, she could have quoted some 'evidence', perhaps by mentioning some international examples, such as the high level of inequality in a market-based economy such as the USA, compared with greater equality in a more government-interventionist economy such as Sweden. It could be argued that the UK is somewhere between the two.

Examiner comments:
Again, definitions (of 'absolute' and 'relative' poverty) would be helpful; but this is quite a good concluding paragraph.

Examiner comments:
It would have been good to see formal definitions of 'income' and 'wealth' here, together with a distinction between the former as a 'flow' and the latter as a 'stock'. There is a reference to the data here, which will be rewarded by the examiner.
Excellent evaluation and good analysis of a problem, using economic ideas.

Overall: Compared with what large numbers of candidates can be expected to write in an attempt to answer this question, this is a sophisticated answer with some important points made, and Helen shows that she understands and can analyse the economics of the issue very well. This answer is well written, logically structured, and makes it to the mid point of Level 4 ('good analysis but limited evaluation'). A little more evaluation might have raised it up into Level 5. This gets 19 marks.

Daniel's answer

Examiner comments:
Absolute poverty is better defined here than relative poverty. Abbreviations like 'OK' and 'govt.' should *not* be used in an answer.

Examiner comments:
It is debatable whether doctors necessarily work longer or harder than factory workers. Daniel misses an opportunity here to discuss the 'incentive' function of incomes.

Examiner comments:
Again, a point is being made about 'incentives', but it is vaguely expressed.

Overall: An insubstantial answer with only basic economic understanding demonstrated. Does not break out of Level 1 ('a very weak answer'). 6 marks.

Examiner comments:
Daniel is talking abo[ut] 'fairness' a bit too much. Economists c[an] not especially well qualified to judge w[hat] is 'just' or 'fair'. It wo[uld] be better for Daniel to use concepts like 'equality' and 'equit[y']

Examiner comme[nts]
These are not particularly good definitions of income and wealth, but at le[ast] Daniel is attempting [to] give definitions.

Examiner comme[nts]
Like Helen, Daniel has introduced this important point, but here it is merely a slo[gan] and Helen develope[d] a lot further.

Absolute poverty is when people don't have enough money for basic necessities such as food and water, like happens in places like Africa where people live on less than a dollar a day. Relative poverty is when people have an OK standard of living but the govt. decides that incomes are unfair. Suppose as well as a minimum wage there was a maximum, or if income was made equal in all jobs, then a doctor would be paid the same as a factory worker which would not be fair. This is because doctors need many more qualifications and work longer hours. Income is what you earn either monthly or weekly for doing a job, wealth is everything what you own such as your house, car, savings. If wealth was evenly distributed then people who had worked hard all their lives to buy a car or house would have them taken away and that would not be fair.

Even though the rich have a lot of assets they still pay a large amount of tax and if they decided not to work so hard the poor would have to pay more tax.

A good way to reduce poverty is 'education, education, education'.

Data-response question

THE EU CONTEXT – ROAMING THROUGH EUROPE

EXTRACT A: UK TARIFF RANGE

The range of prices charged by the main mobile phone network providers in the UK to make a four-minute call home from abroad:

Network	Highest price	Lowest price
A	£5.20	£2.50
B	£4.50	£2.50
C	£4.30	£2.60
D	£4.20	£2.45
E	£2.50	£2.40

EXTRACT B: THE COMMISSION ACTS

The European Commission has announced that it intends to reduce mobile phone roaming charges, the prices charged by mobile phone network companies for international calls.

The companies say that they need to collect the extra revenues to subsidise other services, for example to keep national call costs down or to give 'free' phones to customers. Critics accuse them of 'ripping off' their customers by charging them much more than the actual extra cost of routeing calls between countries. A spokesperson for the EU rejected claims that the high charges were justified by the cost of connecting long-range phone calls, and said that it was 'unnatural' that customers were charged not only for making calls, but also for receiving them when they were abroad. She warned that the EU Commission would consider putting a maximum price on international phone calls, so that they would cost no more than domestic calls. She added: 'At the moment Europe has 27 different markets for mobile phone charges. This clearly is anti-competitive and reduces the efficiency of the Single European Market both for individuals and for businesses'.

Some leading economists have supported the EU stance, and have claimed that the underlying problem is that the market is oligopolistic and anti-competitive. Others argue that technology is changing, and that it will soon be possible for many more people to use the Internet to make phone calls that are very cheap or even free. This, they claim, makes EU action unnecessary, as lower prices will come about quite naturally as a result of market forces.

Comment on two significant features of the data in Extract A
(5 marks)

What evidence is there in the extracts that the mobile phone networks operate as an oligopoly, and what further evidence would need to be collected to prove this?
(10 marks)

Should the UK government support the EU Commission in various methods of reducing roaming charges, or should market forces be allowed to operate? Justify your answer.
(25 marks)

Hot tips

General advice

AQA Economics at A2 uses two types of exam question: data-response and essays. We give you some tips on tackling data-response items below, and some tips on answering essays in the Exam Café section on page 189. This advice is applicable to both papers, ECON-3 and ECON-4.

You should always pay full attention to the following advice.

● Keep an eye on the clock. Reserve some time for reading through the paper at the start (and while you are doing this, marking bits that you need to pay particular attention to with a highlighter pen) reading through your written answers at the end (you might be surprised how many little written errors you can make while working under the pressure of exam conditions).

● Since the data-response and essay questions carry equal marks you should spend a roughly equal amount of time on each.

● Write clearly in ink (preferably black, but blue is okay as well. Do *not* use red, green or purple ink.)

● *Never* use correction fluid. Cross out any mistakes and do them again.

● Use pencil (with a ruler, if appropriate) to draw diagrams. Write labels in ink.

● Follow the *rubric*. Do *not* answer *fewer* or *more* questions than required.

● Pay attention to **command words** (refer to advice on these on page 189 of this book)

● Remember that examiners have to allocate some marks for the *quality of written communication* (known as QWC). Write neatly and clearly, communicate in good clear English, try to spell correctly.

Data-response questions

AQA examination papers ECON-3 and ECON-4 are each marked out of a maximum of 80. There are two data-response questions and **three** essay questions on each paper, each worth 40 marks, and you choose **one** of

each. At A2, there are **three** parts to the data-response question, carrying 5, 10 and 25 marks. Spend time on sub-questions in proportion to the mark allocations. Do *not* spend half an hour on a part worth 5 marks, and only two minutes on a part worth 25 marks. Please note:

● One of the data-response questions will be set in the context of the **European Union**, the other will be set in the **global** context. It follows that during your studies you should take an interest in current events and read as much as you can about the economics of these two contexts.

● In either case, there will be some focus on the UK in the appropriate context.

● Choose your question carefully, on the basis of the **whole** question. Don't be put off by a question because a small part of it is difficult for you; don't be attracted to it if a small part appears easy. Remember that the final part carries the most marks.

● Label sub-questions clearly in the margin: (a), (b), (c).

● Avoid the weakest approach, which is to simply copy out chunks of data without comment.

● Be aware of an 'incline of difficulty': as you move through the questions you should be using higher order skills…

● … and be aware of 'levels of response'. Familiarise yourself with mark schemes (available from AQA). In particular, be aware that about half the marks for part (c) are awarded for the important skill of **evaluation**. So when answering this question *always* reserve some time and space to show your ability to evaluate, for example by making judgements, justifying a policy, or assessing whether advantages outweigh disadvantages. Also see **command words** on page 189.

● Use the data wherever possible, and refer to the data where appropriate.

● Use your knowledge of economic principles.

● Use your pre-existing economic awareness. Improve this from newspapers, television and radio.

The National and International Economy

Welcome to Part 2 of A2 Economics. This introduction includes:

● an overview of what you can expect to study

● a look at the relationship between what you have studied for AS and the requirements of A2

● global and EU contexts.

Overview of Unit 4

Part 2 of your A2 text is devoted to covering all that you need to know to succeed in the examination based upon the AQA specification for Unit 4: 'The National and International Economy'. It is synoptic and draws on work you did for AS, especially for Unit 2. This macroeconomic unit consists of three different but interrelated areas of study:

● *macroeconomic indicators* – the use of data on economic growth, unemployment, inflation and the balance of payments to assess the performance of economies.

● *government policies* designed to affect macroeconomic indicators. These include fiscal, supply-side and monetary policies – you need to be able to model the possible effects of different policies using AD/AS analysis.

● *the international economy* – this includes investigating the possible effects of globalisation, an understanding of the economic gains that greater international trade might bring, and knowing about the balance of payments and exchange rates.

AS and A2

When you took your AS Unit 2 exam, you were required to have an understanding of different macroeconomic indicators, the use of AD/AS analysis to predict what might happen if particular variables changed. Both these areas of study are taken further in Unit 4 and there is a much greater emphasis on the consideration of the consequences of changes in macroeconomic indicators. Much of the work on the international economy will be new to you, although you should already be familiar with the concept of the balance of payments.

You need to have a good idea of the main economic events that have affected the UK, European and global economies over the last 10 years and also be aware of earlier events such as the Great Crash of 1929, the influence of monetarism and the movement towards greater economic integration in Europe.

Global and EU contexts

It is not possible to study and understand macroeconomics without reference to European and global contexts. Increasingly, UK economic policies are directly influenced by EU policies such as the creation of a single European market, the adoption of the euro and common approaches to fiscal policies. Similarly, the shift in economic power from the USA to China, Brazil, Russia and India, and the globalisation of both trade and production have direct effects on the performance of the UK economy.

6 Macroeconomic indicators

On completion of this chapter you should be able to:

- analyse and evaluate the causes of changes in the economic cycle
- analyse and evaluate supply-side factors likely to determine the long-run trend rate of growth
- analyse and evaluate the costs and benefits of economic growth
- use and understand the limitations of national income data to assess living standards
- analyse and evaluate the causes of unemployment
- investigate possible relationships between unemployment and inflation
- analyse and evaluate the causes and economic effects of changes in the price level.

This chapter is divided into four sections, corresponding to the main elements of this part of the AQA specification:

- The economic cycle and economic growth
- Use of national income data to assess living standards
- Inflation and deflation
- Unemployment.

Each of these sections draws on and develops learning that you will have undertaken for AS.

The economic cycle and economic growth

Economic growth is defined as changes in the productive capacity of the economy and is usually measured by changes in GDP over time. Economists distinguish between actual and **potential economic growth** and this can be illustrated by reference to production possibility curves. In Figure 6.1 the movement from PPC_1 to PPC_2 represents an increase in the productive capacity of the economy. This might or might not be realised in reality. Thus, a movement

from point *a* to point *b* represents **actual economic growth** by which an economy has expanded production to a point at which all productive resources are being utilised. Point *c* indicates unused resources.

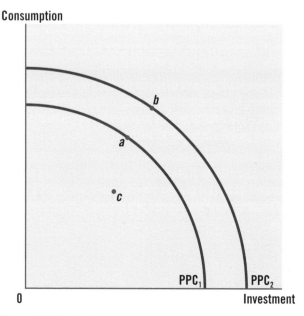

Figure 6.1 Production possibility curve

Most economies enjoy positive economic growth over time, which would be shown by outward movements in the production possibility curve. The historical trend in economic growth is referred to as the long-run trend rate of economic growth. Actual economic growth can be both above and below this trend and these fluctuations are referred to as the **economic cycle.**

In the sections which follow, consideration is given to different theories used to explain the different phases of the economic cycle. This is followed by an analysis of the supply-side factors that are likely to determine the long-run trend rate of growth. Finally, the costs and benefits of economic growth are evaluated.

DEFINITIONS

Economic growth: increases in national output over time, often measured by changes in GNP

Potential economic growth: growth in the productive potential of an economy

Actual economic growth: the extent to which economies grow to their potential

Economic cycle: cyclical fluctuations above and below the long-run trend rate of economic growth

Make sure you understand the diagram in Figure 6.2 by labelling periods of boom, upturn, downturn and recession.

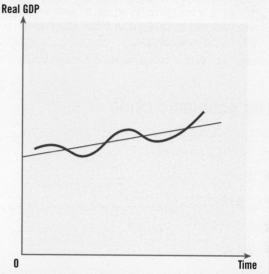

Figure 6.2 The economic cycle

You will have also learned that economic events are interlinked and that in the boom phase, growing demand, increased orders, rising incomes and falling unemployment are all likely to be associated with periods of economic growth. On the other hand, declining economic growth is likely to be associated with falling aggregate demand, rising unemployment, reduced orders and falling incomes.

You will also need to be able use the diagram illustrated in Figure 6.2 to illustrate both positive and negative output gaps.

BUILDING ON AS

For AS you were expected learn about:

● the characteristics of different phases in the economic cycle

● causes of changes in the economic cycle

● what economists mean when they use the terms 'economic growth'

● the difference between short- and long-term economic growth

● factors that influence the long-run trend rate of growth.

STEPPING UP TO A2

The focus in A2 is on:

● being more precise about different stages of the economic cycle

● analysing and evaluating possible explanations of the different phases of the economic cycle

● evaluating the causes and effects of economic growth in more detail

● assessing the costs and benefits of economic growth, especially in relation to environmental issues and to its effects on individuals and the economy

● understanding the possible consequences of inflation and unemployment in greater detail.

You will, as you know by now, be faced with more complex stimulus material and writing one two-part essay in which the emphasis will be on evaluation.

The economic cycle

Economists divide the economic cycle into four recognisable phases:

● boom

● downturn

● recession

● upturn.

BOOM

The **boom** phase can be illustrated using aggregate demand and aggregate supply analysis as is shown in Figure 6.3. In this case, aggregate demand and aggregate supply are in equilibrium at OY_1 and any further increase in aggregate demand would lead to escalating inflation. At the same time, businesses would find order books increasing and may feel the

opportunity to raise prices to boost their short-run profits. It would be expected that the demand for goods and services would be reflected in increases in the derived demand for different types of labour, and boom times could be associated with increased immigration and shortages of labour with particular skills. It is also likely that for short periods of time the rate of growth of the economic cycle will be above the trend rate of growth and this indicates that the economy will '**overheat**'. The two main indicators of this precursor to economic slowdown would be increasing inflation and deterioration in the balance of payments.

DOWNTURN

As noted above, some features of a booming economy, such as increasing rates of inflation, can provide triggers leading to policy responses that could result in a **downturn** in the economic cycle. For example, a government or central bank fearful of inflation might increase interest rates.

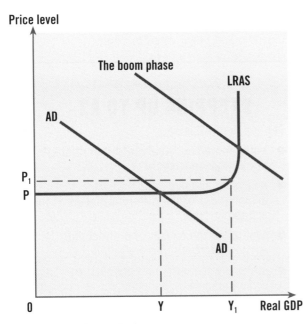

Figure 6.3 The boom phase

ACTIVITY ⋯⋅

Use an aggregate demand and supply diagram to help you illustrate the possible effect of increased interest rates on inflation and economic growth.

Similarly, if prices in the UK are rising more quickly than those in other countries, demand for UK-produced goods and services might fall and the

UK's demand for imported goods and services might rise. The combined effect of these two changes will be a reduction in UK aggregate demand. Whatever the stimulus, falling aggregate demand can lead to declining business and consumer confidence, leading to reductions in both consumption and investment.

The potential impact of falling aggregate demand will be amplified by the multiplier effect described in your AS text and on page 110 of this book. Any decrease in an element of aggregate demand is likely to have a bigger proportional effect on national income. Economies with a relatively low marginal propensity to withdraw are likely to be those with greater fluctuations on the economic cycle.

It is likely that, at this stage of the economic cycle, the government and its central bank will try to influence the economy to ensure that the slowdown in economic activity is kept to a minimum. If the cycle recovers without falling into recession, this is known as a **soft landing.**

The Great Depression of the 1930s led to widespread loss of livelihood

DEFINITION

Soft landing: avoiding *recession* in a time of economic slowdown

RECESSION

A **recession** is characterised by rising unemployment, falling demand, and falling levels of consumer and business confidence. The term is often used rather loosely and can be applied to periods in which the economic growth rate has slowed, but still remains positive. However, economists use the term 'recession' very precisely to describe a situation in which there is negative economic growth for more than two successive quarters. The last time this happened in the UK was in 1991. If negative economic growth persists, it is likely that a significant number of businesses would become bankrupt, leaving unpaid debts. Business failures place additional pressure on the banking system, as loans will not be repaid. Banks will find it necessary to call in loans and restrict credit, setting up a

downward spiral of further business failure. In the worst-case scenario, recession could lead to a **slump** or **depression**, as was seen in the 1930s in many industrialised countries.

However, some of the factors associated with recession could trigger policy changes that might contribute to an upturn, or recovery. Government spending to counter the social ill-effects of recession might provide a stimulus to aggregate demand; falling domestic demand might prompt UK firms to seek new markets abroad; and sooner or later, businesses might reinvest to replace worn-out machinery. Interest rates might fall. Any of these factors could contribute to a recovery in consumer and business confidence leading to the **upturn** phase.

DEFINITIONS

Recession: negative economic growth for more than 6 months

Depression or **slump:** long-term recession

Technological shock: random fluctuation in labour productivity

Upturn: a period in which aggregate demand is increasing

UPTURN

This could follow from the factors identified in the previous section and would be characterised by increasing rates of economic growth, growing business and consumer confidence, rising incomes and falling unemployment. Aggregate demand would increase and, as there would be space capacity in the economy, the output of goods and services would increase without undue inflationary pressures. The recovery phase is represented by the increase in national output from OY to OY_1 in Figure 6.3 on page 108.

Recovery in an economy with relatively low marginal propensity to withdraw is likely to be more rapid, because of the relative significance of the **multiplier effect**. An increase in any of the components of aggregate demand is likely to have a more than proportional effect on national output. Increases in household incomes, associated with increases in the demand for factors of production, will result in further increases in consumption – fuelling a *virtuous* cycle of expansion.

DEFINITION

Multiplier effect: the extent to which a change in a component of aggregate demand can lead to a proportionally larger change in national output

ACTIVITY ⋯⋗

Use aggregate demand and supply diagrams to illustrate a recession deepening into a depression.

ACTIVITY ⋯⋗

Use the NationMaster website to obtain data to plot a graph of economic cycles in the UK and USA between 1990 and 2005. Clearly identify periods of boom, downturn, recession and upturn. Assess the extent to which the two economies might be subject to the same economic cycles.

ECONOMIC POLICIES AND THE ECONOMIC CYCLE

Government economic policies can both potentially dampen and exaggerate fluctuations in the economic cycle. Thus, increasing government expenditure in the boom phase of the cycle is likely to increase aggregate demand, leading to greater inflationary pressure, whereas a similar policy introduced at an appropriate point in the downturn of an economy may well help prevent recession.

Governments tend to argue that economic cycles tend to be global phenomenon whose causes are neither fully understood nor predictable. In this context, government economic policies might be designed to reduce the amplitude of peaks and troughs in economic activity.

MODERN EXPLANATIONS OF THE ECONOMIC CYCLE

The phenomenon of economic or business cycles has long been recognised and numerous theories have been developed to explain fluctuations in economic activity.

Modern theorists tend to support the view that the economic cycle is a global phenomenon over which governments have little direct control and they have focused on the effect of **technological shocks** on economic activity. It is argued that these random changes in the productivity level cause fluctuations around the trend rate of growth of an economy. Examples of such shocks include innovations, bad weather, imported oil price increase, and stricter environmental and safety regulations.

ECONOMICS IN CONTEXT – GLOBAL ECONOMICS

One of the main areas of employment for economists involves trying to predict future patterns of economic activity. The following article focuses upon the interaction between global events and the performance of the UK economy. It was written in the autumn of 2007. Read it and do the Activity that follows.

UK GDP Growth Forecast to Slow Markedly to 1.9% in 2008
Serious Risks to the Downside

- Following the robust GDP growth seen through the first three quarters of 2007, economic activity is forecast to slow markedly from the fourth quarter. Year-on-year growth is expected to fall from 3.2% to 2.8%.
- GDP growth is forecast to slow to 1.9% in 2008, which would be the second-lowest growth rate since 1992.
- Consumer spending seems certain to moderate in the face of the still marked overall rise in interest rates since August 2006, tighter lending conditions resulting from the credit crunch, muted real disposable income growth, heightened debt levels, and a slowing housing market.
- Unemployment seems likely to rise in 2008.
- Meanwhile, exports seem likely to be increasingly hit by slowing global growth and the lagged dampening impact of an extended strong pound.
- Business investment plans are currently being scaled back in the face of the ongoing credit crunch and increased doubts and uncertainty over the economic outlook.
- As a result, we believe that the risks to growth are slanted markedly to the downside. The major downside risks include: 1) the credit crunch is extended and deepens, as problems relating to the US sub-prime

mortgage mess prove even greater than currently believed. The risks to growth from this would be magnified if equity markets suffer sharp falls; 2) the US economy suffers a recession with serious knock-on effects on the global economy; 3) the UK housing market crashes; 4) oil prices rise above US$100/barrel for an extended period and a tipping point is reached, resulting in a major slowdown in global growth.
- Any one of these problems could well cause UK growth to be as low as 1.5% in 2008.
- A combination of them could very possibly lead to recession. This is not our central forecast, but it is a serious risk.
- Consumer price inflation is likely to head up to 2.5% over the next few months as it is pushed up by elevated oil and food prices. Consumer price inflation is forecast to dip back under 2% in the fourth quarter of 2008.
- We expect the Bank of England to cut interest rates to 5.00% by mid-year, and, if the downside risks to the growth forecast materialise, interest rates could very well go down further still.
- Sterling is forecast to fall back significantly against the euro over the coming months, as interest rate differentials become less supportive. The ECB seems set to keep its

key interest rate unchanged at 4.00% for several months to come. However, the pound could well continue to trade above US$2.00 for some time to come, as the dollar is pressurized by concerns over the US economy and further cuts in US interest rates.
- Housing market activity and prices are forecast to cool markedly further over the coming months in reaction to tighter lending practices and stretched affordability pressures. At this stage we do not expect to see a sharp correction. We believe that the downside for house prices will be limited by a lack of supply, the increasing number of households, high employment, and the fact that few vendors are currently having to sell for 'distressed' reasons.

A sharp housing market correction could also be triggered if both sellers and buyers start expecting prices to fall sharply. This could prompt a flood of sellers putting their houses on to the market to try and sell their houses before prices fall markedly; while at the same time, prospective buyers hold off in the expectation that prices will fall. Under such circumstances, a growing surplus of supply over demand would undermine prices.

Source: Global Insight

These shocks can be further subdivided into those that are:

● internal – occurring within a given economy

● external – those that arise outside a given economy

● positive – contributing to economic growth

● negative – leading to falling economic growth

● demand-side – initially affecting aggregate demand

● supply-side – initially affecting aggregate supply.

Those who support this explanation of economic cycles are called 'Real Business theorists' and they argue that the economy would continue along its trend rate of growth were it not for the random occurrence of these shocks. Shocks that are positive lead to increases in productive capacity that can have a lasting effect on long-term growth within an economy and this could account for the overall upward trend rate of economic growth. Real Business theorists also argue that fluctuations in the economic cycle represent the efficient working of the economy in response to random events, and for this reason governments should not intervene to smooth out fluctuations in the economic cycle.

STRETCH AND CHALLENGE

Research the following alternative theories to explain the different phases of the economic cycle:

a Keynesian

b monetarist

c Marxist

d Real Business.

ACTIVITY ⋯⋗

Produce a table which:

a summarises the predictions contained in the commentary above for 2008

b assesses the accuracy of these predictions.

Produce your own forecasts for the forthcoming calendar year.

Economic growth

Long-run economic growth, also called potential growth, refers to increases in the productive capacity of the economy. Economists consider that this is brought about by changes in three interrelated

ACTIVITY ⋯⋗

In late 2007 and early 2008, a series of shocks threatened growth rates in many world economies. These included the collapse in the US sub-prime market, the global credit crunch and – in the UK – the Northern Rock crisis. How far can these events be explained by interest rate policies pursued by the US Federal Reserve?

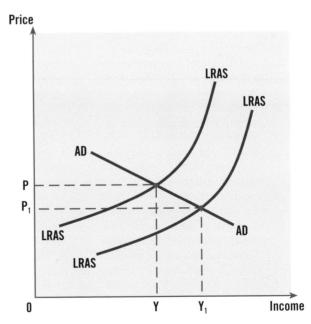

Figure 6.4 The effects of increases in LRAS

supply-side factors: investment, technology and education and training. Thus, increasing investment should enable an economy to produce more; improvements in technology mean that capital is more productive; and better education and training should lead to a more productive workforce. Each of these changes can be represented by a rightward shift in the LRAS curve illustrated in Figure 6.4. This indicates that long-run economic growth can lead to increased output and, potentially, a reduction in the price level. However, it is likely that the government will at the same time boost short-run aggregate demand to further increase GNP up to the point where inflationary pressures become a concern.

> **learning tip**
>
> For A2 you need to be able to analyse the relative importance of
> - investment
> - technology
> - education and training
>
> as determinants of long-run aggregate supply.

INVESTMENT

Traditionally **investment** has been seen as spending by firms on capital – machines used to produce machines. The link between investment and long-run aggregate supply – the productive capacity of the economy – is self-evident. As long as new investment occurs at a greater rate than depreciation, the rate at which capital wears out, it is clear that the productive capacity of the economy will increase. Three other factors make investment a potentially very significant factor leading to economic growth:

- its link to aggregate demand
- the accelerator principle
- possible links to technological change.

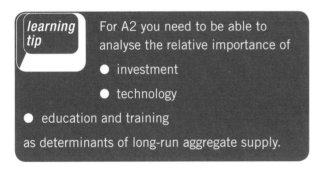

Figure 6.5 The effects of increases in investment

THE LINK TO AGGREGATE DEMAND

Investment, as was explained in the AS part of your course, is a component of aggregate demand. Should investment increase for some reason, aggregate demand increases, as is shown in Figure 6.5.

An increase in aggregate demand will have a multiplier effect on national output, and increasing incomes will lead to further increases in consumption. The positive effects of increasing aggregate demand are likely to be further magnified by increases in investment.

THE ACCELERATOR PRINCIPLE

Increases in aggregate demand, associated with rising incomes and levels of consumption, will provide many firms with higher potential sales. The **accelerator principle** focuses on the relationship between investment and anticipated sales. It is argued that firms will increase productive capacity

---

> **DEFINITION**
>
> **Investment:** spending to increase the productive potential of an economy

> **DEFINITION**
>
> **Accelerator principle:** an explanation of the greater volatility in levels of investment

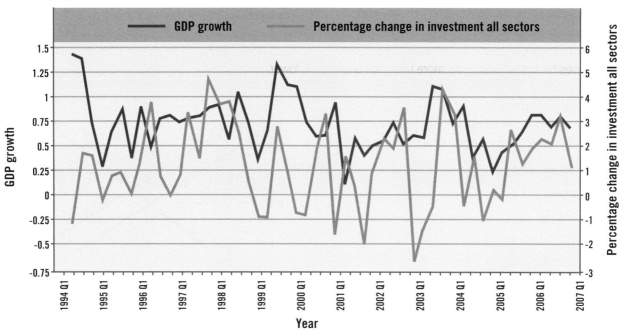

Figure 6.6 Investment and national output

if they expect sales to rise. This means that the changes in investment are related to the rate of change in consumer demand. Investment will tend to increase more than proportionally to any change in demand but, by the same token, if the rate of change in consumer demand is falling, firms will not need so much productive capacity and investment will fall by a greater amount. The relationship between investment and national output is illustrated in Figure 6.6. This shows that changes in investment tend to be much more volatile than changes in national output.

Not all investment is likely to lead to economic growth. The replacement of worn-out machinery – depreciation, for example, maintains the productive capacity of a firm. If national levels of investment are sufficient only to maintain a given level of productive capacity, long-term economic growth will not occur. Economists distinguish between *gross investment*, which is the total of investment in a given time period, and *net* investment which is gross investment less that allocated to cover depreciation.

The theory outlined above envisages a simple positive and quantifiable relationship between net investment and economic growth. However, firms undertake different types of investment. For example,

firms may undertake new investment to enable them to restructure. This could involve 'downsizing', when firms actually reduce their level of productive capacity to focus on more profitable activities. This trend was observable across Europe in the early 1990s, in response to the recession at the beginning of that decade. It is also occurring as more and more European businesses outsource production to China and other east Asian countries. In this context, they might be investing to actually reduce productive capacity.

Economists are, therefore, interested in examining the actual purposes to which investment is directed. This particularly applies to investment that not only increases the productive capacity of an economy but also finances new and better ways of producing goods and services. This is referred to as technological change.

TECHNOLOGICAL CHANGE

The analysis above assumes that investment involves the replacement of capital on a like-for-like basis. In reality, firms investing are more likely to replace old machinery and plant with ones that are technologically more advanced. High rates of investment are therefore likely to be associated with more rapid technological advance. The application of faster and faster, smaller and smaller, computing equipment is occurring at an increasing rate. Those businesses that invest more are more likely to take advantage of these changes and those economies that do so are likely to give themselves a competitive advantage over those whose rates of investment are lower.

DEFINITION

New economic paradigm: suggestion that it is possible for positive economic growth to co-exist with low rates of inflation

STRETCH AND CHALLENGE

What evidence would you look for to evaluate the thesis that the 'fourth industrial revolution' has resulted in the emergence of a new economic paradigm of low inflation, high growth and low unemployment to replace the traditional economic cycle?

ECONOMICS IN CONTEXT – GLOBAL ECONOMICS

ARE WE THROUGH WITH BOOM AND BUST?

Looked at historically, the UK has passed through a number of different phases of economic development. The initial stages of the industrial revolution in the late eighteenth century were partly fuelled by developments in water power – canals to transport goods more cheaply and water mills to produce textiles and other goods in greater volumes at lower cost.

This process accelerated with the development and application of steam power to trains, ships and all types of factories, leading to a further leap forward in productivity and output. In the late nineteenth and early twentieth century, technological changes involving the use of electricity as an energy source provided further impetus for technological change.

The late twentieth and early twenty-first century has seen the development of the microprocessor as a means of revolutionising all types of productive activities, leading again to increased output and lower costs. For example, all kinds of published materials can be produced using digital techniques requiring fewer employees, and enabling the rapid inputting and transfer of data.

Similarly computerised stock control systems allow firms to carry smaller stocks, while at the same time decreasing the response times for increases in demand for goods and services. There are many other ways in which information and communication (ICT) applications have simplified and speeded up productive and distributive systems. Some people have called the development of microchip technologies the fourth industrial revolution.

In most of the 1990s, relatively high rates of economic growth in the USA and the rest of the developed world and a lack of any periods of extended recession prompted some economists and commentators to suggest that developed economies were moving into a new state in which they were able to sustain positive economic growth, low rates of inflation and low rates of unemployment. This has been called a **new economic paradigm**. Some economists have argued that this is the result of major technological shifts associated with the greater use of ICT and related technologies.

EDUCATION AND TRAINING

Traditional theories of economic growth emphasised the importance of investment in physical plant and machinery to increase the long-run productive capacity of an economy. Although attention has always been paid to the skills, attitudes and abilities of the workforce, from the 1960s a number of economists suggested that investment in education and training can lead to larger increases in national output than equivalent increases in physical capital. These theories were first developed by Theodore Schultz in relation to agricultural production and then extended to apply to the US economy as a whole. Economists use the term **human capital** to emphasise the importance of this type of investment, which is becoming increasingly significant because of structural changes in economies associated with technological changes and globalisation.

DEFINITION

Human capital: the productive capacity of people

In the UK and other developed economies, there is a greater emphasis on technological advances that require workers with improved skills. At the same time, productive processes that require less skilled workers are increasingly being undertaken in the developing world, where labour costs are lower. This means that the UK and other developed countries now rely more heavily on the production of goods and services that are technologically more advanced and require more highly skilled workers. UK politicians are fond of pointing to the poor record of the UK in terms of education and training when in comparison with other countries, and Tony Blair famously won the 1997 election behind the slogan 'education, education, education'.

learning tip

You could be asked to answer part of an essay question about economic growth. Look closely at the '*command*' word: it could be *explain/evaluate/assess* different causes of economic growth. If you are asked to explain, you need to write about investment, technology and education and training; if to evaluate or assess, you are being asked to ask which factor is most important – the analysis above should lead you to the conclusion that all three factors are important.

ACTIVITY ····⁝

Conduct further research into the success of the Asian Tigers – assess how far the factors associated with their high growth rates support or contradict the explanations of economic growth provided earlier in this text.

ECONOMICS IN CONTEXT – GLOBAL ECONOMICS

ASIAN TIGERS

In order to have a better understanding of those factors that contribute to economic growth, economists have focused attention on the economic performance of the four Asian Tiger countries: Taiwan, Singapore, Hong Kong and South Korea. All achieved double-digit economic growth through most of the 1980s and 1990s. Five factors are said to explain their success:

● land reform to ensure a fairer distribution of agricultural land

● export-led growth
● high expenditure on education
● very high savings ratios
● authoritarian governments.

Although the currency crisis of the late 1990s slowed growth in these countries, and although India and China are major competitors, the Asian Tigers continue to grow and prosper.

learning tip

The use of the command 'assess' in a question tells you that there is unlikely to be a straightforward or unambiguous answer. Use phrases like: 'There is some evidence to suggest that ...', 'on the other hand ...', 'one factor shared by all Asian Tigers is ...', 'a factor that seems only to apply to South Korea is ...'

Benefits and costs of economic growth

learning tip

There is a brief mention in your AS course of the benefits of economic growth in terms of enabling more people to enjoy higher living standards and the costs of economic growth in terms of negative externalities and the big CC – climate change.

This is taken further in A2, as you are required to:

● *analyse and evaluate the various benefits and costs of economic growth*

● *discuss issues of sustainability*

● *evaluate the impact of economic growth on individuals, the economy and the environment.*

BENEFITS OF ECONOMIC GROWTH

Economic growth can lead to:

● *increased prosperity* – even the relatively low rate of economic growth of around 2 per cent led to a doubling on income in the UK over a 30 year period. In the Asian Tiger countries (Taiwan, Singapore, Hong Kong and South Korea), GNP has increased more than threefold over the same period. Higher incomes enable greater material prosperity and give more and more people living in poorer countries access to goods and services that we in developed countries regard as normal goods.

● *reduced poverty* – increased national incomes can result in a reduction in absolute poverty. Better employment prospects, greater spending on health, education, food and clean water all contribute to the potential reduction in poverty. Economic growth can allow governments to spend more on services that benefit the poor without redistributing income from the rich to the poor. Reductions in poverty lead to longer and healthier lives. There is a high correlation between incomes and life expectancy. You can expect to live for a little over 39 years if you live in Swaziland but a Japanese woman will on average live to the age of 86.

● *better quality of life* – higher incomes not only allow greater prosperity, they can enable people to enjoy a better quality of life than would be the case if their incomes were lower. It could be argued that economic growth enables economies to be more considerate to environmental dangers – better-off countries tend to have stronger anti-pollution legislation than poorer countries.

● *greater political power* – economic power and political power go hand in hand. The strongest political power in the world is the USA – but for how long? Rapid growth in China is likely to lead to a shift in political power. This may provide a dangerous phase in global relationships. Historically, loss of political power has been associated with increases in conflict.

Costs of economic growth

There are also strong arguments against ever-continued economic growth:

● **Sustainability** is a major issue that brings us right back to the economic problem of reconciling unlimited wants with scarce resources, first introduced at the beginning of your AS course. Some economists argue that we are now seeing the effects of unsustainable economic growth. The price of crude oil has now passed the $100/barrel mark and this can be seen as a clear signal that demand

DEFINITION

Sustainability: economic growth that does not deplete non-renewable resources

The high price of wheat is a sign that demand is outstripping supply

is outstripping supply. Prices of other commodities, such as wheat, gold, and platinum, are also at record highs.

● *Negative externalities* are also generated by increasing rates of economic growth. The scientific evidence of global warming is now accepted by all countries. There is less consensus as to how CO_2 emissions might be limited. The challenge facing all of us is whether or not it is possible to take measures that will actually reduce the emissions that are causing global warming.

● *Increased inequalities* – economic growth can result in a redistribution of income from those who have least to those who have most. In the UK, the gap between the richest and poorest has actually widened over the last decade of steady economic growth. The expanding economy has provided opportunities for the well-off to become even better-off, while those suffering greatest social deprivation are excluded from the benefits of economic growth.

● There are indications that there is a positive correlation between increasing prosperity and increasing mental ill-health. It can be argued that economic growth bring about greater stresses in relationship to spells of unemployment and to work pressure, as workers are expected to be more flexible and mobile. Economic growth can provide a threat to traditional ways of life that provide social cohesion, which many individuals find difficult.

learning tip

Getting you to weigh up the costs and benefits of economic growth is the kind of question that examiners like to test you with. There is no right or wrong answer, but what they will be looking for is that you can develop two or three of the costs and two or three of the benefits, and that you come to a conclusion at the end. If you only present one set of arguments, you will be limiting your chances of getting a good mark.

You could also be asked to assess the impact of economic growth on individuals or the economy or the environment – you will use similar arguments but you will need to relate these to the context specified in the question.

learning tip

Part a) essay questions on growth and economic cycles are likely to ask you to explain the possible causes of different phases of the economic cycle and how one phase may lead into another.

Part b) questions are more likely to ask you to evaluate, or assess, the effectiveness of different policies, especially supply-side reforms, in promoting economic growth.

Use of national income data to assess living standards

BUILDING ON AS

For AS you were required to know:

● how data – such as GDP, retail price indices, unemployment and the balance of payments on current account – is used to measure the performance of an economy, and how index numbers are used.

● how to use this data to compare the performance of different economies.

You would have learned that GDP-per-capita data is used by economists to give an indication of how well-off, or badly-off, a particular economy might be. On this basis, the UK was ranked the twenty-seventh richest country in the world, but it was suggested that caution was needed if this data was going to be used to inform judgements about relative living standards. Thus, you needed to know that it was also important to understand that incomes could be distributed very unequally, making it difficult to generalise about the living standards of all those living in a given country.

STEPPING UP TO A2

For A2 you need to know about other ways of measuring and comparing living standards and you will be required to be more critical about the ways in which these measures are constructed and used to make judgements about living standards.

Using national income data to judge living standards

You should already be familiar with the problems of using GDP as a macroeconomic measure in a developed economy such as the UK. GDP accounts for the value of goods and services produced in a given period of time. 'Real' data will exclude the effects of inflation and per-capita measures will take account of the size of a country's population. Even so, real GDP per capita:

● can be distorted by recording and accounting problems

● fails to indicate differences in the quality of life

● does not identify gender differences.

These factors apply in varying degrees to all countries, but there are particular issues relating to developing economies. For them, economic growth is vital, but this does not necessarily raise living standards for all. In a worst-case scenario, it is possible to consider economic growth occurring in the context of gross inequalities of income resulting

in the production of luxury goods rather than basics for survival. This growth could be unsustainable, involving the once-and-for-all consumption of non-renewable resources, whereas the mutual support offered by poorer groups and extended families would not be recognised. Finally, if government and civil services are weak, it is likely that official statistics would be incomplete. This extreme scenario illustrates the shortcoming of relying on GDP as a measure of living standards. Nonetheless, this and related data shown in Table 6.1 is useful.

	GNI per capita ($)
Burundi	100
Syria	1,750
Cuba	900–3500 (estimate)
China	2,010
Brazil	4,730
UK	40,180
Luxembourg	76,010

Source: World Development Indicators, World Bank

Table 6.1 Gross national income per capita, 2006

GNI stands for gross national income per capita and is a similar measure to GDP used by the World Bank in making comparisons between different countries.

> **learning tip**
> *Gross national product* is worked out by adding up the added value of the production process in a country. *Gross national income* refers to the aggregation of incomes that are derived from the productive process. In theory they should be the same, but difficulties in accounting can lead to differences.

Although it is not possible to make judgements about living standards using this data alone, the underlying significance of GNI must never be underestimated. If per-capita income figures are low, as is the case with Burundi, it follows that poverty, suffering and starvation will be major problems and that such countries are always going to be faced with massive problems in terms of financing development programmes. This data also indicates global inequalities – people living in Luxembourg are likely to be 760 times better-off than inhabitants of Burundi. Finally, the broad estimate for Cuba indicates that the Cuban government may collect data in different ways or might be reluctant to release data.

It is important to consider the nature of the economic growth being experienced. If long-term economic growth is going to occur, it needs to be sustainable, that is, achieved in a way that does not reduce future populations' ability to produce more. Some developing nations, particularly in Africa, have in the past achieved relatively high levels of growth but at the opportunity cost of using up non-renewable resources.

Limitations in national income data

Different countries collect statistics about national income in different ways, and the official statistics in all economies tend to underestimate the level

nting is a 'hidden' economic activity

of economic activity at any one time. This is partly because national statistics do not always record economic activity, especially if it occurs informally or does not generate a money income. If I employ a gardener, his or her contribution to the economy will – if he is taxed at source or declares his income to the tax authorities – be measured by the payment or income received. If I choose to do the same work myself, or if his income is not declared, the economic activity will not be recorded and not show up in national income data.

This argument can be extended to economies that official statistics indicate are much poorer than the UK. Those growing their own food, or hunting or fishing are engaged in economic activity, but it is unlikely to show up in official statistics.

A bigger problem is that there are economies hidden within economies in which illegal activity and tax evasion take place. A fascinating area of study for some economists involves trying to assess the relative size of hidden or unofficial or informal economies. One approach used by economists investigating the size of the hidden economy in the former communist states of eastern Europe is to focus on electricity consumption. It is argued that there is a very close correlation between electricity consumption and GNP, making it possible to make alternative estimates of GNP based on electricity consumption. These studies show that the hidden economy in some eastern European countries is as much as 30 per cent of the official economy. These estimates compare with 10 per cent for the USA and over 50 per cent for the Sudan.

It should be noted that there are likely to be significant differences in the make-up of different hidden economies. Thus, corruption is highly significant in the Sudan, whereas tax avoidance is one of the main influences in eastern Europe, and in the USA the size of the illegal trade in drugs is probably not taken into account in the 10 per cent figure mentioned above.

The significance of hidden economies is not just that official statistics probably underestimate levels of economic activity, but that economic policies and objectives are far harder to meet. For example, in the

Sudan, a minority of those who dominate the hidden economy are very rich and much of their wealth is illegally transferred from the Sudan to countries such as Switzerland. This **capital flight** means that one of the poorest countries in Africa is starved of funds that could be used to finance economic development.

> ### DEFINITION
>
> **Capital flight:** the export, often illegal, of cash and valuable assets from poor countries

The quality of life

Two measures, infant mortality and life expectancy, are commonly used to give a quick notion of the quality of life in different countries. This is illustrated in Table 6.2.

	Infant mortality (deaths/1000 before 5th birthday)	Life expectancy (years at birth)
Burundi	190	44.6
Brazil	33	71.2
China	27	71.8
Cuba	7	77.3
Luxembourg	5	79.2
Syria	14.5	73.8
UK	6	78.9

Source: World Development Indicators, World Bank

Table 6.2 Infant mortality and life expectancy, 2005

Infant mortality is expressed in terms of the number of children who die before they reach their fifth birthday per 1000 of the population; this is regarded as a very useful measure, as it acts as a proxy variable for many other factors – quality of health care, clean water, the diet of mothers, and so on. The data for Burundi indicates that almost 1 in 5 children born die before their fifth birthday. This confirms the serious difficulties faced by its people, whereas the data for Cuba indicates the priority given to health care in an otherwise poor country.

Life expectancy data shows less variation, but data from Burundi and other sub-Saharan African countries provides chilling evidence of the impact of conflict, HIV/aids and malaria.

Gender differences

There are different ways in which gender inequalities might be measured. The World Bank currently includes measures of males and females aged 15 and above who are literate. The data for the same countries as identified above is shown in Table 6.3.

	Literacy in males and females aged 15 or more (%)	Literacy in females aged 15 or more (%)
Burundi	67	52
Brazil	88	89
China	95	87
Cuba	97	97
Luxembourg	unknown	unknown
Syria	88	74
UK	unknown	unknown

Source: World Development Indicators, World Bank

Table 6.3 Gender differences in literacy rates, 2005

It is argued that gender inequalities can provide a significant explanation of slower rates of development. The education of women can be seen as an important strategy in raising living standards. Better-educated and more powerful women are more likely to limit birth rates and, it is argued be able to contribute more to the economic well-being of developing countries.

The Human Development Index

This alternative and more comprehensive set of measures of economic development developed by the United Nations Development Programme focuses on the human impact of various economic factors. It is assumed that development should focus on three aspects of human development:

● life expectancy at birth

● access to knowledge and learning

● standard of living.

The most recently available HDI index is reproduced in Table 6.4. The HDI for Iceland is 0.968, which gives the country a rank of 1st out of 177 countries with data.

Countries are ranked according to these three variables. The Human Development Index is an index number using the value of 1 to represent the highest level of human development. Thus, Iceland scores 0.968. It is 3rd in terms of life expectancy at birth, 13th when it comes to the proportion of the population enrolled in education and 5th in terms of purchasing power parity – as a measure to the standard of living related to the cost of living. By these measures, Sierra Leone has the lowest human development index.

Compared to national income measures, the HDI produces a different ranking of countries with Iceland at the top and Sierra Leone at the bottom, but it still fails to take into account other factors that might be regarded as important measures of human development, such as income and gender equalities,

political freedoms and human rights. Other measures try to capture these differences.

STRETCH AND CHALLENGE

Use the NationMaster website to find ways of measuring differences between countries in terms of:

● gender inequalities

● carbon footprints

● human rights.

How far do these correlate to measures of economic well-being identified earlier in this section?

Other indicies

The measures used by both the World Bank and the United Nations have been criticised for failing to take account of the environmental impacts of economic growth and development. The New Economics Foundation has developed the 'Happy Planet Index' which is based on life expectancy, life satisfaction and the carbon footprint of individual economies. The measure produces totally different outcomes to the HDI, but can be criticised because it depends in part on the subjective valuations as revealed in surveys about happiness. Nonetheless the outcomes of this approach to measuring living standards make interesting reading.

HDI value	Life expectancy at birth (years)	Combined primary, secondary and tertiary gross enrolment ratio (%)	GDP per capita (PPP US$)
1 Iceland (0.968)	1 Japan (82.3)	1 Australia (113.0)	1 Luxembourg (60,228)
2 Norway (0.968)	2 Hong Kong (81.9)	11 France (96.5)	3 Norway (41,420)
3 Australia (0.962)	3 Iceland (81.5)	12 South Korea (96.0)	4 Ireland (38,505)
4 Canada (0.961)	4 Switzerland (81.3)	13 Iceland (95.4)	5 Iceland (36,510)
5 Ireland (0.959)	5 Australia (80.9)	14 Sweden (95.3)	6 Switzerland (35,633)
6 Sweden (0.956)	6 Spain (80.5)	15. Belgium (95.1)	7 Hong Kong (34,833)
177 Sierra Leone (0.336)	177 Zambia (40.5)	172 Niger (22.7)	174 Malawi (667)

Source: UNDP

Table 6.4 Human Development Index, 2005

ACTIVITY

Use the Happy Planet Index website to learn more about the Happy Planet Index and assess how far this is a better measure of living standards in different European countries.

learning tip

There is a range of indicators that can be used to judge living standards in different countries. The World Bank uses measures that focus on more economic dimensions to development, whereas the UN focuses more on social factors. Both organisations generate amazing amounts of data that is easily accessed. Whatever measures are used, this data shows the worst living standards in the world are to be found in sub-Saharan Africa. These indicators also show that over 50 countries in the world are becoming worse off than they were in the past.

In your exam, national income data can be used as the basis for both stimulus- response and essay style questions. For the former, you could be given sets of different measures of living standards for different countries and be faced with a mix of questions asking you to identify trends, and make simple comparisons. The higher tariff questions are likely to ask you to assess the limitations of using data in this way, and also you might be expected to explain differences by reference to aggregate demand and aggregate supply.

Essay questions are likely to be more straightforward along the following lines:

'Evaluate the usefulness of national income statistics in helping measure living standards in different countries.'

Inflation and deflation

BUILDING ON AS

For AS you needed to know about:

- how inflation is measured by the CPI and RPI
- how these indices are derived
- the meaning of cost-push inflation
- the meaning of demand-pull inflation
- why governments give a high priority to keeping inflationary pressures under control.

STEPPING UP TO A2

For A2 you need to learn more about:

- problems with the measurement of inflation by the RPI and CPI
- more detailed understanding of the consequences of changes in the price level
- the causes of inflation, especially monetarist theories
- the possible trade-off between levels of unemployment and changes in the price level.

As with the rest of A2, you need to do more analysis and evaluation, to assess the impact of rising and falling prices on individuals and on the economy as a whole.

ACTIVITY

Use aggregate demand and supply diagrams to illustrate:

a cost-push inflation

b demand-pull inflation

c the possible difference between Keynesian and neoclassical approaches to understanding inflation.

learning tip

It is really important to make sure that you revise your AS work on inflation. If you don't, you will find the next sections tough going.

Measuring inflation

From your studies at AS, you will know that there are two main measures of inflation, the Retail Price Index and the Consumer Price Index. They are constructed in similar ways and are based on using the Family Expenditure Survey to measure changes in prices of a basket of goods bought by the average family. This data is weighted to account for the relative importance of different items of expenditure and is then used to construct a series of index numbers with a base of 100. These enable us to have a quick understanding of how prices might have changed over the last year. Thus, a change in the CPI from 112 to 115.5 indicates that prices have risen by 3.5 per cent. A change in the index from 130 to 140 would represent an annual change of 10 per cent in prices.

The data contained in these indices is very much about a notional household – there is no such thing as an average household and different groups in society will have different experiences of inflation, according to individual patterns of expenditure. For example, the poor and the old spend a higher proportion of their incomes on heating, and their personal rates of inflation are likely to be higher than those reported in the CPI.

ACTIVITY ····❖

Use the National Statistics website to find out how the UK government has changed the weighting given to goods and services contained in the 'typical basket of goods'. Choose two examples of items now excluded and two new inclusions and explain why these changes have been made.

STRETCH AND CHALLENGE

Go to the National Statistics website and use the 'personal inflation calculator' to calculate inflation rates for the following:

a   a typical university student

b   an old age pensioner

c   a high-income family

d   a low-income family.

Explain the significance of any differences you may have discovered.

The effects of inflation on individuals

It follows from the previous section that it is not easy to generalise about the effects of inflation on individuals. Each one of us spends our income in different ways, allocating different proportions of spending on the purchase of different proportions of different goods and services. Prices do not change uniformly, and this too means inflation will have different effects on different individuals. Nonetheless, it is possible to make some generalisations about the impact of changes in the price level.

In the last 100 years in the UK economy, periods of rising prices have been far more common than falling prices. Some individuals have benefited from these times of from inflation.

● Borrowers can benefit if the value of the assets that they have bought with borrowed money rises by less than the rate of inflation. Typically in the UK, houses increase in price by more than the rate of inflation. Twenty years ago I borrowed £30,000 to buy my house and, although I have paid twice that sum in terms of mortgage repayments, my house is now worth £400,000. I have benefited from inflation, as the value of my most significant asset has increased by more than the general rate of inflation over that time period.

● Similarly if an individual is lucky enough to have a job and career generating an income that increases by more than the rate of inflation, they will become better-off. This applies to members of strong trade unions or professional groups. Moreover, the earnings of some occupational groups are directly linked to rising prices. Estate agents, who charge a fee directly related to house prices, and those earning commissions expressed as a percentage of the price of sales are likely to earn more during periods of inflation.

● Generally speaking, some degree of inflation is good for all of us, because it is more usually associated with an expanding and growing economy.

● Those who are relatively well off are likely to benefit more from periods of inflation than the poor. They are likely to own more assets that gain in value, and are more likely to benefit from increasing profits and incomes.

However, if some gain, others are likely to lose.

● If you borrow to buy an asset that then falls in value, you will be a loser. This happened to some house buyers who borrowed to purchase houses at what turned out to be the end of the last housing boom in the early 1990s. House prices suddenly fell and some individuals were left owing more on their mortgages than was represented by the value of their homes. This issue of **negative equity** was very serious as it could lead to homelessness. If borrowers fell behind on their mortgage repayments, lenders could repossess their homes, which would then be sold. This further depressed house prices.

● If increases in your income do not keep up with inflation, your standard of living will fall. You will have to pay more for the sample bundle of goods and services and your **real income** will fall. Increases in state pensions and other welfare benefits tend to lag behind increases in the price level, and this means that often the least well-off in society suffer more significantly during periods of inflation.

● If inflation gets out of hand, more of us are likely to be losers. Daily increases in prices associated with **hyperinflation** mean that we will all tend to be worse-off at the end of the day than at the beginning. Savings rapidly lose their value and in the worst-case scenario, inflation can lead to social breakdown and political instability.

● The poor will tend to suffer as income is redistributed to the better-off.

DEFINITIONS

Negative equity: situation in which debts are greater than the assets that secure them – typically housing

Real income: a measure of income that excludes inflation

Hyperinflation: very rapid rates of inflation

 learning tip You could be asked to evaluate the effects of inflation on different groups of individuals.

The effects of inflation on the economy

As indicated earlier, some degree of inflation in an economy, associated with rising levels of economic activity, can be seen to be beneficial to an economy. However, any increase in the price level that exceeds the trend rate of growth of an economy is likely to have a harmful effect on economic performance. The following factors contribute to the detrimental effects of inflation:

● Expectations – psychological factors play an important part in stimulating and sustaining periods of inflation. Anxieties and worries about increasing rates of inflation, its effects, and the ultimate fear of hyperinflation are particularly significant, as such expectations about future levels of inflation fuel the cost–price spiral outlined in your AS course. Expectations can lead firms to increase prices, and encourage workers to push for higher pay rises. These changes result in a rising price level.

● If inflation rates are higher in the UK than in other nations with whom we compete on world markets, the relative price of our exports will rise and the relative price of imports will fall. Both effects tend to worsen the balance of payments. This can also set up an undesirable train of events. A deteriorating balance of payments might lead to a fall in the value of the pound.

● Inflation could ultimately contribute to falling levels of national output. Business costs, in terms of keeping price lists and other material up to date, will increase, and more resources are likely to be devoted to minimising the harmful effects of rising prices. The instability associated with periods of inflation increases the risks faced by businesses, and this could result in reductions in investment. This, coupled with potential decreases in consumer confidence, is likely to lead to reductions in aggregate demand and a fall in national output. The effect of this reduction in aggregate demand will be falling national output, but inflationary pressures are also likely to fall – the opportunity cost of rising inflation could be falling national output.

Different theories of inflation

As the preceding section shows, concerns about inflation have been a major issue for both economists and politicians. For older generations, there is a clear link between the chaos caused by hyperinflation in Germany in the 1920s and the rise of Hitler. In more recent years, run-away inflation in countries such as Argentina, the former USSR and Zimbabwe have had serious social consequences that can lead to the breakdown of societies. Although the UK has not suffered such excesses, inflation in the early 1980s peaked at around 18 per cent; it almost reached 10 percent in 1990.

Over the last 50 years, four different theories have been used to account for inflation:

- demand-pull
- cost-push
- monetarist
- the triangle model.

DEMAND-PULL

You covered the mechanics of this theory when you studied for AS. It is easy to understand and in its simplest form it suggests that prices in an economy will rise if the demand for goods and services exceeds the supply. Its earlier formulations were associated with J.M. Keynes, who pointed out that inflationary pressures were particularly likely to occur when factors of production in an economy were fully employed. This situation is illustrated in Figure 6.7. This shows that an increase in aggregate demand from *AD* to *AD₁* will push up prices from *OP* to *OP₁*. If resources are already fully employed, the rise in inflation will be greater and there will be no increase in national output.

Important research was undertaken in the 1950s by a New Zealand-born economist called A.W. Phillips, who collected historical data on changes in wage rates and levels of unemployment. Changes in the wage rate were plotted on the vertical axis and changes in levels of unemployment on the horizontal. Changes

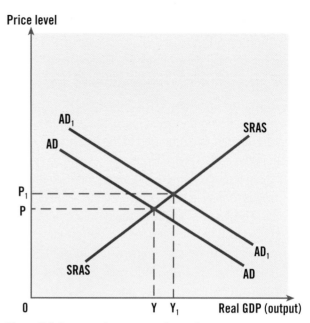

Figure 6.7 Increased aggregate demand

in wage rates were taken as a proxy variable for changes in the price level, or inflation, and levels of unemployment represented the existence or otherwise of unused resources in the economy. Phillips showed that there was an inverse relationship between changes in wage rates and levels of unemployment. In other words, if unemployment was high, the increase in wages was relatively low, and vice versa. This relationship is illustrated in Figure 6.8.

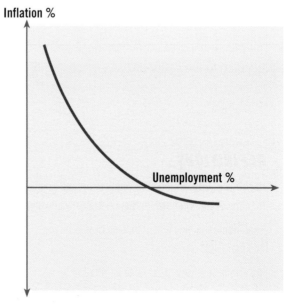

Figure 6.8 Short-run Phillips curve

The findings of his research were interpreted to provide evidence to support demand-pull theories of inflation and governments were provided with not just a possible explanation of inflation but also suggestions as to what policies to pursue to deal with inflation. The logical outcome of applying this theoretical understanding of inflation was that there was a trade-off between unemployment and inflation. If a government was worried about increasing rates of inflation, it should decrease aggregate demand by using monetary or fiscal polices. This would lead to a movement up the Phillips curve, showing an increase in unemployment but at the same time a reduction in the rate of increase of wage rates.

COST-PUSH

During the 1960s, there was a tendency for unemployment and inflation to both increase and this data was interpreted by some economists to suggest that demand-pull theories might not fully explain inflation. They suggested another simple cause of inflation. Increases in the price level could be caused by increased costs of production. Some economists argued that trade unions could force up the costs of production and that firms operating in less competitive markets were able to pass on increases in their costs in the form of high prices for goods and services. The logical outcome from this theory in terms

of government policy would be to limit the ability of trade unions to push for higher wages. The impact of cost-push pressures on the price level is illustrated in Figure 6.9, where rising costs of production shift the aggregate supply curve upwards to the left, leading to rising prices and a fall in national output.

Cost-push theories were given further credence in the 1970s when the price of oil increased fourfold. In this case, costs of production of an important energy source and raw material were forced up, and passed on to consumers in the form of higher prices, thus triggering an inflationary spiral.

MONETARIST

The 1970s were a turbulent time for the UK economy. Inflation increased, industrial relations were extremely poor, strike activity increased, and there were shortages of electricity. The balance of payments account deteriorated and unemployment hit the 1 million mark for the first time since the 1930s. Both Labour and Conservative governments struggled to develop effective economic policies.

Traditional cost-push and Keynesian demand-pull theories of inflation were increasingly challenged. The relatively stable relationship shown by the Phillips curve no longer appeared to apply, as inflation

Figure 6.9 Cost-push inflation

Price level (vertical axis), *Real GDP (output)* (horizontal axis). Curves labelled SRAS₁, SRAS, AD. Points P_1, P on vertical axis; Y_1, Y on horizontal axis.

Leicester Square, London, during the refuse collectors' strike of 1979

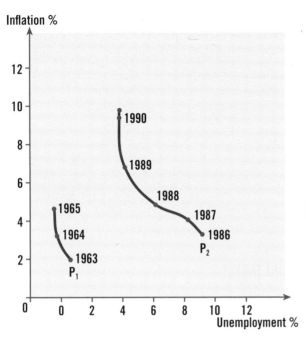

Figure 6.10 Shifting Phillips curve

and unemployment both appeared to be rising at the same time. This was called **stagflation**, and is illustrated in Figure 6.10. In this diagram, it appears that new relationships between rising wage levels and unemployment are occurring that would not be predicted by the Phillips curve and that high levels of inflation could be associated with higher levels of unemployment.

To some, this suggested that the correlation between unemployment and inflation did not exist. Another explanation was that periods of inflation lead workers, and producers, to expect further increases in inflation. In order to maintain their standard of living, employees would demand higher incomes. This could lead to the development of an expectations-augmented Phillips curve, which could be illustrated by P_2.

DEFINITIONS

Monetarism: theory or theories explaining inflation in terms of monetary factors

Stagflation: the co-existence of low rates of economic growth and relatively high inflation

However, the existence of stagflation and fundamental economic problems of the UK economy, and to a lesser extent in the US, in the 1970s gave right-wing, free-market economists much more influence on economic thinking and government policies.

DEFINITION

Quantity theory of money: theory that explains changes in the rate of inflation by reference to changes in the money supply

QUANTITY THEORY OF MONEY

At this time in the 1970s, the theories and writing of one economist, Milton Friedman, became very influential. He argued that rising inflation could be explained by increases in the money supply. This became known as **monetarism**. He based his theory on the **quantity theory of money**, which had been developed in the 1920s by Irving Fisher. He argued that there was a direct relationship between changes in the money supply and changes in the price level. This was expressed in the Fisher equation of exchange:

$$MV \equiv PT$$

Where M stands for the money supply, V the velocity of circulation of money, P the price level and T the volume of transactions. Friedman argued that both the velocity of circulation of money (the rate at which money changed hands in an economy) and the level of transactions could be treated as constants, which left a simple relationship between the money supply and the price level, expressed as:

$$M = P$$

In other words, any change in the supply of money will lead directly to a change in the price level. Friedman produced historical data that appeared to support his hypothesis.

Friedman appeared to offer politicians a different explanation of inflation that produced different policy options. In the mid-1970s, the then Labour government tried to restrict the money supply by placing controls on the amount of bank lending. These policies appeared to have a limited effect, and in 1979, when the Conservatives were returned to power, they used increases in interest rates up to 17 percent to limit the amount of borrowing in order to reduce the supply of money. The effects of this, coupled with cuts in government expenditure and a rising exchange rate, were to plunge the economy into the deepest recession since the 1930s. The UK economy only started to recover in the mid-1980s.

THE TRIANGLE MODEL

The 1990s and early part of the twenty-first century have shown different behaviour in terms of macroeconomic variables. As you will have learned, from the early 1990s rates of inflation in the UK and other developed countries have been relatively low and unemployment has fallen. This has lead to new explanations about inflation. These build on, rather than discard, earlier theories. One example is the **triangle model** developed by the American economist Robert Gordon. He has argued that inflation is three-dimensional, consisting of:

● demand-pull, whereby increases in government expenditure and consumption that cannot be supported by trend rates of growth will cause inflation

● supply shock inflation, which is a renaming of 'cost-push inflation' to account for external shocks such as oil price rises that can lead to increases in costs that are then passed on to customers in higher prices

● built-in inflation, which takes into account the possible contribution of expectations of both workers and firms. Periods of inflation are likely to trigger a wage–price spiral as both sets of economic agents attempt to defend themselves against the adverse effects of inflation.

DEFINITION

Triangle model: theory of inflation that combines demand-pull, cost-push and the role of expectations

learning tip For the examination, make sure you can assess the validity of different theories of inflation.

ACTIVITY ····⋮

The MPC of the Bank of England has set both an upper limit for inflation and a lower limit. The European Central Bank has set just an upper limit. Use the Internet sites of both institutions to research the possibility that each has a different approach to inflation.

Deflation

Deflation refers to a period in which prices are actually falling. As noted earlier, such periods are much less common in almost all economies than are periods of inflation. The last significant period of deflation in the USA was from 1930 to 1933, when prices fell on average by 10 per cent per year. This was a period of severe recession characterised by:

● rising unemployment
● falling share prices
● widespread bankruptcies
● banking failures
● social unrest.

DEFINITIONS

Deflation: falling price levels

NAIRU: the non accelerating inflation rate of unemployment, also known as the *natural rate of unemployment*.

Natural rate of unemployment: according to Milton Friedman and others, a rate of unemployment at which inflation is stable and not affected by changes in government policy; another name for NAIRU

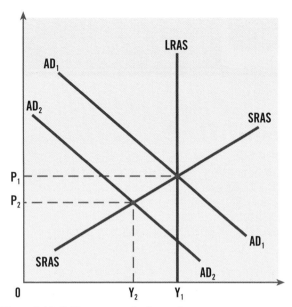

Figure 6.11 Falling aggregate demand

In many ways, deflation can be seen as the reverse of inflation and historically it has been the result of continued periods of recession in which aggregate demand is falling. All or any of the factors listed above can be both the cause and consequence of falling aggregate demand. The 1930s recession was famously triggered by banking failures, falling stock market prices and the collapse of consumer confidence. The latter resulted in falling consumption and aggregate demand, which in turn resulted in business failure and massive job losses. This process is illustrated in Figure 6.11, where aggregate demand falls from AD_1 to AD_2 leading to a reduction in national output from OY_1 to OY_2 and a falling price level from OP_1 to OP_2.

Government policies to deal with deflation

Deflation is not the mirror image of inflation in every respect. Typically, governments use interest rates to limit inflationary pressures. In a period of deflation, the nominal rate of interest falls to zero and the real rate of interest becomes equal to the actual rate of deflation. It becomes more profitable to hold cash than other forms of assets. Governments lose the power to use cuts in the interest rate to stimulate the economy and boost aggregate demand.

It took a long time to reverse the deflation of the 1930s and involved increased government spending

ECONOMICS IN CONTEXT – GLOBAL ECONOMICS

ECONOMICS IN REVERSE

The Japanese economy in the 1990s suffered periods of deflation following a long period of relatively rapid economic growth. Different economists provide different explanations of what caused this period of deflation and the difficulties the Japanese government has had in trying to boost aggregate demand.

It has been argued that growth in the 1970s and 1980s lead to significant increases in both corporate and government debt, which could be sustained as the Japanese economy continued to grow. However, in the 1990s there was a collapse in over-inflated property prices, which lead to falling asset prices and banking insolvencies. Prices fell and government attempts to stimulate the economy by cutting interest rates and boosting government spending failed to stimulate consumer confidence. At the same time, the Asian Tigers were growing and China was beginning a period of rapid economic growth. Japanese business culture, in which workers enjoyed great job security, did not appear flexible enough to cope with the combination of competitive pressure and domestic stagnation, and it is only in the last few years that there have been signs of recovery in the Japanese economy.

and increases in aggregate demand that eventually contributed to rising consumer confidence, leading to a more sustained increase in aggregate demand.

STRETCH AND CHALLENGE

Find out more about the macro economic performance of the Japanese economy over the last two decades and write a report forecasting its performance over the next five years.

Unemployment

BUILDING ON AS

For AS you needed to know about:

- how unemployment is measured
- how unemployment can be caused by both demand and supply-side factors
- the four different types of employment – cyclical, frictional, structural and seasonal
- the links between the output gap in relation to economic growth and unemployment pages

You should be able to draw two aggregate demand and aggregate supply diagrams to illustrate the following. The first should show how falling aggregate demand can lead to rising unemployment and the second should illustrate how increases in aggregate supply can lead to falling unemployment.

You should also be able to draw a production possibility curve diagram to show a movement from a situation in which the labour force is being under-utilised to one in which there is full employment.

STEPPING UP TO A2

You have to analyse and evaluate/ assess the impact of unemployment on individuals and the economy. You also need to have an understanding of what some economists call real wage unemployment, the 'natural rate of unemployment' and NAIRU. You will also need to have a deeper theoretical grasp of the possible relationship between unemployment and inflation.

ACTIVITY ····⋮⋮

Undertake research to assess how far each of the causes of unemployment identified in your AS course contributes to unemployment in the area in which you live.

Effects of unemployment on individuals

Unemployment leads to:

- *lower incomes and lower standards of living* – this consequence is compounded as those without work might be forced to borrow at exhorbitant rates of interest and are faced with increased heating and lighting costs as they are likely to spend more time at home. Some studies indicate that the cost of living for those on low incomes is actually higher than for those who are better-off.

- *reduced self-esteem* – we often judge each other by what we do – those who are unemployed may have less status and may blame themselves for their situation. This can lead to falling self-confidence and a sense of fatalism. This is particularly the case with the long-term unemployed, and there is considerable evidence to suggest that the longer an individual remains out of work the less likely it is that they will work again. Such workers can become unemployable.

- Unemployment tends to have a disproportionate effect on different groups within society – unskilled Afro Caribbean men and those with ethnic origins in Bangladesh have the highest rates of unemployment. This can contribute to social exclusion, dislocation and racial conflict.

- Long-term unemployment is associated with increased incidence of domestic violence, mental illness, hard drug use and criminal behaviour.

Effects of unemployment on the economy

For the economy, unemployment represents:

- a loss of productive capacity. If there are unemployed, the economy is not using its resources to the full.

● reduced aggregate demand because of lower levels of consumption. This is likely to further reduce levels of economic activity in an economy.

● higher levels of unemployment likely to lead to increased welfare payments, and reduced levels of government revenue through income and other taxes. These factors are likely to push government budgets towards deficit.

● negative externalities associated with racial conflict, increases in crime, mental illness and incapacity, all of which place additional costs on the rest of society.

The natural rate of unemployment

In the previous section on inflation you were introduced to the work of A.W. Phillips, who investigated the extent to which there might be a relationship between changes in the price level and changes in levels of unemployment. This work led economists to believe that there might be a trade-off between unemployment and inflation, giving governments a choice between keeping inflation low and tolerating an increase in unemployment, or stimulating aggregate demand and accepting increased rates of inflation This interpretation was questioned in the 1970s, when both unemployment and inflation were seen to increase.

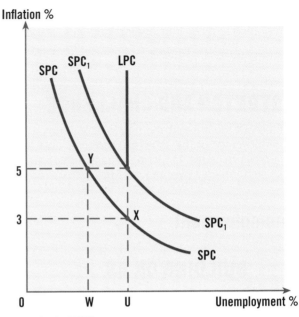

Figure 6.12 NAIRU

Friedman and others argued that in the long run there was no trade-off between unemployment and inflation but that there was a 'natural' rate of unemployment at which inflation would be stable and which could not be affected by changes in government policy. They distinguished between short-run Phillips curves and the long run, which would be set by this **natural rate of unemployment**. This is illustrated in Figure 6.12, in which the natural

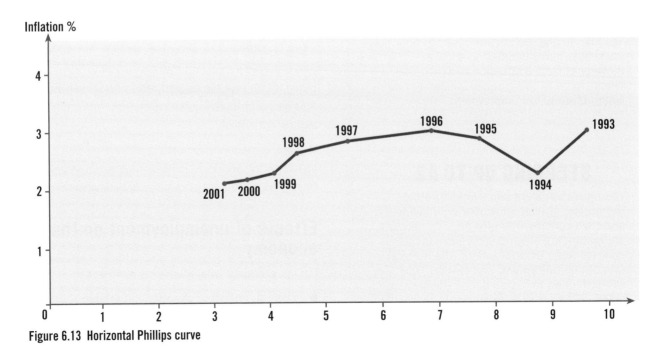

Figure 6.13 Horizontal Phillips curve

rate of unemployment – also known as **NAIRU** (non-accelerating inflation rate of unemployment) – is represented by the vertical line at *OU*. Friedman argued that it was only possible to increase employment in the short run, say by cutting interest rates, leading to a movement along *SPC* from *x* to *y* and a short-term reduction in unemployment to *OW*. However, it is argued, this will cause an increase in inflation from 3 per cent to 5 per cent, which will raise expectations of future inflation, which in turn would result in a new short-run Phillips curve SPC_1, representing a return to the natural rate of unemployment at *OU*.

There are considerable differences between economists in accepting the existence of a long-run Phillips curve as described by Friedman. Indeed, data on changes in inflation and unemployment from the 1990s implies that it is possible to have both low rates of inflation and falling unemployment. This is illustrated in Figure 6.13.

ACTIVITY ····⬖

Use the website of the Office for National Statistics to access inflation rates and unemployment rates for each of the last 25 years. Plot this data, measuring inflation on the vertical axis and unemployment on the horizontal. Analyse the data you have collected. What evidence does your data show to confirm or deny the relationships between the two variables identified by A.W. Phillips and Milton Friedman?

7 Managing the national economy

On completion of this chapter you should be able to:

- use the aggregate demand and supply model to analyse possible conflicts in policy objectives
- understand how monetary and fiscal policies have changed in recent years
- evaluate the possible economic consequences of budget deficits and failures
- analyse and evaluate the microeconomic significance of taxation
- assess the success of fiscal rules
- evaluate the contribution of supply-side policies to both the macro- and microeconomy
- discuss how the Bank of England can affect the money supply and rate of interest
- understand different money markets
- consider how changes in the exchange rate might influence policy objectives.

This chapter is divided into five sections relating to the main elements of this part of the AQA specification. They relate to the different types of economic policies that governments might use in an effort to influence macroeconomic variables:

- Macroeconomic models and policies
- Fiscal policy
- Supply-side policies
- Monetary policy
- Exchange rate policy.

You should already be able to use aggregate demand and aggregate supply diagrams to indicate the likely impact of fiscal, monetary and supply-side policies.

BUILDING ON AS

The list of learning objectives above might appear to be daunting, but if you succeeded in getting a good understanding of government fiscal, monetary and supply-side policies for AS, you will have a solid foundation in understanding and knowledge to tackle the demands of the A2 specification.

STEPPING UP TO A2

There is some additional content in terms of taxation and money markets, but the main difference is one of sophistication. This is reflected in the kinds of questions you are likely to be asked. For example, at AS you are expected to understand how supply-side policies might affect macroeconomic policy objectives, but at A2 you will be expected to evaluate their effectiveness. The data-response questions are likely to be based on more complex stimuli, and you need to practise and develop your essay-writing skills.

Macroeconomic models and policies

Governments formulate economic policies to tackle a range of policy objectives. Although priorities might change, the UK government and those of most developed economies seek to maintain macroeconomic stability by:

● ensuring that short-run economic growth is consistent with the long-term trend rate of growth

● using supply-side policies to promote long-term economic growth and improve international competitiveness

● ensuring that inflation stays within published targets

● reducing unemployment

● ensuring that other macroeconomic objectives are not constrained by balance of payments issues.

These can be analysed by using the aggregate demand and supply analysis you will have learned about for AS

Short- and long-term economic growth

The relationship between short-term and long-term economic growth can be illustrated using aggregate demand and aggregate supply analysis. In Figure 7.1, the movement from *LRAS* to *LRAS₁* represents long-term economic growth – in other words, an increase in the productive capacity of the economy.

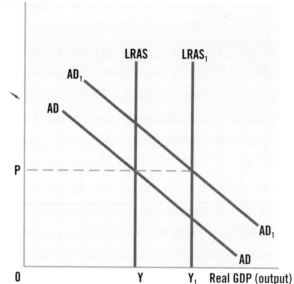

Figure 7.1 Aggregate demand and aggregate supply

Over the last decade, the UK economy has grown by around 2.5 per cent per annum. The shift in aggregate demand from *AD* to *AD₁* could represent government policies to try to ensure that short-run economic growth keeps up with longer-term trends in the economy. In this case, the MPC of the Bank of England might have decided to reduce interest rates to boost aggregate demand to increase national output from *OY* to *OY₁*.

The same outcome could have been achieved by the use of fiscal measures, by raising government expenditure, or cutting taxation, or a combination of both. However, over the last decade the government has preferred to rely on the MPC to use interest rates to try to ensure short-term economic growth is consistent with long-term trends.

ACTIVITY ⋯⋰

Use aggregate demand and supply analysis to illustrate what might happen to the price level and national output if the MPC of the Bank of England:

a set interest rates too high in relationship to long-term trend rates of economic growth

b set interest rates too low in relationship to long-term trend rates of economic growth.

Conflicts between policy objectives

Governments can easily be faced with potentially conflicting policy objectives. They may have to choose between:

● reducing inflation or reducing unemployment – policies to reduce inflationary pressures such as raising interest rates or reducing government spending are likely to not only reduce upward pressures on prices but also reduce the level of economic activity and the demand for labour. There could, therefore, be a trade-off between cutting inflation and reducing unemployment.

● improving the balance of payments or increasing GNP. As noted in your AS course, imports tend to increase more than proportionally with increases in national output and incomes. It follows that using fiscal, monetary or monetarist polices to reduce aggregate demand in the UK will have a more than proportional effect in terms of reducing imports. Moreover, falling domestic demand might provide an incentive for UK-based firms to increase their exports.

● increasing levels of investment or increasing consumption. Expenditure on new plant and machinery to boost the long-term productive capacity of the economy carries with it the opportunity cost of reductions in current levels of consumption. The same applies to firms, as they can be faced with the choice between retaining profits for investment or increasing dividends to shareholders.

Changing economic policies

UK growth rates from 1950 to 2007 are illustrated in Figure 7.2. Some economists have suggested that the UK is now experiencing a new economic paradigm (see page 115), in which economic growth rates have become more stable, and that extreme fluctuations in the economic cycle can now be avoided by appropriate government intervention. It has been argued that the 1950s and 1960s were a period of stop–go economic policies with which the governments of the time, both Labour and Conservative, used fiscal policies to stimulate the economy and then applied monetary restraints to cool the economy when it became overheated.

From the mid-1970s to the early 1990s, monetarist policies were pursued first by the Labour government and then by the Conservatives led by Margaret Thatcher. This appeared to coincide with much greater volatility in terms of economic performance. The economy appears to have stabilised from the mid-1990s onwards, and since 1997 the MPC of

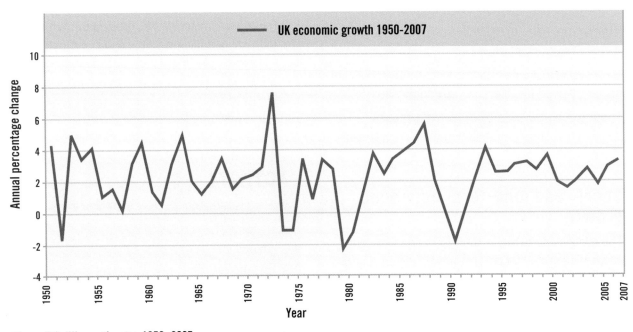

Figure 7.2 UK growth rates 1950–2007

the Bank of England has set interest rates, and more attention has been paid to the implementation of supply-side policies to boost long-term economic growth.

ACTIVITY

Use the University of Pennsylvania's Centre for International Comparisons website to obtain data on changes in the rate of economic growth between 1980 and the present in at least three European countries.

What evidence is there to support the views that:

a there are regular cycles of economic activity

b the performance of the economies in the 1980s showed greater volatility

c the performance of the economies since 1994 has shown much greater stability?

Fiscal policy

BUILDING ON AS

For AS you needed to know the meaning of the terms budget deficit and budget surplus, the different items of government expenditure, and have some understanding of different taxes. You were also introduced to the principles of fiscal stability and the implications of membership of the EU for **fiscal policies**.

STEPPING UP TO A2

For A2 you need to know more about the impact of budget balances and imbalances. You need to learn about policies that could be used to rectify budget imbalances, principles of taxation and understand the extent to which EU membership is bringing about convergence in terms of the fiscal policies followed by different members of the EU.

Budget deficits, surpluses and the golden rule

A **budget deficit** occurs when the government's expenditure plans exceed expected revenue. Such a budget is said to be expansionary, as government spending is an element of aggregate demand. The impact of a budget deficit on the national economy will depend upon the availability or otherwise of spare capacity in the economy. This is shown in Figure 7.3, where a planned budget deficit increases aggregate demand from AD to AD_1, resulting in an increase in national output from OY to OY_1 and no increase in the price level. Should the deficit be such that aggregate demand shifts further to the right, national output would reach a point where it could not increase because of a lack of productive capacity but prices would rise significantly.

DEFINITIONS

Fiscal policies: using changes in government revenue and expenditure to achieve macroeconomic policy objectives

Budget deficit: when governments plan to spend more than they plan to raise in revenue

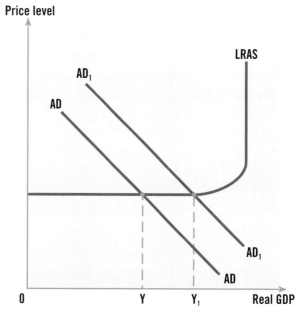

Figure 7.3 **Increasing aggregate demand**

Should the government plan to raise more in terms of revenue that it plans to spend, a **budget surplus** occurs. This provides governments with a policy option that might be used to reduce aggregate demand to lessen inflationary pressures and/or to improve the balance of payments.

DEFINITION

Budget surplus: when governments plan to raise more revenue than they plan to spend

---

ACTIVITY ····⋮⟩

Use aggregate demand and supply analysis to illustrate the successful use of a budget surplus to limit inflationary pressures without having an adverse effect on national output.

The golden rule

As you will have learned for AS, the UK government tends not to rely on fiscal policies to manipulate aggregate demand in order to manage macroeconomic performance. Although fiscal measures tend to have an automatic stabilising effect, evening out fluctuations in the economic cycle – welfare payments increase and tax receipts decrease in the downswing while welfare payments fall and tax receipts rise in an upswing – the active use of fiscal measures is now seen to be too crude a tool to influence economic performance. It is not easy to turn on and turn off government expenditure, and frequent changes in taxation increase risk and uncertainty in the economy.

For these reasons, the UK government tries to use fiscal policy to:

● create macroeconomic stability – since 1997 the government has, by publishing longer-term budget plans, attempted to reduce the risks and uncertainties that could be attributed to changes in government fiscal policies by aiming to balance the budget over the period of the economic cycle. This has become known as the **golden rule** of fiscal policies.

● ensure that the government borrows only to finance investments aimed at increasing the productive capacity of the economy, and refrains from borrowing to finance current expenditure – the running costs of government.

● bring about supply-side changes to increase the productive potential of the economy – this involves the use of both planned revenues and expenditure to improve levels of education and training, to encourage more of the population to seek work, and subsidies to improve the transport infrastructure of the economy.

● attempt to reduce inequalities – as you will have learned in the sections on income and wealth inequality (see pages 70–76), successive governments have found it very difficult to reduce inequalities in the UK economy. The current government has hoped that increased spending on education, particularly in the pre-school period, will lead to reductions in long-term inequalities.

DEFINITION

Golden rule: maintaining a balanced budget over the economic cycle

---

ACTIVITY ····⋮⟩

Evaluate the extent to which Labour governments since 1997 have used fiscal policies to:

a   create macroeconomic stability

b   improve the productive capacity of the economy

c   reduce inequalities in income and wealth.

Functions of taxation

The UK and other governments use taxes:

- to finance government expenditure
- to redistribute income
- to try to remedy different forms of market failure
- to provide incentives to firms and consumers
- as part of fiscal policies to achieve macroeconomic policy objectives.

GOVERNMENT EXPENDITURE

It may seem obvious, but the primary function of taxation is to finance government expenditure. Should planned revenue be less than planned expenditure, governments have two options:

- to sell off or privatise publicly owned assets – a policy pursued by Conservative governments in the 1980s. It is estimated that £100 billion was raised in this way. However, these were one-off earnings which, obviously, cannot be repeated.

- to increase government borrowing – the danger of this is that additional demand for credit will push up interest rates, which could have an adverse effect on the economy. Moreover, increased borrowing increases the size of the national debt and this can lead a country to default on the EU Stability and Growth Pact.

Since 1998 and the introduction of the UK code for fiscal stability, the government has effectively committed itself to financing expenditure from government taxation revenue.

ACTIVITY ⋯⋖

Assess the extent to which the EU has succeeded in promoting greater fiscal harmony between member states.

THE REDISTRIBUTION OF INCOME

Traditionally, **progressive taxes** have been used as a means by which income can be re-distributed from the better-off to the less well-off. It can be argued that inequalities in society would be reduced if taxation levied on the better-off were spent on those aspects of government expenditure that benefit the worse-off.

DEFINITIONS

Redistribution of income: making one section of society better-off at the expense of another

Progressive taxation: taxes that take proportionally more from the better-off

Numerous studies suggest that inequalities are hard to remove. This is shown by the article on poverty and wealth maps.

ECONOMICS IN CONTEXT – EUROPEAN ECONOMICS

STABILITY AND GROWTH PACT (SGP)

This was one of the outcomes of the Maastricht Treaty agreement to promote greater economic integration and the development of a single market in the EU. The Germans, in particular, were worried that inflationary pressures would be increased if member states did not actively seek to limit the size of their annual budget deficits and national debts. It was agreed that the former would be limited to 3 per cent of a country's GDP and that national debt should not exceed 60 per cent of GDP.

A system of sanctions and fines was developed, but the EU found it difficult to enforce these, especially when broken by France and Germany. In 2005 the SGP was reformed, making it much less prescriptive. While member states were expected to work to the same targets, greater allowances were made for the particular problems faced by particular countries.

ECONOMICS IN CONTEXT

POVERTY AND WEALTH MAPS REVEAL INEQUALITY AT 40-YEAR HIGH

A new way of comparing poverty and wealth trends across Britain shows inequality has reached levels not seen for over 40 years. This is according to research released today (17 July) by the Joseph Rowntree Foundation. A second report, published simultaneously, has found that the public believes the gap between rich and poor people is too large.

Researchers working on the first report found that households in already-wealthy areas have tended to become disproportionately wealthier and that many rich people live in areas segregated from the rest of society. At the same time, more households have become poor over the last 15 years, but fewer are very poor.

Allowing more detailed comparisons than previously possible, the report contains comprehensive maps which are based on census and survey data illustrating the changes in poverty and wealth across Britain from 1968 to 2005.

The widening gap between rich and poor has meant that 'average' households (neither poor nor wealthy) have been decreasing in number. The report raises questions about what Britain will look like in 10 years' time if trends continue as they have.

Danny Dorling, who led the research, said: 'Most interesting and certainly unexpected when this work began is the geography of those households who are neither rich nor poor. Over time it has become clear that there is less and less room in the south for them; they have either moved elsewhere, or become poor.'

The second report, from Michael Orton and Karen Rowlingson, studies people's attitudes to inequality. It found that over the last 20 years, a large and enduring majority of people have considered the gap between high and low incomes too large. However, people are more likely to think that those on higher incomes are overpaid, than to believe that those on low incomes are underpaid.

This report also found that despite most people considering the gap between rich and poor people to be too large, attitudes to wealth redistribution are complex. The authors conclude that, while the public believes economic inequality is a problem, there is no clear public consensus about how this problem should be tackled.

Michael Orton said: 'There is evidence that a high level of inequality may cause real socio-economic problems. There is widespread acceptance that some occupations should be paid more than others: but the gap between high and low paid occupations is far greater than people think it should be.'

Source: From the press release 'New poverty wealth maps of Britain reveal inequality to be at 40-year high', published in 2007 by the Joseph Rowntree Foundation. Reproduced by permission of the Joseph Rowntree Foundation

Poverty, wealth and place in Britain 1968 to 2005 by Danny Dorling, Jan Rigby, Ben Wheeler, Dimitris Ballas, Bethan Thomas, Eldin Fahmy, Dave Gordon and Ruth Lupton

The taxation system can also be used to **redistribute income** from the relatively poor to the relatively rich. Thus, spending on roads and the expansion of airports, which might be funded through taxation, will tend to benefit the better-off at the expense of the poor.

THE REMEDY OF MARKET FAILURE

You should have a good understanding of various government options that can be used to try to remedy market failure. Taxation can be used to try to ensure that the marginal social cost of a product or service is equal to its marginal social benefit. Similarly, the production and consumption of demerit goods can be limited by taxation, while lower or zero rates of taxation can be used to encourage the production and consumption of merit goods.

INCENTIVES TO FIRMS AND INDIVIDUALS

The existence of different types of allowances and different rates of taxes provides governments with opportunities to use both carrots and sticks to encourage particular forms of behaviour. Thus, companies are allowed to offset investment in new plant and machinery against taxation, and individuals can reduce their income tax by putting more money aside for retirement.

MACROECONOMIC OBJECTIVES

As you will have learned for AS, changing rates of taxation can have a significant effect on aggregate demand, which can in turn have an impact on levels of national output and the price level. However, as indicated earlier, the UK government prefers to use other policy measures to achieve macroeconomic objectives.

Principles of taxation

The study of taxes has long been a subject to engage economists. Adam Smith, the so-called 'father of economics', started the ball rolling in 1790 when he identified the four qualities that a 'good' tax should have:

● It should be *cheap* to collect, relative to the amount collected.

● The timing of collection and amount to be paid should be *clear and certain*.

● The timing of payment and means of collection should be *convenient* to the taxpayer.

● It should be *fair* in the sense that the amount to be paid should vary according to the ability to pay of the taxpayer.

It would be hard to argue with Smith's four qualities but economists have added the need for a tax to:

● be *flexible*, especially in respect to changes in the price level

● be *efficient* in the sense that the tax has the least loss of economic efficiency and in an ideal world should actually increase economic efficiency

● be *compatible* in terms of fitting in with taxes used by other countries, especially, in the case of the UK, other members of the EU

● not have a negative effect on *incentives*.

ACTIVITY ····⋮⋗

Compare the relative merits of progressive and regressive taxation.

Types of taxes

The UK collects a range of taxes, some of which are not even called taxes. The contribution of each of the main taxes to government revenue is shown in Figure 7.4.

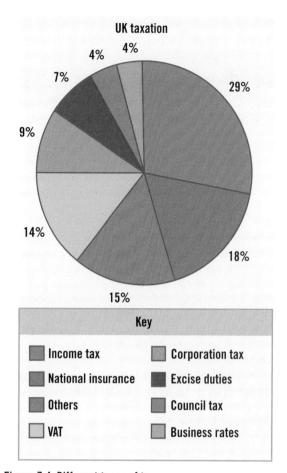

Figure 7.4 Different types of taxes

INCOME TAX

The most significant source of government revenue is income tax, which in the tax year 2007 to 2008 is expected to raise £157 billion. As you will have learned for AS, income tax for most taxpayers is a progressive tax, as the proportion paid increases along with income. Currently, if you are single and you earn £12,000 a year, you would pay around £1,130 in tax – 9.4 per cent of your income. If you were also single and earned £50,000 a year, you would pay around £11,500 in income tax – nearly 23 per cent of your income.

The rate of income tax was in three bands, 10, 22 and 40 per cent. Recently the government decided to phase out the lowest band, leading to vigorous economic and political debate. Most taxpayers fall into the middle category, but if your tax exceeds £34,600, any additional income is taxed at 40 per cent. Income tax probably satisfies Adam Smith's criteria outlined above, especially as for most people it is deducted from their earnings by their employers. This makes it cheap for the government to collect. It is clear when it has to be paid and the amount paid takes into account the ability of the taxpayer to pay.

Some economists argue that progressive taxes such as income tax act as a disincentive to those prepared to work harder, or longer, or to take greater risks. This applies particularly to those who fall in the highest tax bracket who pay 40 per cent of additional earnings in income tax. Right-wing economists have argued that a flat rate tax, where all taxpayers pay the same percentage of their incomes, is cheaper, fairer and provides a greater incentive to work harder.

ECONOMICS IN CONTEXT – GLOBAL ECONOMICS

FLAT RATE TAXES TAKE THE EAST BY STORM

It all started in Estonia, breaking free from political and economic domination by the former USSR. Soon after independence, they followed the advice of free-market economists and introduced a 24 per cent flat rate tax. Since then, their example has been followed by a host of eastern European countries, including Russia (13 per cent), and Romania (16 per cent).

It has been argued that it reduces the incentive to avoid paying tax, encourages the unemployed back into work and the employed to work harder.

Some US politicians, especially conservatives, are campaigning for flat rate taxes as a cure for the ills of the US economy.

However, research undertaken in Russia by the British think-tank, the Institute for Fiscal Policy, indicates that there may be some reduction in tax avoidance, but that the flat rate tax has had no effect on the labour supply or work effort.

ACTIVITY ⋯⃗

Use the Internet to assess how far flat rate taxes have become more popular politically.

NATIONAL INSURANCE

When is a tax not a tax? When it is called National insurance, which in 2008–09 is projected to produce £95 billion in government revenue. All employees earning between £90 and £770 per week have to pay 11 per cent of their taxable earnings in the form of national insurance contributions. Employers also have to contribute 12.8 per cent of their employees' earnings in the form of national insurance contributions.

When unemployment, sickness benefits and pensions were first introduced, they were financed by national insurance contributions. However, the direct link between contributions and benefits has now been lost.

ACTIVITY ⋯⃗

Assess the extent to which national insurance meets the criteria for a 'good tax' explained on page 141.

VALUED ADDED TAX (VAT)

Unlike national insurance and income tax, VAT is an indirect tax, which has only to be paid when value has been added to the production of goods and services. At one level, VAT is a **regressive tax**, as it has to be paid at the same rate irrespective of the ability of the taxpayer to pay. However, VAT is not applied to all goods. Some so-called essential items such as children's clothing, food and water are zero rated. VAT on domestic fuels is set at 5 per cent, but all other goods and services are taxed at 17.5 per cent.

DEFINITION

Regressive tax: a tax taking proportionally more in taxes from the poor than from the rich

VAT was introduced in 1973 to bring UK taxation more in line with that of other European countries.

It was also argued that it is less distorting to the price mechanism, as it is levied at each stage of the production process, and fairer than sales taxes, which are paid only by the final customer. VAT currently earns the government around £80 billion in revenue but is administratively complicated. Many small businesses find it difficult to cope with, especially when they fall in arrears.

CORPORATION TAX

This is a tax on company profits and in 2007–08 it is expected that this will generate £50 billion in government revenue. Businesses earning more than £1.5 million in profits have to pay corporation tax at 30 per cent, with a lower rate of 20 per cent for small companies.

The government levies a high tax on alcohol and tobacco products

ECONOMICS IN CONTEXT – EUROPEAN ECONOMICS

HARMONY OR DISHARMONY?

One of the major issues facing the members of the EU, with their desire to create a single European market, is tax harmonisation. As far as VAT is concerned, rates vary from 0 to 25 per cent, with 17 different rates for different types of foodstuffs in different member states. These different rates obviously affect the cost of living in different EU countries and some consumers take advantage of lower rates in neighbouring countries.

A much bigger problem for the EU is represented by the different rates of company taxation. Some countries fear that businesses will move to countries where taxes on profits are lower, while others argue that creating common levels of company taxation takes away economic power from individual countries.

It is not surprising that the Irish and Baltic governments with low rates of company taxation are against tax harmonisation, while France and Germany, with relatively high rates, are in favour. The UK government has also been hostile to plans to harmonise taxes as it believes that relatively low business taxes provide the UK with a competitive advantage compared to other member states.

ACTIVITY ⋯⋗

Evaluate the arguments for and against greater harmony between company taxation rates across Europe.

EXCISE DUTIES

The £40 billion raised in excise duties in the UK each year includes taxes on the production of alcohol, hydrocarbons, aggregates, tobacco, the provision of air travel, land fill and insurance, as well as the climate change levy. The purposes of this group of taxes are varied. Arguably, alcohol and tobacco are demerit goods and higher rates of taxation may deter consumption, as well as generating revenue for the government. Others of these taxes could be described as 'green', as they are designed to reduce the negative externalities associated with land fill, air travel, quarrying and climate change, but as with all aspects of taxation there is considerable controversy as to their effectiveness.

OTHER TAXES

Council tax, used to fund the police and local councils, accounts for a further £21 billion of government taxation, and business rates, which go to the national government, a slightly smaller amount. Capital gains taxes, charged mainly on profits made from buying and selling of shares and inheritance tax, and death duties each raise around £3 billion.

ACTIVITY

Assess the effectiveness of the UK's taxation structure in terms of reducing:

a inequalities

b negative externalities

c unemployment.

Supply-side policies

BUILDING ON AS

From AS you should have an understanding that supply-side policies include both interventionist and market-based approaches designed to increase the long-run aggregate supply within an economy. Interventionist policies include government funding of education and training, support for research and development, and government funding for infrastructure changes, while market-based approaches designed to reduce government intervention include privatisation, cutting marginal rates of taxation and reducing welfare benefits. Supply-side policies are usually initiated by governments but can also be provided by the business sector. You should understand that these policies are not universally accepted by all economists and there is considerable debate as to the effectiveness of both interventionist and market-based policies.

STEPPING UP TO A2

You are expected not only to have an understanding of the strengths and weaknesses of individual supply-side policies but also to put these into the context of the impact of both fiscal and monetary measures. You need to recognise that, at any one time, there will be a range of policy initiatives at work and it is often difficult to pick out cause and effect. You also need to recognise that supply-side measures can have microeconomic as well as macroeconomic effects.

learning tip It may be crude but right wing governments and economists tend to favour market based supply-side policies whereas those on the political left are more likely to argue for interventionist policies.

ACTIVITY

Use aggregate demand and supply analysis to show the possible supply side effects of:

a government support for the London Olympics in 2012

b reduction in the time during which job seeker's allowance is paid

c failure of the private sector to invest in training.

As noted earlier, the main objective of supply-side policies is to increase the long run productive capacity of the economy, as would be shown by an outward shift in the long-run aggregate supply (LRAS) curves. The present government uses a mix of market-focused and interventionist measures. Four approaches are designed to increase the flexibility of the economy, to make UK businesses more competitive and, in so doing, make the UK economy more dynamic and capable of responding to change:

● tax reform

● privatisation

● market reform

● anti-trade union legislation.

However, the government is not content to rely on these right-wing approaches to increasing long-term aggregate supply. It places great importance on intervention through the following policy measures:

● education and training

● infrastructure developments

● partnership and collaboration, especially with the trade union movement.

Tax reform

Tax reform and tax cuts are at the heart of supply-side, right-wing economics. Their theoretical basis is associated with Arthur Laffer, an economic adviser to the US President Ronald Reagan from 1981 to 1989. It is said that Laffer sketched on a dinner napkin a possible relationship between tax rates and revenues. He argued that a zero tax rate would result in zero tax revenues as would a 100 per cent tax rate. Laffer sketched a curve, illustrated in Figure 7.5, which shows that tax revenues will increase along with increasing tax rates, reach a maximum and then decline along with further increases in tax rates. Most economists would agree with the principle that increasing tax rates beyond a certain point will lead to a reduction in tax revenues, but actually finding that point has proved to be very difficult.

Some empirical work in the USA has indicated that tax revenues will fall with marginal tax rates of around 65 per cent, but supply-side economists point to a possible causal link between relatively low flat-rate taxes and high rates of economic growth in the Baltic states.

Research in the UK into the incentive effects of tax cuts indicates that cutting marginal rates can encourage some workers to work harder but that significant increases in tax allowances in the 1988 budget only increased the total number of hours worked by 0.5 per cent. Similarly, cutting the top marginal rate of taxation from 60 to 40 per cent had a minimal effect in encouraging the better-off to work more hours.

Privatisation

Privatisation – the sale of assets from the public to the private sector – was a key supply-side policy largely started by the Conservatives in the 1980s but effectively carried on by Labour governments from 1997 onwards. It was argued that under public ownership companies such as British Telecom, British Steel and various local water boards had no financial incentive to cut costs. Many were monopolies not subject to competition and as such were likely to be productively inefficient. In a 15-year period starting in 1979, over 40 businesses were privatised, and in many cases rationalisation and widespread redundancies have forced down average costs of production and increased productive efficiency.

In some markets, especially those that can be described as natural monopolies, the drive to cut costs of production and increase profits has been at the expense of the consumer, and in the most extreme example, rail safety has suffered, resulting in the effective nationalisation of Railtrack.

It is possible to evaluate the microeconomic impacts of privatisation by assessing changes in prices paid by consumers, the quality of service, levels

Government revenue

Figure 7.5 Laffer curve

Tax rate (per cent) — 0, t, 100

Recent rail crashes have been attributed to privatisation

of investment, and so on in particular industries. On this basis, it might be possible to conclude that the privatisation of British Airways, British Telecom and British Steel has benefited customers, whereas it is perceived that customers are charged higher prices for poorer rail services, and less reliable water supplies. However, making such comparisons and being clear about cause and effect is not always easy. For example, it is arguable that increased charges for water are necessary to provide investment which should have been, but was not, undertaken under public ownership.

Moreover, it is hard to make clear judgements about the macroeconomic effects of privatisation over time. Greater productive efficiency represents the better use of existing resources – short-run growth in aggregate supply. Long-run aggregate supply is affected by a range of factors. For example, many privatisations coincided with technological improvements arising from the use of microprocessors – it is hard to assess the relative contribution of these different drivers of change.

As most businesses which were in public ownership have now been privatised, the scope for extending this policy further is limited. One way in which the UK government has sought to benefit from perceived private sector expertise has been through the 'Private Finance Initiative' (PFI), which has been used to build roads, schools and hospitals. These projects are funded and managed by private sector businesses and then rented back to the public sector. New building is undertaken without the use of government expenditure, which is meant to encourage greater efficiency during the construction stage, but the public sector then becomes liable for paying rents for a long time – often 30 years – into the future. There is considerable argument and dispute between economists as to the merits of such initiatives. Those involving the modernisation of London's underground have been particularly problematical.

ACTIVITY ····⦂

Choose a PFI project and assess its economic strengths and weaknesses.

Market reforms

For the last 30 years, both Conservative and Labour governments have pursued policies which are designed to make markets more competitive by:

● encouraging greater labour mobility

● deregulating markets

● encouraging competition.

Successive governments have increased the incentives for the unemployed to seek work. It is now more difficult for the unemployed to qualify for welfare benefits, and more pressure is put upon claimants to seek work. Similar changes are planned to encourage those who are classified with disabilities to seek work.

Finally, reducing regulations and controls on markets frees them up and encourages markets to be more responsive. It is argued that more dynamic markets contribute to long-run economic growth.

Anti-trade union legislation

Both Labour and Conservative governments have since the 1970s taken steps to reduce the power of trade unions. They have made it harder to go on strike and have outlawed secondary activity, which limits the opportunities for one union to support the actions of another. Trade unions appear to have much less influence than they did 30–40 years ago. Membership has declined significantly and the

Union leader Arthur Scargill led the miners' strike of 1984–85

number of working days lost to strike activity has decreased. This decline in influence has coincided with the decline of employment in industries such as coal mining, steel making, and printing, where union membership was relatively high. The failure of the miners' strike in 1984–5 was seen as a victory for the supply-side economics championed by Margaret Thatcher. Employers may now feel more powerful in terms of their relationship with the union movement, and workers are arguably more flexible in taking on new roles and responsibilities than they might have been in the past.

Some economists believe that the successful implementation of labour market reforms can make a major contribution to reducing the non-accelerating inflation rate of unemployment (NAIRU) or natural rate of unemployment (see page 132). If trade union power is diminished, it is argued, workers will be less likely to be successful in pushing for higher wages to help them keep up with inflation. This dampens inflationary expectations and leads to a reduction in NAIRU, showing that higher levels of employment/lower levels of unemployment can be consistent with lower rates of increases in the price level.

Education and training

When elected in 1997, Tony Blair famously responded to questions about economic policies with the words 'education, education, education'. A whole series of reports have highlighted potential weakness in terms of education and training in the UK compared with those countries that are seen to be our competitors. One of the main surveys of international education standards is the Programme for International Student Assessment (PISA) studies undertaken by the Organisation for Economic Co-operation and Development (OECD). The studies compare achievements of 15-year-olds in science, maths and reading. They tend to show students in Finland reach the highest standards, closely followed by Hong Kong, South Korea and the Netherlands. The authors point out that there are more variations in achievement within countries than there are between countries. Nonetheless, data such as this is used by politicians to both praise and criticise the successes and failings of government policy.

ECONOMICS IN CONTEXT – GLOBAL ECONOMICS

This major review of skills training in the UK was published in December 2006. It was enthusiastically endorsed by the Prime Minister, who recently argued that the skills gap was more important than the arms race. The principal recommendations of the Leitch report were as follows.

THE LEITCH REPORT

- the UK commits to become a world leader in skills by 2020
- 95 per cent of working-age adults to have basic skills in both functional literacy and numeracy – rising from 85 and 79 per cent respectively in 2005
- more than 90 per cent of adults to be skilled to GCSE level or to vocational equivalents – rising from 69 per cent in 2005
- the number of apprentices in the UK to increase to 500,000 by 2020
- more than 40 per cent of adults skilled to graduate level and above – up from 29 per cent in 2005
- government, employers and individuals to all engage and invest more in skills development and significantly increase training in the workplace
- if insufficient progress has been made by 2010, the government should introduce a statutory right for employees to access workplace training.

Infrastructure changes

These are examples of interventionist supply side-policies and involve the government funding major investments that have significant positive externalities. Improvements to transport systems and energy supplies are often sited as examples of ways in which government funding can be used to increase the long-term productive capacity of the economy. Cheaper and more reliable transport and energy supplies can be a benefit to both consumers and businesses, but such projects usually involve very significant inputs of finance, from which the returns only accrue in the very long run. This makes major investments such as the Severn barrage, improved north–south rail links, or more motorways less attractive to the private sector, which may seek quicker returns in other forms of investment.

There are, however, problems with major infrastructure projects, associated with the length of the planning processes and the tendency of governments to underestimate eventual costs. For these reasons, the UK government tends to favour partnership arrangements with the private sector, much in the same way that private finance initiative (PFI) has been used to fund the building of new hospitals and schools.

Partnership and collaboration

Successive Labour governments have largely embraced many of the supply-side policies first initiated by Conservative governments in office prior to 1997. One such is a tough anti-trade union policy. At the same time, Labour has encouraged a more positive relationship with the union movement. One area of collaboration that has been successful has been the engagement of trade union officials in the promotion of learning in the workplace. This has resulted in employers and unions working together to ensure that employees develop skills that benefit both workers and employers – leading to greater productivity and expanding the productive capacity of the economy.

Monetary policy, the money supply and interest rates

BUILDING ON AS

For AS you should have learned that the UK government uses a mix of fiscal, supply-side and monetary policy to achieve both macro- and microeconomic policy objectives. There are overlaps, but the current strategy is that supply-side policies are used to try to boost the long-term aggregate supply; that in terms of fiscal policy the government budget is kept in balance over the period of the economic cycle; and that in terms of monetary policy the monetary policy committee (MPC) of the Bank of England has the responsibility for setting interest rates to ensure that inflation is kept at a target level of 2 per cent, while ensuring that the economy expands in line with long-term trend rates of growth.

These policies appear to have been successful, as the UK economy has grown steadily over the last 20 years, inflation has been kept low, and the booms and slumps associated with the economic cycle have been avoided.

STEPPING UP TO A2

There is more emphasis in A2 on understanding how money markets work and the effect they have on interest rates, together with a more detailed understanding of the policy measures used by the Bank of England to achieve monetary policy objectives.

In terms of likely questions there is also a greater emphasis on evaluation, for example, 'Evaluate the extent to which the MPC have helped the government achieve its macroeconomic policy objectives', for which you have to consider monetary policy in the wider context of macroeconomic policies.

ACTIVITY ·····

Use aggregate demand and supply diagrams to show the effects on prices and national output if the government succeeds in promoting:

a growth in long-run aggregate supply

b fiscal balance

c setting interest rates to maintain long-run trend rates of growth.

Money markets

You already know that **interest rates** can be seen as the cost of borrowing and lending money. Clearly, variations in interest rates will have effects on consumers, businesses and a whole range of macroeconomic indices.

DEFINITION

Interest rates: the cost of borrowing and lending money – always expressed as a percentage

ACTIVITY ·····

Assess the extent to which falling interest rates impact on:

a consumer spending

b investment

c government borrowing

d the exchange rate

e the CPI.

In AS the focus was on the MPC meeting on a monthly basis to set the 'bank rate' in order to achieve government inflation targets. For example, in April 2008 the bank rate was cut from 5.25 to 5 per cent. You will be aware that, for the economy as a whole, there is a range of other interest rates. At the moment, if I borrow money I might be lucky enough pay around 7.3 per cent to the bank of Scotland, around 16 per cent on my credit card and up to 10 times that to a pawn shop.

There is a series of interconnected markets for money and credit and they work in much the same way as any other market. There are those that demand and those that supply, and not surprisingly the demand for money tends to have an inverse relationship with the rate of interest. And, also not surprisingly, the supply of money to any particular money market is likely to have a positive relationship to changes in interest rates. This means that we can use demand and supply analysis to explain what might happen in an individual money market. This is shown in Figure 7.6, which shows how the current typical rate of 16 per cent for borrowing on a credit card has been determined. Should credit card providers attempt to charge a higher rate, say 20 per cent, they would lose some customers, and presumably those offering lower rates would find it difficult to cover the costs of the services they provide, which will include provision for bad debts.

Money markets range from 'home credit' – which involves loans at a cost of 150 per cent or more, on which the repayments are collected on a weekly basis – to the now infamous 'sub-prime market' in the USA, which involves mortgage lending to those on low incomes. Although these markets may appear to be miles apart, money or credit is very mobile, and for this reason it is possible for the Bank of England in the UK to be both influenced by and to influence changes in individual money markets anywhere in the world.

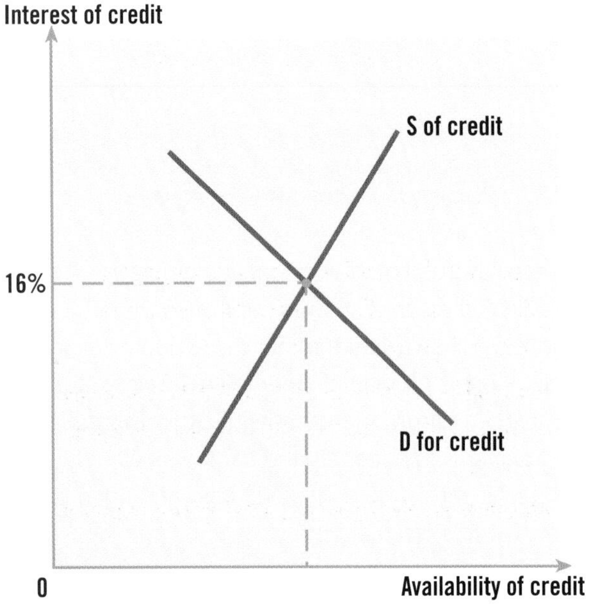

Interest of credit

16%

S of credit

D for credit

0   **Availability of credit**

Figure 7.6 The money market

Monetary policy

Monetary policies include those government and central bank actions designed to influence macroeconomic performance. The interconnectedness of money markets outlined in the previous section provides the government with different opportunities to influence money markets to pursue monetary policy objectives. These focus on:

- the supply of money
- interest rates.

THE SUPPLY OF MONEY

In your work for AS and in earlier sections of this book you will have learned that monetary economists, in particular, have put considerable emphasis on controlling the money supply as a means of controlling inflation. Friedman demonstrated that there appeared to be a direct causal relationship between changes in the supply of money and changes in the level of prices. Some Keynesian economists have questioned the validity of this causal relationship, preferring to suggest that both the supply of money and inflation can be explained more effectively by reference to the relationship between aggregate demand and aggregate supply. They suggest that, should aggregate demand exceed aggregate supply, both the supply of money and inflation are likely to rise.

Between 1950 and 1985, successive governments attempted to use different policy measures to directly control the supply of money. In order to make this work, it was important to define what actually constituted the money. This may sound silly, but governments found this very hard to achieve and more than eight different definitions were used.

The overwhelming majority of transactions which take place in the economy do not involve exchanges of cash. Rather, they rely on credit, which can take many forms. Governments discovered that if they defined the money supply in a particular way, usually to restrict its growth and bring down inflation, banks and other financial intermediaries were able to develop new lines of credit that enabled them to evade government controls. One economist likened attempts to control the money supply as squeezing an inflated balloon. Nonetheless, the government does have some influence, rather than effective control, over the money supply, and this arises because of the interdependence of the money markets and the need for banks and other financial institutions to have a bankers' banker: the Bank of England has three ways of influencing the supply of money:

- open market operations
- direct controls
- formal and informal influences.

OPEN MARKET OPERATIONS

Government borrowing is financed by the issue of long-term and short-term government securities, known as gilts or bonds and treasury bills. These are held as assets by banks, and the Bank of England can affect the asset structure of banks by buying and selling bonds and bills. Should the government sell securities, banks will transfer cash to the Bank of England, which reduces their ability to lend to others. Conversely, if the government buys back securities and treasury bills, cash holdings of banks increase as does their ability to lend. Buying and selling in this way is referred to as open market operations, and it provides a way for the government to try to affect the amount of credit which banks are able to extend to customers; in other words, influence the money supply.

DIRECT CONTROLS

In the past, governments have used direct controls on banks in order to try to influence the availability of credit/supply of money. They have tried to use powers to force banks to make additional deposits at the Bank of England, or to keep a higher proportion of their reserves in the form of cash. Both measures are designed to limit the growth in the money supply. Direct controls were not successful and it was thought that they had long been abandoned. However, in 2008, the government actually used nationalisation to try to solve the Northern Rock banking crisis.

FORMAL AND INFORMAL INFLUENCES

Although banking and banking institutions have been part of the process of globalisation, the City of London remains a world financial capital and is also the home of the Bank of England. Financial institutions based in the City often have similar

objects – not least macroeconomic stability, and each advises and consults the other. The government is reliant on financial expertise from the banking sector, which in turn is reliant on government contracts. In this context the Bank of England is able to wield considerable power and influence.

Although the government and the Bank of England monitor different measures of the money supply, they do so in order to inform their overall judgement as to the performance of macroeconomic variables.

Interest rates

The government, through the Bank of England, has much more influence on interest rates than it does on the money supply, because of its role as **lender of last resort.**

In almost all countries of the world, central banks have the role of acting as a banker to the banking system, and this includes acting as lender of last resort. If a bank in the UK is short of cash, it can turn to the Bank of England and borrow. This is a common occurrence, as transactions between banks will often generate short-term imbalances. Should a UK bank be short of cash it can sell assets, usually treasury bills or government bonds, to the Bank of England in return for cash. The Bank of England will then sell back the assets it has been sold in a given period of time – usually 14 days. The rate of interest charged on this transaction is technically called the **repo rate** and this is determined by the MPC, and changed or confirmed on a monthly basis.

DEFINITION

Monetary policies: policies involving changing the interest rate and/or the supply of money to achieve macroeconomic policy objectives

Lender of last resort: role of the central bank in terms of always being prepared to lend to commercial banks – at a price

Repo rate: the rate of interest charged by the central bank

ECONOMICS IN CONTEXT – GLOBAL ECONOMICS

GREAT CRASH RE-RUN?

In the Great Crash of 1929, share prices collapsed first in Wall Street then around the world. The crash followed a series of banking failures and a period of great optimism in the USA in terms of increasing prosperity and rising share prices. The Great Depression which followed involved massive increases in unemployment, falling incomes and social and political turmoil.

Economic events of 2007 and 2008 could lead us to consider the possibility of a re-run. Fifteen years of economic growth have contributed to complacency, optimism about rising share prices, and a belief that we will all continue to become better-off.

The reality is that much of this optimism is based on shaky foundations and the reckless expansion of credit. Borrowing is cheap, inflation is low and both consumers and sections of the private sector have built up large amounts of debt. Government controls on banking have been relaxed and some economists have talked about a new economic paradigm of prosperity for almost everyone (see page 115).

However, the fears about the consequences of banking failure and fragility of the US and other economies have been brought into sharp focus by the failures of the sub-prime mortgage market in the USA, the nationalisation in the UK of Northern Rock, and speculative attacks on both US and UK plcs. These resulted in the collapse in share price of investment bank Bear Sterns from $160 in 2007 to $2 in March 2008, leading to immediate intervention from the Federal Reserve Bank to enable the ailing bank to be taken over by Morgan Stanley – in other words the US government cannot afford to let banks fail – they fear a domino effect of potential business and financial failures reminiscent of events in Wall Street 80 years ago.

There are other repo rates, as the banks use a similar system to lend and borrow cash between one another over a short period of time. This is called the Libor (London inter-bank offered rate) and on 1 January 2008 banks in the UK were prepared to lend to each other for one month at a rate of 5.746 per cent.

ACTIVITY ···⋮

Use the Internet to collect data on changes to the bank rate and LIBOR between mid-2007 and mid-2008. What does this data tell you about the performance of the UK economy? Has the crisis caused by the US sub-prime market been resolved? Explain your conclusions.

THE MPC AND INTEREST RATES

The monetary policy committee (MPC) of the Bank of England meets monthly. It reviews a range of economic indicators and concludes with a recommendation about the bank rate. The minutes of the meetings are publicly available and as an A2 student you should find that they provide an excellent insight into the kinds of discussions that take place and the factors that the committee takes into account when making this important decision about monetary policy. In December 2007, the committee considered:

● the state of financial markets in the UK following the Northern Rock crisis

● international economic considerations, especially in respect of the performance of trading partners

● money, credit, demand and output in the UK, focusing on the potential trade-off between inflation and economic growth.

It then reached the conclusion contained in the section which follows.

ECONOMICS IN CONTEXT

EXTRACT FROM THE MINUTES OF THE MPC MEETING, DECEMBER 2007

The Committee discussed a number of policy options. Continued upward pressure on prices and costs in the near term and elevated inflation expectations suggested that no change in Bank Rate might be appropriate to keep inflation on track to meet the target.

But the worsening financial market turmoil, and the consequent tightening of credit conditions, had increased the downside risks to activity and inflation in the medium term. Signs of slowing growth in the industrial world were already apparent. That suggested a substantial loosening in policy might be needed. However, a large reduction in Bank Rate now would increase the upside risk to inflation.

On balance, the Committee thought that the downside risks to the economy and inflation in the medium term from the deterioration in financial market conditions outweighed the potential upside risks to inflation from short-run cost pressures. The level of interest rates, following a marked tightening in policy last year, was already restrictive, and the expected slowdown in domestic demand should act to dampen inflationary pressures.

That put the Committee in a good position to act pre-emptively to reduce the risks stemming from the tightening of credit without losing credibility among wage and price setters.

Against that background, the Committee judged that an immediate decrease in Bank Rate of 25 basis points was necessary to meet the inflation target in the medium term.

The Governor invited the Committee to vote on the proposition that Bank Rate should be reduced by 25 basis points to 5.5 per cent. The Committee voted unanimously in favour of the proposition.

ACTIVITY

Use the Internet to access and print off a copy of the minutes of the latest meeting of the MPC.

a Highlight all data discussed by the MPC to make its judgement about the bank rate.

b Use a table to classify this data in terms of suggesting the need for an upward or downward revision in interest rate.

c Explain the conclusion reached by the MPC. Was it unanimous? Why do you think this was?

d Assess the extent to which decisions by the MPC are influenced by European or global economic factors.

Exchange rate policy

BUILDING ON AS

You will have touched on the importance of exchange rates for AS and should have a good understanding of the related topic – the balance of payments.

STEPPING UP TO A2

You need to know how the exchange rate is determined and this also provides a good opportunity to apply demand and supply analysis to a particular series of markets. You also need to have an understanding of the relationship between interest rates and exchange rates, and how changes in the exchange rate might be an influence on policy objectives such as price stability and unemployment. As with other concepts in A2, examiners expect you to have a deeper and more sophisticated understanding. If you are going to do well, they will expect you to understand the inter-relatedness of different economic concepts. Looking at the possible relationship between interest rates and the exchange rate and other macroeconomic variables provides a good opportunity for you to show off these skills.

Determination of exchange rates

Exchange rates can be set by governments or by markets, but in both cases the basic influences which determine the level at which one currency

Exchange rates are ultimately determined by demand and supply

might be exchanged for another are those of demand and supply. In other words, the value of the pound at a particular period in time is determined by the forces of demand and supply of pounds to the foreign exchange market. As will be considered in later sections, governments may intervene in foreign exchange markets in pursuit of particular macroeconomic policy objectives.

DEFINITION

Exchange rate: what one currency is worth in terms of another

The demand for pounds

Your understanding of the balance of payments should provide you with a good framework for understanding who demands pounds. If a foreign resident wishes to purchase a good or service from a UK resident, it is likely that at some time their purchase will result in an increase in demand for pounds. The demand for pounds is therefore a derived demand. Similarly, if a foreign resident

chooses to purchase assets or stocks from a UK resident, their decision will eventually trigger an increase in demand for pounds. The same thing will happen if foreign residents decide to take a holiday in the UK or enjoy foreign travel with a UK-owned air or cruise line company. All these potential consumers of UK-produced or -owned goods, services or assets will be affected by changes in the exchange rate. If they can buy pounds more cheaply, it is likely that their demands for UK-produced goods, services and assets will increase – all of these will appear to be cheaper to the foreign resident. Therefore, it is possible to construct a demand curve for pounds, and this is illustrated in Figure 7.7.

In this diagram the price of pounds is indicated in terms of dollars. Currently the pound is worth around $2. If its value falls, say, to $1.75, all those foreign residents using dollars to buy pounds can now get more for their money and their demand for pounds is likely to increase, as shown by the movement from *a* to *b* and the increase in quantity demanded from *OQ* to *OQ$_1$*.

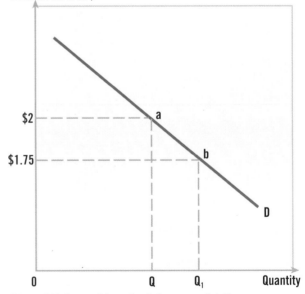

Figure 7.7 Demand for pounds in terms of dollars

exchange rates is to think clearly: Who demands pounds and who supplies them to the foreign exchange market? If you choose to holiday in the USA, you will supply pounds for conversion into US dollars. Conversely, a US resident coming to the UK will be demanding pounds – the foreign exchange market links and resolves these two transactions.

The supply of pounds

The supply of pounds can be analysed in a similar way. UK residents purchasing goods, services or assets owned by foreign residents will trigger a process by which pounds will be supplied to be turned into a foreign currency. If you decide to holiday abroad using a foreign-owned company, you will effectively be supplying pounds to a foreign currency market. If the pound falls in value, you will have to supply more pounds to purchase the same amount of foreign currency and this increase in the price of your holiday may deter you from holidaying abroad, or lead you to find a cheaper substitute.

Therefore, a fall in the value of the pound leads to a fall in the quantity supplied of pounds. Conversely, if the pound increases in value, foreign-produced goods and services will appear to be cheaper and the supply of pounds is likely to rise. This relationship between the supply of pounds and the exchange rate is illustrated in Figure 7.8.

Determination of the exchange rate

When the demand for pounds and the supply of pounds are combined, it is possible to show how the equilibrium will be determined. In this example, the equilibrium is given when the pound is worth $1.95. Any value above this will result in an excess supply of pounds, which will result in a downward pressure on the exchange rate; and any value below the equilibrium will result in upward pressures on the exchange rate. This is illustrated in Figure 7.9.

Should British goods become more attractive to foreign residents, their demand will increase, increasing the derived demand for pounds. This would be illustrated by a rightward shift in the demand for pounds illustrated in Figure 7.10, leading to an increase in the exchange rate to $2.10.

Figure 7.8 Supply of pounds in terms of dollars

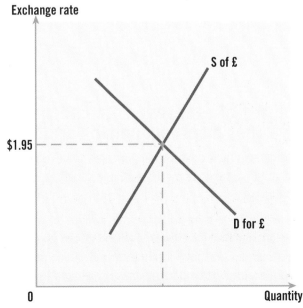

Figure 7.9 The market for pounds

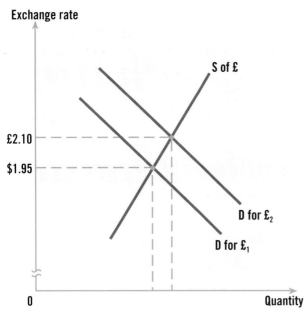

Figure 7.10 Increased demand for pounds

Impact of exchange rate changes on other macroeconomic variables

Changes in the exchange rate are likely to have an impact on a range of macroeconomic variables, including:

● *exports* – a rising exchange rate is likely to lead to a fall in demand for exports of UK-produced goods and services, as they will appear to have become more expensive compared to those produced by our competitors. Foreign orders for UK-produced goods and services are likely to fall. However, if the exchange rate falls, exports are likely to rise, and a falling exchange rate can appear to be a good way of stimulating demand for UK-produced goods.

● *imports* – a rising exchange rate is likely to lead to an increase in demand for imported goods and services, as they will appear to be relatively cheaper, whereas a falling exchange rate will make imports more expensive and demand for them is likely to fall. This reinforces the effect of a falling UK exchange rate benefiting UK-based producers, and imports become relatively more expensive.

● *balance of payments* – the effects of changes in the exchange rate on the balance of payments are more complicated. Remember that the balance of payments is about revenue flow, not the physical flow of goods. A falling exchange rate will make UK-produced goods relatively cheaper, leading to increases in domestic and overseas demand, but the balance of payments will only improve if the total revenue spent on UK-produced goods and services rises. For this to happen, the combined elasticities of demand for exports and imports need to be greater than −1 – in other words, the combined demands need to be relatively elastic.

If, however the combined elasticities are less than −1, a falling exchange rate will actually lead to a worsening in the balance of payments, as the amount of revenue generated by exports and import substitution will actually fall. Net outflows from the balance of payments will increase and this could lead to a deficit in the balance of payments.

● *employment* – the employment effects of changes in the exchange rate are determined by the effects on imports and exports. On the basis of the analysis above, a rising UK exchange rate is likely to lead to a fall in aggregate demand, which will in turn lead to a fall in national output. This means that the demand for labour in the UK will fall and unemployment, other things being equal, is likely to rise.

On the other hand, a falling exchange rate is likely to stimulate exports and the demand for import substitutes, leading overall to an increase in aggregate demand and, should capacity be available in the economy, an increase in employment levels and reduction in unemployment.

● *inflation* – given the analysis above, a rise in the exchange rate is likely to lead to a reduction in inflationary pressures and a falling exchange rate can be potentially inflationary.

The relationship between the elasticities of demand for exports and imports, changes in the exchange rate and balance of payments effects is known as the **Marshall Learner condition**. This analysis indicates that, if the combined elasticities of demand for exports and imports is less than –1 (that is, relatively inelastic) then a falling exchange rate will actually have an adverse effect on the balance of payments. If, however, the combined demand for imports and exports is relatively elastic a fall in the exchange rate will have a positive effect on a country's balance of payments.

DEFINITION

Marshall Learner condition: the requirement that the combined elasticities for imports and exports need to be relatively elastic if a fall in the exchange rate is going to benefit the balance of payments

learning tip Studies of the UK economy indicate that if the combined elasticities for imports and exports exceed the value of –1, this means that a rising exchange rate has an adverse effect on the balance of payments and a falling one benefits the UK balance of payments. Don't forget this – it is key to understanding other exchange rate effects.

Clearly, changes in the exchange rate can have major impacts on other macroeconomic variables, especially levels of employment and the rate of inflation. Moreover, changes in the exchange rate can also have microeconomic consequences. The effects of changes will be stronger in those industries reliant upon exports or faced with competition from imports.

The demand for the outputs of these firms will be affected by exchange rate changes and these firms will also be faced with increasing risks and costs associated with changes in the exchange rate.

Policy changes

The preceding analysis could prompt governments to try to influence the exchange rate in order to achieve other macroeconomic policy objectives:

● They may wish to promote stability in foreign exchange markets.

● Reducing the exchange rate could raise employment levels in the UK.

● Raising the exchange rate could reduce inflationary pressures in the UK.

In the past, UK governments have tried to influence the exchange rate in pursuit of one or more of the above objectives. The principal way that this was achieved was through the use of gold and foreign currency reserves. The Bank of England demands currencies from and supplies them to foreign exchange markets. It could boost its reserves by buying in more gold and foreign currency. This would increase the supply of pounds and potentially reduce the exchange rate. This is illustrated in Figure 7.11. Conversely the Bank of England could try to boost the exchange rate by selling gold and foreign currency

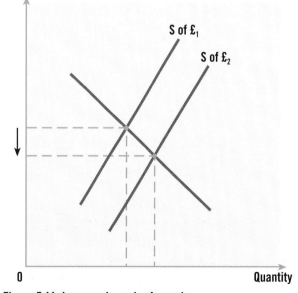

Figure 7.11 Increased supply of pounds

from its reserves, thereby increasing the demand for pounds.

In the past, UK governments have pursued policies aimed at influencing the exchange rate. However, as you will have read in your AS text, the events of Black Wednesday on 16 September 1992, when the government lost £3.4 billion (Treasury estimate of 1997) in trying to maintain an over-valued pound, have for the time being brought an end to active intervention. This does not mean that the government and the Bank of England ignore the exchange rate –

relatively high rates are a check on inflation, relatively low rates boost employment and businesses prefer to operate in a climate of exchange rate stability.

ACTIVITY ····⫶

Use the Internet to track changes in the UK/US and UK/Euro exchange rates over the previous three years and assess the effects on both macro- and microeconomic variables.

8 The international economy

On completion of this chapter you should be able to:

- understand globalisation and its consequences for developing and developed countries
- distinguish between comparative and absolute advantage in trade and understand the importance and limitations of these concepts
- understand the reasons for changes in the pattern of trade between the UK and the rest of the world and the importance of this pattern to both developed and developing countries
- evaluate the arguments for and against free trade and protectionism
- understand the significance of short- and long-term capital flows on the balance of payments
- analyse and evaluate measures that may be taken to deal with balance of payments deficits or surpluses
- evaluate different exchange rate systems
- understand the main features of the European Union (EU) and its impact on the UK economy.

This chapter is divided into five sections relating to the main elements of this part of the AQA specification, which relate to different aspects of the international economy:

- Globalisation
- Trade
- The balance of payments
- Exchange rate systems
- The European Union.

learned in the last chapter about the determination of exchange rates. This all needs to be carried forward to help you understand the concepts in this chapter.

STEPPING UP TO A2

Globalisation is one of the themes of this chapter. You are expected to develop a better understanding of some of the issues relating to economic growth in developing countries. New theories include those underpinning arguments about free trade and exchange rates. Although you will be aware of the implications of membership of the EU for the UK economy, you will need to ensure that you have a basic understanding of its institutional structure, the importance of the single European market enlargement and the single European currency.

BUILDING ON AS

Unlike Chapters 6 and 7, much of the content of this chapter will be new to you. You should, from AS, have an understanding of the balance of payments. You will have

Globalisation

Globalisation refers to the historical processes by which more and more aspects of more and more people's lives are being shaped as a result of global rather than national developments. There are social, cultural and political dimensions to globalisation. In economics, the process involves the production and selling of goods and services on a global basis, accompanied by a reduction and possible elimination of the barriers that previously may have prevented the free movement between different countries of:

- goods and services
- capital
- technology.

Arguably, globalisation might also involve the free movement of *labour* on a world basis, but national boundaries, some would argue, present massive barriers to the free movement of labour. The extent to which impoverished and oppressed people attempt to overcome these barriers indicates the strength of those pressures, which could result in a freer movement of labour on a global basis. Within individual countries, globalisation has been associated with growing urbanisation.

> **DEFINITION**
>
> **Globalisation:** production and distribution of goods and services on a global scale

> **ACTIVITY** ···⌁
>
> Assess the extent to which the USA has been successful in limiting the free flow of labour from Central and South America.

Causes of globalisation

There are a number of key factors that have contributed to globalisation. These include:

- greater inter-government co-operation

- the ever-increasing growth of multinational corporations
- improvements in communications
- technological changes.

Inter-government co-operation

In many ways, the Second World War provided the impetus for greater economic and political co-operation between countries, as shown by the development of the United Nations, a range of international financial institutions such as the World Bank, trading blocks such as the EU, and a desire to avoid the economic and social conflicts that had contributed to a world war. One objective that has been pursued for the last 60 years has been the removal of tariffs and barriers to trade. Although many still exist, there are significantly fewer barriers to trade than there were, and the World Trade Organisation (WTO) continues to try to reach agreement about the further removal of trade barriers. Similarly, members of the EU have argued their way to creating a single European market,

The first General Assembly of the United Nations was held in London in 1946

involving the removal of barriers to trade within Europe. The economic rationale for these changes is described in the sections which follow on free trade.

Growth of multinationals

Multinationals or transnational firms are those that produce and market their products in more than one country of the world. Globalisation is directly associated with the growth of multinational firms and it is said that some 500 companies control nearly 25 per cent of the total value of the world's economy. Although estimates vary, between 30 and 50 of the world's largest economies are actually multinational companies. The world's top 10 are shown in Table 8.1.

> **DEFINITION**
>
> **Multinational:** company producing and selling in a number of different countries

Clearly oil producers and motor vehicle manufacturers dominate this list, but, according to some estimates, Wal-Mart has now overtaken Exxon as the largest corporation. Interestingly, the top 20 now include financial services companies.

Multinational firms are both a cause and an effect of globalisation. They are able to influence governments to reduce barriers to trade and they provide a means by which both capital and technology can be easily transferred between countries.

Improvements in communications

There have been great improvements in both the physical transportation of goods and the effectiveness of communications between countries. The cost of transport of goods by both sea and air is not only relatively lower than it was 50 years ago; it is also quicker and more reliable.

Electronic and digital changes have revolutionised communication between countries. Typically, components can be designed in Europe and produced on computer-aided manufacturing (CAM) machine tools in China or other eastern countries with virtually no human contribution. It is perhaps surprising that Microsoft is currently only the 63rd largest corporation in the world.

	Company	Activity	Revenue ($/year*)	HQ
1	ExxonMobil	Oil and gas	375.9	USA
2	Wal-Mart	Retailing	345.0	USA
3	Royal Dutch Shell	Oil and gas	318.8	Netherlands/UK
4	BP	Oil and gas; alternative fuel	265.9	UK
5	General Motors	Automobiles; trucks; financial services	206.5	USA
6	Toyota Motor	Automobiles; trucks; robotics; financial services; biotechnology	205.0	Japan
7	Chevron	Oil and gas	204.9	USA
8	Total	Oil and gas	193.2	France
9	Daimler	Automobiles; trucks; financial services	190.4	Germany
10	ConocoPhillips	Oil and gas	188.5	USA

* data from 2006 and 2007

Source: Wikipedia

Table 8.1 World's top 10 multinational companies

Technological changes

Improvements in communications are closely related to technological changes which have reduced the importance of some locational factors that previously tied particular productive processes to particular geographic locations, for example, reliance on coal for energy supplies. The widespread use of electricity gives companies greater freedom in choosing locations where labour or other costs are lowest. The rate of technological transfer, the speed by which new ways of making things can pass from country to country, has also increased significantly.

Consequences of globalisation

All countries in the world operate within a global economy and those in the developing world are particularly dependent on the import and export of key commodities and products. The impacts of globalisation are hotly disputed, as poorer countries are often in conflict with governments of developed economies and the growing anti-globalisation movement shows that many in both developed and developing countries are concerned about the effects of globalisation.

Those who argue in favour of globalisation focus on:

● The rise in standards of living for those in countries that accept globalisation. The World Bank, which tends to support globalisation, has produced data showing that growing globalisation has been associated with reductions in absolute poverty. It claims that East Asian countries, including China, which have embraced globalisation have in the 20 years up to 2002 halved the numbers of those living on less than $2 a day. The existence of such a causal relationship is challenged by the anti-globalisation movement. On the other hand, the numbers falling below this poverty line in sub-Saharan Africa, which can be seen to be more resistant to globalisation, has actually increased.

● As far as the UK is concerned, relatively free movement of the labour force has resulted in an increase in immigration, which is said to have contributed to an expansion in the productive capacity of the economy.

● Globalisation has resulted in falling prices for many manufactured goods and this has helped

reduce inflation. Moreover, greater international competition is likely to have the same effect.

● More rapid technology transfer means that new ways of making things can now be shared and enjoyed more quickly in more countries of the world.

Anti-globalisation arguments come from both the political left and right:

● The main argument is that globalisation actually creates greater inequalities in both the developed and developing world. The manufacturing sector in the UK has been badly hit by international competition, resulting in long-term unemployment for those workers unable to find alternative jobs. Similarly, in the developing world, those who depend on agriculture have been badly affected by cheap imports from the developed world. Poverty and deprivation associated with urbanisation in the third world are often blamed on the collapse of domestic agricultural production.

● It is argued in many developing nations that the World Bank and WTO actually act in the interests of the developed world, especially the USA. It has been suggested that the developed countries are only really interested in opening up new markets for their products, rather than undertaking tariff reductions that are fair to all countries. The EU, USA and Japan heavily subsidise their farming industries, while at the same time being reluctant to reduce their tariffs on manufactured goods from the developing world. Those in the anti-globalisation movement argue that countries in the developed world are not really committed to raising living standards for all, and that trade liberalisation is essentially one-sided. Developing nations are expected to reduce tariff barriers, but these changes are not reciprocated by the developed nations.

● Multinational companies, especially mining and logging companies, are accused of ignoring the negative externalities caused by their activities, especially in those countries that are dependent on the exploitation of particular raw materials.

● Finally, those on the right wing of politics complain of immigration and the loss of national identity associated with the free movement of labour and the growth of global branding.

ECONOMICS IN CONTEXT – GLOBAL ECONOMICS

THE ETHICS OF MNCS

The record of multinationals in promoting development is very mixed. They have been responsible for mining raw materials from poor countries that have received very little in return. Multinational companies (MNCs) can be very powerful and capable of extracting very favourable terms for investment in particular countries, such as freedom from local taxation, and in some cases their activities can be very destabilising for the developing countries, for example, oil exploration in Columbia and Ecuador. They use transfer pricing, which involves understating the value of production or sales to reduce tax liabilities in countries with higher tax regimes as a technique for understating the profits made from activities in particular countries.

On the other hand, external finance is required. The extraction of resources is often beyond the means of poorer countries and some MNCs are more ethically inclined than others. When governments are strong enough to negotiate wide-ranging agreements with MNCs, they can help ensure that they share more fairly in the profits of the particular activity, that local people are trained to take senior as well as lower level jobs, and that other ethical considerations are included.

ACTIVITY ⋯⁖

Select a developing economy and investigate the role of globalisation – for good or ill? You may wish to consider economic growth, the balance of payments, technology transfer, transfer pricing and sustainability.

Trade

One of the key aspects of globalisation considered in the previous section was the reduction of tariff and other barriers which would otherwise limit trade between different countries. The theoretical basis of the idea that freer trade could be to the benefit of all countries was developed in the early nineteenth century by an English economist, David Ricardo, who was heavily influenced by Adam Smith.

The key explanation in understanding why countries may benefit from freer trade is known as the model of absolute and comparative advantage.

Absolute advantage

A country is said to have an **absolute advantage** in producing a product or products when it is more efficient at producing it/them than other countries. Putting it in more technical terms, it means that a country can produce more of the product from each unit of resource than other countries – it has an absolute advantage.

This is illustrated in Figure 8.1, which is based on the assumption that there are 10 workers in the UK and 10 in Malaysia. Each UK worker could produce 6 tanks, giving a total possible production of 60 tanks. Each UK worker could produce 10 toys, and if all did so, 100 would be made. This is illustrated by the UK production possibility curve (PPC) in Figure 8.1, which shows that UK workers could produce either

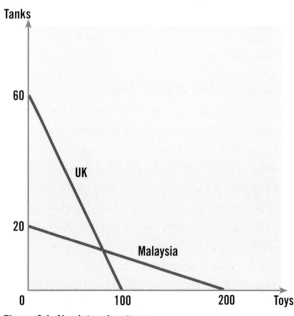

Figure 8.1 Absolute advantage

60 tanks or 100 toys or any other combination along *PPC– UK*.

In this example, the 10 Malaysian workers are less productive in terms of tank production but more productive when it comes to toys. They could produce a total of 20 tanks or 200 toys, or any combination shown by *PPC- Malaysia* in Figure 8.1 The PPCs show that the UK has the absolute advantage in the production of tanks whereas Malaysia has the absolute advantage in toy production.

The implication of this simple analysis is that both countries could become better-off if specialisation and trade took place. The total production of both tanks and toys would be increased if the UK specialised in the production of tanks and Malaysia in the production of toys.

This analysis provides a good argument for the use of specialisation and trade to promote economic growth in both countries, but it depends on the existence of absolute advantages.

> **DEFINITION**
>
> **Absolute advantage:** exists when one country can produce goods and services more efficiently than another

Comparative advantage

The notion of absolute advantage is easy to understand. However, the world and its economies are somewhat more complicated. Because of superior productivity, there is a whole range of goods and services in which the UK has an absolute advantage, and for many poorer countries there can be few if any products or services that can be produced with an absolute advantage.

The principle of **comparative advantage** provides an even stronger argument in favour of freer trade to promote economic well-being, even though one country may have an absolute advantage in the production of a range of goods and services. A country is said to have a comparative advantage in the production of a good or service if it can produce it at a lower opportunity cost compared to another country.

> **DEFINITION**
>
> **Comparative advantage:** applies when one country can produce goods and services at lower opportunity costs than another

The application of the theory of comparative advantage can be used to show that both countries can benefit from specialisation, as long as there is a difference in their relative efficiencies. This is illustrated in Figure 8.2, which is also based on the assumption that both the UK and Malaysia have a workforce of 10 workers. In this example *PPC–UK* shows that 60 tanks, or 1,200 toys, or any combination of the two along the curve could be produced, whereas Malaysian workers could make 20 tanks or 800 toys, as shown by *PPC–Malaysia*. The PPC for the UK lies to the right of that for

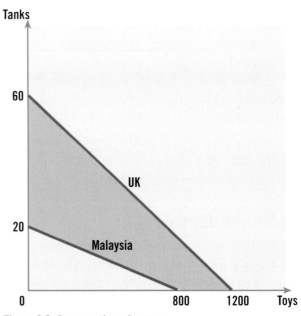

Figure 8.2 Comparative advantage

Malaysia, showing the UK has an absolute advantage in the production of both items.

However, the UK has a comparative advantage in the production of tanks. It can produce three times as many tanks as Malaysia, but only one and a half times as many toys. In other words, the opportunity cost of producing an additional tank is lower in the UK than in Malaysia. One UK-made tank has the opportunity cost of 20 toys as opposed to the opportunity cost in Malaysia of 40 toys. Malaysia's comparative advantage is in the production of toys. It can produce two-thirds as many toys as the UK but only a third as many tanks and it has a lower opportunity cost in the production of toys. The gradients or slopes of the two PPCs are different, illustrating different opportunity costs.

> **learning tip**
>
> Hopefully the reasoning in the text is clear. If not, you may have to read and make notes from this section more than once to make your learning secure. For those of you who like visual prompts to help your learning, practise drawing the diagrams in this section.

The benefits of greater specialisation are shown in Table 8.2, which shows the situation if the UK concentrates mainly on tank production, devoting 8 workers to tank production and 2 to toy production and Malaysia specialises completely in toy production.

	Tanks	Toys
UK	48	240
Malaysia		800
Total	48	1,040

Table 8.2 Output after specialisation

Specialisation in this context has also caused total output of both tanks and toys to rise. Both countries will benefit from trade if the exchange rate lies between their respective opportunity cost ratios. In

other words, the ratio at which toys and tanks are exchanged needs to lie within the shaded area in Figure 8.2, for example, an exchange rate is one tank for 30 toys.

	Tanks	Toys
UK	35	630
Malaysia	13	410
Total	48	1,040

Table 8.3 Possible consumption after specialisation and trade

> **ACTIVITY** ⋯⟶⋮
>
> Use PPC diagrams to illustrate the advantages of UK specialisation in the provision of financial services and Chinese specialisation in the production of textiles.

Limitations in applying the theory of comparative advantage

Theory of comparative advantage demonstrates that, if there are differences in relative productivity, there are real advantages to countries if they apply the

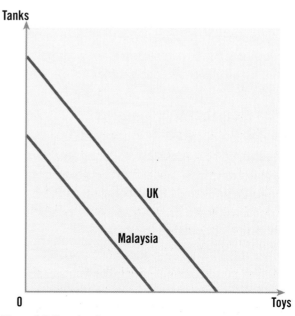

Figure 8.3 No advantage

principle of comparative advantage and specialise in the production of goods and services for which they have a comparative advantage. There are, however, potential limitations in the application of the comparative cost model:

● First, if the opportunity cost ratios for the two goods produced in the two countries are the same, as shown in Figure 8.3, where the PPCs are parallel, there are no gains to be made from specialisation and trade.

● It is often expressed, as here, in terms of a few countries and a few products. In the real world, as there are many countries and many products, and as situations are always changing, it is more difficult to work out where comparative advantages lie.

● As noted above, for both countries to benefit, the exchange rate must be favourable to both countries.

● The principle ignores transport and other costs of trade.

● It assumes free trade, that is, no tariffs or quotas.

● It fails to account for externalities associated with the development of particular industrial sectors, such as high technology industries.

Costs and benefits of greater trade

To some extent these arguments are similar to those about globalisation. Some argue that we all benefit, while others argue that the developed world gains at the expense of the developing world.

BENEFITS OF GREATER TRADE

The principle of comparative cost shows that as long as opportunity costs for producing goods within countries vary, and as long as exchange rates are 'fair', countries benefit from specialisation in the production of those goods and services for which they have a comparative advantage:

● World Bank data used earlier on page 162 indicates that if countries can take advantage of comparative costs, economic growth and further economic development will take place.

● More goods can be produced, products become relatively cheaper, inflationary pressures are reduced, and national outputs and incomes can rise.

COSTS OF GREATER TRADE

The two major costs to greater trade are:

● negative externalities, especially global warming, associated with greater energy use and the depletion of non renewable resources

● potential increase in inequalities, as specialisation involves structural changes in economies, such as the decline of primary and secondary industries in the UK and the relative decline of the agricultural sector in developing countries.

> **learning tip**
> Give yourself plenty of practice getting used to the style of part a) and part b) essay questions. Generally speaking, part a) questions require an explanation. For example, 'Explain how the principle of comparative advantage can be used as a justification for the removal of trade barriers.'

Changing trade patterns

Over the last 50 years the pattern of UK trade exports has changed, as is shown in Figures 8.4 and 8.5. A number of trends are evident:

● increased percentage of total exports going to European countries

● similar increases to North America

● significant declines in the relative importance of export markets in other parts of the world, especially Commonwealth countries.

Figures 8.6 and 8.7 show how patterns of imports have changed over the last 50 years.

These show that:

● imports from Europe have increased significantly

● imports from the USA have declined in relative significance

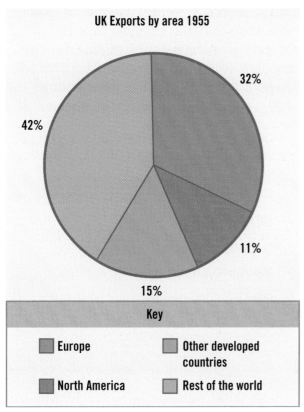

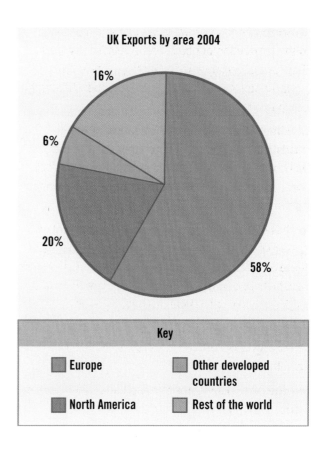

Figures 8.4 and 8.5 Changing patterns of UK trade exports

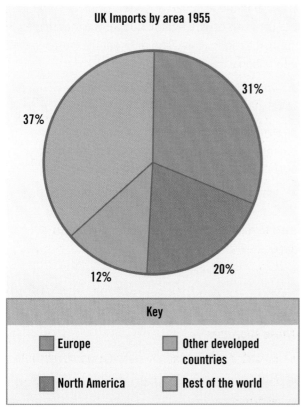

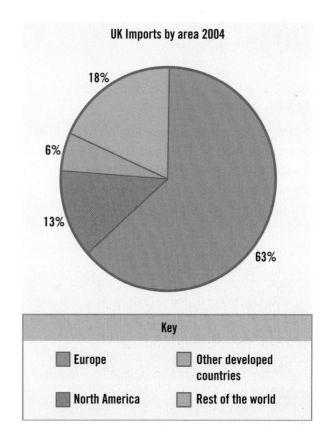

Figures 8.6 and 8.7 Changing patterns of UK trade imports

● imports from the rest of the world, especially Commonwealth countries, are in relative decline.

These changing patterns in UK trade are both a cause and an effect of growing European integration. Fifty years ago, manufacturing still dominated the structure of UK industry. This tended to lead to imports of raw materials from other parts of the world and the export of finished goods back to those countries. The structure of trade has changed significantly as:

● trade in services has increased significantly

● relatively more trade now takes place between developed countries.

ACTIVITY ···⦂

The data above does not illustrate more recent trends associated with the rapid growth in some Asian economies, especially China. UK imports from China totalled £13.2 billion in 2005, while exports stood at £3.4 billion. The UK was the biggest investor in China from the EU.

Assess the impact of these changes on:

a   the UK economy

b   the Chinese economy.

Trade barriers

In spite of the economic arguments in favour of freer trade, all governments face very strong pressures to restrict trade. For example, in 2003 the US steel industry, faced with increased competition, successfully lobbied the Bush government to impose **tariffs** of 30 per cent on steel imports. The efforts to save jobs in the USA were short lived, as some steel imports were routed through Canada (part of the North American Free Trade Area) and action against the USA was taken by the EU and other countries. More recently, in 2004 the EU and China were locked into what became quickly known as the 'bra wars' when the EU blocked imports of cheap Chinese-made clothing, as it was claimed that their **import quotas** had been exceeded.

The governments of developing nations are also faced with protectionist pressures, especially as a result of competition from large corporations in the developed world. It has been argued that tariffs are needed to protect the growth of '**infant industries**' too small to enjoy the economies of scale which benefit their competitors.

DEFINITIONS

Tariffs: taxes on imports

Import quotas: physical restrictions on imports

Infant industries: newly established industries that cannot compete with larger competitors

As noted earlier, the developed economies of the world respond to pressure from farming groups to offer **export subsidies** to protect the jobs and incomes of those in the agricultural sector. Until recently, 50 per cent of the EU's annual budget was devoted to support to agriculture. The different measures to limit international trade include:

● *import quotas* – actual limits on exports or imports of specified products

● **exchange controls** – often used by developing nations, especially when their currencies are not acceptable as international means of exchange

● **embargoes** – prohibitions on imports, often used for political reasons; for example, the USA has tried to restrict the export of computer-based applications

DEFINITIONS

Export subsidies: government subsidies to encourage exports

Exchange control: government intervention to limit the exchange of one currency for another

Embargo: prohibition on imports of specified goods or services

● *tariffs* (import or export taxes) – traditionally favoured by governments, as they generate additional revenues

● *export subsidies*, as mentioned above

● deliberately complicated and confusing regulations over imports, for example, in the language of documentation, different standards, and things as apparently trivial as delays at borders.

Trade conflicts

While the application of comparative and absolute cost theory provides a powerful case for freer trade to the benefit all nations, there are enormous conflicts between countries and trading blocks, limiting agreements over freer trade. The EU and the USA are keen to open markets for their exporters, but they are much more reluctant to open their own markets and many developing countries feel discriminated against.

The World Trade Organisation

The main body with a role overseeing world trade and promoting freer trade is the World Trade Organisation, formed in 1995 and replacing the General Agreement on Tariffs and Trade (GATT). The WTO seeks to reduce tariffs and other restrictions on international trade and provides a means by which countries can settle their trade disputes. The WTO, which currently has 136 member countries, seeks to promote trade liberalisation through a series of negotiations (which are often referred to as rounds). For example, the Uruguay round achieved agreement to reduce trade barriers in textiles. Recently, the WTO admitted

China as a new member, after a number of years of discussion and conflict.

The role of the WTO has been criticised by developing countries, which argue that industrial countries are favoured. For example, tariffs on tobacco have been reduced to 4 per cent, while tariffs on tobacco products remain at 40 per cent. Developing countries argue that the differential has nothing to do with health concerns, but is concerned with keeping industrial processing, where higher profits are made, in the developed countries. They also claim that the WTO, by allowing industrialised countries to impose restrictions to prevent **dumping**,

DEFINITION

Dumping: pricing exported goods at less than their cost of production

ECONOMICS IN CONTEXT – GLOBAL ECONOMICS

THE BRIC THESIS

Forget about the ailing US economy. The EU has had its day. Economic power is shifting away from the USA and Europe to the BRIC countries – Brazil, Russia, India and China. It is argued that these four will grow and dominate world markets by 2050. Rather than obsessing about the ailing US economy as the driving force behind economic trade and well-being, we should focus on where economic power is going to lie.

This thesis is variously attributed to investment bankers, Goldman Sachs and Russian president Vladimir Putin, but the argument is clear. Based on present rates of economic growth, collectively – and perhaps individually – these countries are likely to overtake the USA as the world's most powerful economy. China and India will dominate the global production of goods and services, while their raw material and energy needs are most likely to be met by Brazil and Russia.

is, in reality, discriminating against developing countries.

Free international trade provides a number of potential benefits to both developed and developing countries. Most importantly, free trade can lead to higher levels of output, and to increased income and employment levels for all. However, it can also pose problems for countries, especially if they cannot trade on equal terms. Countries impose a range of import restrictions, including tariffs and quotas in order to protect their economies and industries.

ACTIVITY

How far do you agree with the BRIC thesis? What are the implications for UK-based firms?

The balance of payments

BUILDING ON AS

To get through your AS examination, you were expected to have a good knowledge of the composition of the current account of the balance of payments. You will probably have developed some insights into the possible links between the balance of payments and other macroeconomic variables. You will find that aggregate demand and aggregate supply analysis provides a useful way of linking these different parts of the specification. The previous chapter involved developing a better understanding of exchange rates and this is very relevant for an improved understanding of the balance of payments.

STEPPING UP TO A2

A2 demands a more detailed understanding of the capital and financial accounts of the balance of payments, especially of the significance of short- and long-term capital flows and the special role of the City of London in the international trade in financial services.

You also need to have a more detailed understanding of the impacts of deficits and

surpluses in the balance of payment, both on individuals and on the global economy. Finally, don't forget that you will be expected to analyse and evaluate different measures to deal with deficits and surpluses.

The balance of payments account

The **balance of payments accounts** are a series of records meant to record all transactions that occur between residents of this country and those living in other countries. They are divided into three sections, which are further subdivided to account for different types of transactions:

● The *current account* made up of the balance on the trade of goods – which in the UK is almost always in deficit – and the trade in services (including income earned on overseas assets owned by UK residents) – which is usually in surplus but has not since 1997 been large enough to prevent a deficit in the current account of the balance of payments.

● The *capital account* – this is not very significant and consists of debt forgiveness and the purchase and sale of fixed assets.

● The *financial account,* which is a record of both short-term and long-term monetary transactions, including both direct investments and purchases and sales of stocks and shares. These flows are very important to the UK economy. Long-term investments known as foreign direct investment (FDI) have made an important contribution to the performance of the UK economy. It is argued that the supply-side changes outlined on page 144 in the previous chapter have made the UK an attractive destination for FDI investment, particularly from non-EU countries wishing to gain access to European

DEFINITION

Balance of payments accounts: records of financial transactions between one country and the rest of the world

markets. Short-term investments, often referred to as 'hot money' because they can be more volatile and potentially damaging if they are withdrawn, can also make an important contribution to keeping the balance of payments in balance.

Finally, there is a section called 'net errors and omissions', which is a balancing item included to ensure that the balance of payments actually balances.

> **learning tip**
>
> The last bit probably confused you – just remember accounts always have to balance – ask an accountant. It's how they balance that is interesting – see the Global economics section on page 173.

ACTIVITY ⋯⋗

Use the Internet to collect evidence that will enable you to assess the validity of the claim that the City of London is the financial capital of the world.

Balance of payments deficits

If the balance of payments is looked at before considering 'net errors and omissions', it is almost inevitable that it will be in surplus or deficit. The balance is made up of thousands and thousands of individual transactions – there is no means by which the two sides of the accounts will automatically balance. If it is in deficit, it simply means that we owe those living in other countries more than they owe us. UK residents have incurred debts, which will have to be paid in some way. Ultimately, the responsibility for maintaining the balance of payments account in balance lies with the government. In the short term the government can:

● use its reserves of gold and foreign currency – releasing these onto foreign currency markets could bring the account into balance

● borrow from an institution like the International Monetary Fund, which was set up to help governments overcome short-term budget deficits

● borrow from another government – perhaps one with a surplus

ECONOMICS IN CONTEXT – GLOBAL ECONOMICS

CITY OF LONDON – STILL THE FINANCIAL CAPITAL OF THE WORLD?

According to the Lord Mayor of the City of London:

● 32 per cent of all world currency trading takes place in London (more than NYSE and NASDAQ combined).

● 90 per cent of world trade in metals, 23 per cent of world aviation insurance, 25 per cent of all marine insurance, and almost 50 per cent of all ship brokering is in London.

● London has the most liquid financial market and is the most international.

● London is the largest investment banking centre in Europe, dealing with half of all European investment banking activity. Most investment banks are headquartered or have a major office in London.

● 610 foreign companies are listed on the London Stock Exchange.

● London has international experience – it has the most foreign banks of any financial centre (255 in March 2007); New York has 228 and Paris 217.

● rely on other governments, speculators and multinational companies to hold pounds as part of their reserves – this is feasible as long as the pound is not expected to fall in value and because the pound is widely held and used to finance international trade.

Any, some, or all of these measures could solve a short-term budget deficit, but each will be much harder to maintain in the longer term: reserves are not infinite, nor would the IMF, or other governments, have infinite patience. Sooner or later, a persistent balance of payments deficit that is not being corrected will result in a fall in the value of, in this case, the pound.

In the long term, curing a balance of payments deficit is more problematical. A government could:

● raise interest rates in order to try to make the UK more attractive to foreign investors. Raising interest rates is likely to also lead to a fall in aggregate demand, which should result in a fall in national output and reduction in demand for imports (see page 174).

● use other means to reduce aggregate demand, such as raising taxation or cutting government expenditure, with the intention of reducing the demand for imports and increasing the incentive for UK firms to export more.

● 'allow' the value of the pound to fall (see page 155) – this will eventually make UK exports cheaper and sales abroad should increase, while increasing prices of imports should reduce their demand – both factors contributing to an improvement in the balance of payments. The danger of an engineered 'devaluation' is that other countries, not wishing to lose their competitive advantage, may imitate this policy.

● introduce barriers to trade, such as tariffs and quotas, in an effort to reduce outflows of currency to pay for imports and encourage domestic production. This might be the only option for a fragile developing economy but is not realistic for a developed economy such as the UK, as it would violate agreements made as a member of the EU and of WTO.

ACTIVITY ····⁙

Evaluate the potential effectiveness of both short-term and long-term measures to remedy a balance of payments deficit.

Balance of payments surpluses

As noted in your AS, this might not appear at first sight to be a problem. However, surpluses can be problematical both because of the possible effect on other macroeconomic variables and because of their long-term effect on other countries. One country's surplus is likely to be another country's deficit. If the UK balance of payments were in surplus, it would mean that foreign residents owe UK residents more than they are owed. There are a number of solutions that could be applied if it is expected that the surplus is likely to be short lived. The government could:

● add to its reserves of gold and foreign currency – this would bring the account into balance and provide some greater security for the future, should the government need to finance a short term balance of payments deficit

● lend to an institution like the International Monetary Fund – which is partly how this institution was designed to work. Such lending could help other countries overcome their own short-term budget deficits.

● lend to other governments – perhaps one with a deficit.

● discourage other governments, speculators and multinational companies from holding pounds as part of their reserves.

Any, some, or all of the measures outlined above could solve a short-term budget surplus, but each will be much harder to maintain in the longer term. Sooner or later, a persistent balance of payments surplus that is not being corrected will result in an increase in the value of, in this case, the pound.

In the long term, curing a balance of payments surplus is more problematical. A government could:

● cut interest rates in order to try to make the UK more attractive to foreign investors. Cutting interest

ECONOMICS IN CONTEXT – GLOBAL ECONOMICS

HOW DOES THE UK GET AWAY WITH PERSISTENT DEFICITS?

Although the current account of the UK's balance of payments has been in deficit since 1997, this is not necessarily a major problem. The short answer is that residents in other countries have considered that the UK is a good place to invest, and this is shown by transactions in the Financial Account of the balance of payments. As noted earlier, the UK has been a major destination for FDI.

The pound is an alternative world currency to the dollar. As will be explained in the following section, the dollar has been seen as a weak international currency – the expectation is that its value will fall. The pound has been seen by some holders of international currencies to be a good alternative. Thus, weaknesses in the dollar have been to the pound's advantage.

Short-term capital movements have also been important. As long as speculators believe that the pound will hold or improve its value, they have an incentive to buy pounds. Conversely, as soon as they perceive that the value of the pound is likely to fall, they will have an incentive to sell pounds, thereby ensuring that the value of the pound will fall.

What will happen to the dollar? Does it matter?

This is the million-dollar question of enormous significance to not just the USA but the also rest of the world. Around 40 per cent of world trade is undertaken by the USA. The dollar is the leading world currency, used by many nations to conduct trade and to keep in reserves. Figure 8.8 charts the value of the dollar in terms of both the pound and the euro, two alternative world currencies.

This shows that over six years, the dollar has lost almost one-third of its value, falling from 69p in 2001 to around 50p at the end of 2007. The fall against the euro has been more dramatic, from around €1.14 to 75 cents.

Many factors have contributed to this significant change, not least persistent deficits in the US balance of payments. The last time that it was in surplus was in 1991, and in the autumn of 2007 the US deficit stood at $179 billion. It might well be that the recent fall in the value of the dollar will stimulate US exports and check imports, and there has been some relative improvement in the US deficit following successive falls in the value of the dollar. Two critical factors leave the future state of the US balance of payments, its economy, and the state of the world economy in doubt:

- the extent to which other countries, especially China, which has an enormous favourable balance of trade with the USA, are prepared to hold dollars in their reserves
- the willingness or otherwise of the US government to take other actions to rectify the persistent deficit. Policy measures could include raising interest rates and reducing the size of the US budget deficit (not to be confused with the balance of payments deficit), both of which are likely to raise unemployment, reduce national output and cut incomes.

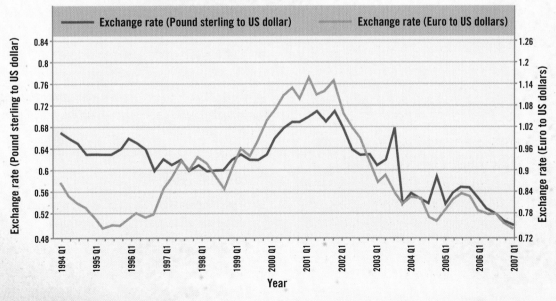

Figure 8.8 Changing exchange rates

rates is likely also to lead to an increase in aggregate demand, which should result in a rise in national output, an increase in demand for imports resulting in an increase in their price. For both reasons such a policy might also lead to an increase in inflationary pressures, which might not be welcomed.

● use other means to increase aggregate demand, such as cutting taxation or increasing government expenditure, with the intention of increasing the demand for imports and reducing the incentive for UK firms to export more. The outcome of this measure could also be to increase inflationary pressures within the economy.

● 'allow' the value of the pound to rise (see page 156) – this will eventually make UK exports more expensive and sales abroad should fall, while reducing prices of imports should increase their demand – both factors should help to cure a persistent surplus. The cost of an engineered 'revaluation' could be an increase in unemployment in the UK, and falling national output and incomes.

● reduce barriers to trade, such as tariffs and quotas, in an effort to increase imports and outflows of currency to pay for imports and expose domestic production to greater foreign competition. The opportunity cost of such a policy could be falling national output, levels of income and employment.

ACTIVITY ⋯⋗

Discuss the extent to which a persistent balance of payments surplus might be economically undesirable.

STRETCH AND CHALLENGE

Evaluate the effectiveness of the following potential policies to improve the US balance of payments:

a   allowing the value of the dollar to fall

b   increasing borrowing from abroad

c   increasing US interest rates

d   reducing US government expenditure

e   raising US taxes.

Exchange rate systems

There are basically three different systems for the determination of exchange rates:

● floating

● fixed

● dirty.

Floating rates

How exchange rates are determined in foreign exchange markets was outlined on pages 153–156 in the previous chapter. You will have also learned that since 1992 the UK government has not actively intervened in foreign exchange markets. This means that the pound has been part of a '**floating exchange rate system**' which simply means that its value is determined by market forces. This system is attractive, as it means that:

● governments can concentrate on other macro policy objectives

● governments avoid losses at the hands of speculators (see page 172–73)

● in theory the floating exchange rate should ensure that the balance of payments is kept in equilibrium.

There are potential drawbacks:

● An increasing value of the pound will usually mean that imports become cheaper and exports more expensive.

● A falling value of the pound will lead to increases in the price of imports, which can be inflationary.

● Volatility in foreign exchange markets increases the risks and costs for both importers and exporters.

DEFINITION

Floating exchange rate: a system by which market forces are left to determine exchange rates

Fixed rates

As their name implies, **fixed exchange rates** are set and maintained by governments, which use gold and

ACTIVITY ···⁞

Use demand and supply analysis to show how a floating rate for the pound measured in terms of the yen will be affected by:

a a rise in imports from Japan

b increasing UK interest rates

c inflation rising more slowly in Japan than in the UK.

DEFINITION

Fixed exchange rates: government intervention to fix exchange rates

foreign currency reserves in much the same way that stocks of agricultural products are used to smooth out fluctuations in the prices of foodstuffs. Thus, if for some reason the demand for pounds rises, as illustrated by the shift from D_1 to D_2 in Figure 8.9, under a floating system the exchange rate would rise from OX_1 to OX_2 to re-establish equilibrium between the demand and the supply of pounds.

In order to maintain the fixed rate at OX_1, the government would have to buy foreign currency and add it to their reserves, thus increasing the supply of pounds to this foreign exchange market. This intervention is represented by the shift in supply from S_1 to S_2.

Should market forces be pushing the rate of exchange downwards from OX_1 to OX_2, as shown by an increase in supply of pounds from S_1 to S_2 in Figure 8.10, this could be associated with an increase in demand for imports. In this case, the government would have to use its reserves to buy pounds, boosting the demand for pounds from D_1 to D_2 to maintain the rate at OX_1.

This second scenario cannot be maintained over a long period of time, as sooner or later the government would run out of reserves – foreign currency reserves will always be much less than the potential volume of pounds in circulation. In these circumstances, the government will almost certainly have to consider changing the value of the pound. In this case, devaluation would be required. This could restore stability to the foreign exchange markets, but speculators would gain, as they could buy back pounds more cheaply than they might have sold them.

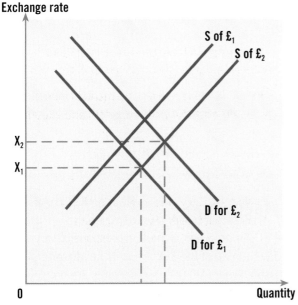

Figure 8.9 Government intervention in foreign exchange markets (rising pound)

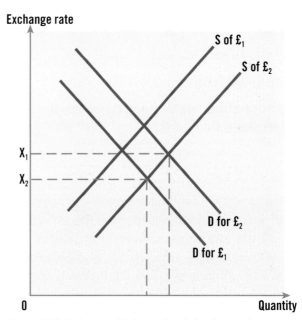

Figure 8.10 Government intervention in foreign exchange markets (falling pound)

In short, the advantages of fixed rates are that:

● exchange rate stability reduces the risks and costs of importing and exporting

● the domestic economy is protected from inflationary pressures associated with falling rates

● the domestic economy is protected from falling employment levels and national output which might be associated with a rising rate.

The disadvantages are:

● the need for large reserves of gold and foreign currency

● the fear of speculative pressures affecting the value of the currency upwards or downwards

● the requirement to sacrifice other macro policy objectives in order to maintain a given exchange rate.

Dirty systems

A **dirty exchange rate** system is one in which the government tries to manage or influence freely floating exchange rates. In this context, the UK government might be prepared to encourage increases in the exchange rate to keep down inflation rates, or encourage falls to boost incomes and employment.

DEFINITION

Dirty exchange rate: government manipulation of exchange rates

In the late 1980s, the UK government intervened in foreign currency markets to keep the pound in close relationship with the deutschmark. This policy of trying to manage the exchange rate, also known as *dirty floating*, manages to combine the weaknesses of the fixed rate systems but none of the advantages of having market-determined rates.

ACTIVITY

Use the Internet to research the impact of Asian currency crisis of 1999. Choose one of the countries affected and:

a explain why it occurred

b assess the role of speculation as a cause of the crisis

c evaluate how far can it be explained by a fixed or dirty exchange rate system

d explain the longer-term effects of the crisis on exchange rate systems in the country you have chosen.

The European Union

BUILDING ON AS

You probably have already debated the merits of the EU adopting the euro, assessed the impact of enlargement, and argued the effects of migration. For AS you will have looked at the Common Agriculture Policy (CAP) and the attempts of the EU to reduce expenditure to support farmers.

STEPPING UP TO A2

You need to have a basic understanding of how the EU has developed and how its institutions work, especially the European Commission and the European Central Bank. Other topics are:

● the EU as a customs union

● the single European market

● economic and monetary union.

EU institutions

The EU Commission is the body responsible for day-to-day running of the EU. It has its headquarters in Brussels, where 25,000 civil servants are employed. The Commission consists of 27 commissioners – one per member state appointed to be responsible for different policy areas, for example, enlargement,

The European Parliament chamber in Brussels

the environment and transport. The Commission is responsible for initiating possible legislation for consideration by the Parliament and for carrying out the decisions made by the Parliament and the Council of Ministers.

The Parliament consists of 785 members of the European Parliament (MEPs) in proportion to the populations of member states, and sits in both Strasbourg and Brussels. Members are directly elected for a five-year term of office and have the power to approve or reject legislative changes, appoint or sack commissioners, and decide on the EU's budget.

The Council of Ministers is made up of ministers from the EU's member states, who meet periodically. The actual make-up of the Council can depend upon the

topic under discussion. For example, meetings about the CAP will be attended by agriculture ministers. The presidency of the Council rotates between member states each six months. The Council has the power to make EU laws and decide the budget.

> ## ACTIVITY ···⟨
>
> Access the Eurostat website to identify and explain how the EU is attempting to tackle three economic issues considered important by the EU Parliament.

The development of the EU

The origins of the EU are both political and economic. At the end of the Second World War, there were strong moves to avoid future conflict by encouraging greater co-operation between European countries. Although it is said that the former UK Prime Minister, Winston Churchill, coined the phrase 'United States of Europe', the UK was not heavily involved in these political and economic moves. The EU was preceded by the European Coal and Steel Community, which was created in 1951 to encourage co-operation in this vital sector of the European economy.

In 1957, six countries, Belgium, France, Italy, Luxembourg, the Netherlands and West Germany, signed the Treaty of Rome to form the European

ECONOMICS IN CONTEXT – EUROPEAN ECONOMICS

POLES APART

Discussions about the reform of EU institutions never seem to go away, and it is easy to be sceptical of the bureaucratic nature of proceedings that to UK observers can appear to be long-winded and inefficient. Two points should be born in mind. First, the UK and especially the English political system is highly centralised and adversarial in nature. Question time in the House of Commons gives a flavour of this approach. In many European countries, especially where one party does not have an overall majority, party politics is more consensual, and talks and discussions will continue until agreement is reached. The second point is that the EU institutions have to

try to resolve political differences on an enormous scale. National as well party, sectional and ethnic interests often conflict, making it difficult, to say the least, to arrive at agreed policies.

These clashes and conflicts of interest partly explain the sometimes uneasy relationship that exists between the Parliament, its Commission and the Council of Ministers. Most parliaments have more powers, and some suggest that the Commission has too many and that the leading European powers have all been guilty of highjacking meetings of the Council of Ministers in order to pursue national interests.

Economic Community (EEC), which came into existence on 1 January 1958. This was a customs union. The name changed to the European Community (EC) in 1967. The UK, Ireland and Denmark joined in 1973. Since then, 18 more countries have joined, and three countries, Turkey, Macedonia and Croatia have been accepted as potential members.

The EU can be seen to have passed through four stages of development:

- customs union
- common market
- single market
- enlargement.

Customs union

This represents a relatively simple level of integration between economies and was the form of the earliest association, the European Economic Community (EEC) created in 1958. A **customs union** is an agreement to remove trade restrictions between member states, while at the same time creating common barriers to trade with non-member countries.

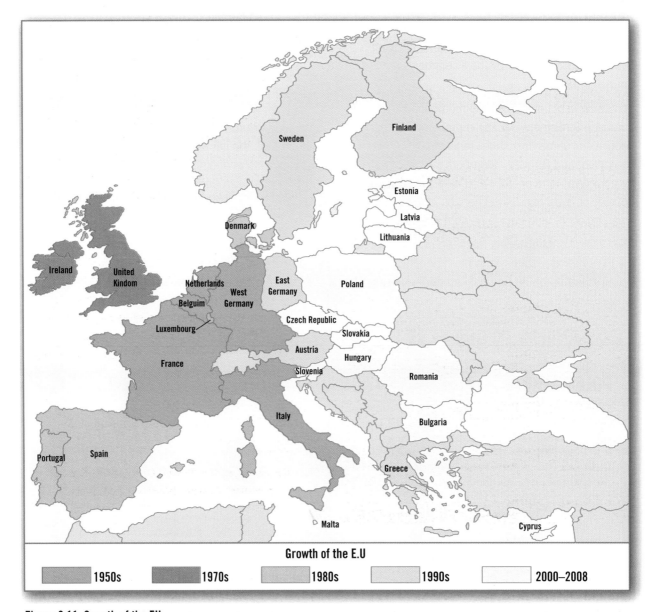

Growth of the E.U

| 1950s | 1970s | 1980s | 1990s | 2000–2008 |

Figure 8.11 Growth of the EU

Belgium	1957
France	1957
(West) Germany	1957
Italy	1957
Luxembourg	1957
Netherlands	1957

Denmark	1973
Ireland	1973
UK	1973

Greece	1981

Portugal	1986
Spain	1986

Austria	1995
Finland	1995
Sweden	1995

Cyprus	2004
Czech Republic	2004
Estonia	2004
Hungary	2004
Latvia	2004
Lithuania	2004
Malta	2004
Poland	2004
Slovakia	2004
Slovenia	2004

Bulgaria	2007
Romania	2007

Table 8.4 Member states and years of accession to the EU

> **DEFINITION**
>
> **Customs union:** a group of countries that trade freely with each other, yet maintain common tariffs in respect of trade with other countries

The effect of this is to both create trade between member states and to divert trade away from other countries that might have supplied goods and services more cheaply than member states. One of the reasons why the UK showed little interest in joining the original six member states was that joining the customs union would have meant diverting imports away from existing trading partners – principally fellow members of the Commonwealth and the USA.

When the UK eventually joined in 1973, it no longer enjoyed cheap imports of meat and diary produce from countries such as New Zealand, but the hope was that more new trade would be created within the EEC to compensate for the loss of cheap imports.

The Common Market

This represents a closer degree of integration whereby labour and capital are also freed from restrictions on their movement between member states. Creating a **common market** usually involves the removal of what are called non-tariff barriers and the creation of common safety standards for member countries.

> **DEFINITION**
>
> **Common market:** a group of countries between which the movement of capital, labour and goods is not restricted

The main legislative measure designed to develop the common market was the Single European Act (SEA), which came into force in July 1987. It was designed to remove all internal barriers to the movement of goods, services, capital and labour. It also involved the removal of customs controls between member states, stopping favouritism in the allocation of government contracts, reducing subsidies paid by individual governments, and ensuring that qualifications are mutually recognised.

Progress in implementing the SEA has been slow, and 20 years later there are still many barriers to the free movement of services, whereas goods are traded much more freely. According to EU regulations, if a particular good can be sold in one member country, then it should be freely traded by other member states. However, a service provider has to satisfy the individual requirements of each member state if that service is to be freely traded between all states.

The single market

This occurs when member countries form a **single market** – something like Winston Churchill's United States of Europe. In such a market, there is free movement of goods, services, capital and labour and this further develops the concept of a common market in respect of the trade in goods and services. It is argued that a single market requires:

- a single European currency
- common fiscal and monetary policies
- agreement as to regional, social, transport and environmental policies.

DEFINITION

Single market: a market with a common currency and economic policies

The movement towards a single European market was boosted by the agreement, in February 1992, of member states to the Maastricht Treaty. This, in line with the origins of the EU, was partly political and partly economic. Members agreed to move towards common foreign and security policies and also agreed to:

- 'convergence criteria' to achieve closer economic integration
- the creation of the European Central Bank
- the introduction of the euro as a single European currency
- increased co-ordination of monetary and fiscal policies.

ECONOMICS IN CONTEXT – EUROPEAN ECONOMICS

WILLING PARTNERS?

'Agreed' as the word is used in the preceding sections is perhaps too strong a term. As noted earlier, the UK has never been an enthusiastic member of the wider European community. How far this reflects patriotic and anti-European sentiments in the UK and how far this reflects genuine economic concerns is very difficult to assess. The arguments about greater integration can be summed up as follows:

- The EU is the UK's main trading partner.
- Economic theory suggests that freer movement of resources and freer trade leads to greater economic growth.
- The single European market is designed to achieve these objectives.
- The costs of greater integration are a loss of national sovereignty over monetary, fiscal and other political and economic factors.

For those in favour of greater UK involvement in European integration, the potential economic benefits outweigh the costs of the loss of sovereignty. Those opposed to such moves are not prepared to sacrifice UK independence.

ACTIVITY

Use the Internet to research different attitudes in the UK towards greater European integration. How far can you categorise these different attitudes? Try to distinguish between economic and political arguments.

ACTIVITY ···⋮

Assess the economic justification for the creation of common fiscal and monetary policies if a single European market is to be created.

Convergence criteria

One of the main fears of the EU countries was that the movement to a single market would give advantages or disadvantages to particular member states. Such might be the case, for example, for a country whose currency was seen to be undervalued compared to other members, as would one running a large budget deficit. For these reasons, the countries party to the Maastricht Treaty agreed to four **convergence criteria** in order to being each economy more in line the others. They agreed to try to ensure that inflation rates were within 1.5 per cent of the average rate of the three lowest rates in the EU. Similarly a target was set for interest rates to be no more than 2 per cent above the average rate of the lowest three countries. As noted earlier on page 139, governments had to try to ensure that they kept their national debts to less than 60 per cent of their GDP, and that budget deficits should not exceed 3 per cent of GDP. Finally, each agreed in addition to maintain stable exchange rates.

DEFINITION

Convergence criteria: in the context of the EU, these are tests that have to be satisfied if an individual member country is to adopt the euro

These measures were designed to pave the way towards the creation of a single currency and, 10 years after the Maastricht agreement, the euro was established and adopted by 11 member states, not including the UK, Greece, Sweden and Denmark.

The European Central Bank (ECB)

This body came into being at the same time as the euro, and was responsible for setting a common interest rate for those countries adopting the euro. Its governing council meets monthly to determine the bank's interest rate. The ECB also has the power to manage euro exchange rates and has control of part of the reserves of the central banks of member countries, which could be used to influence the value of the euro. However, as with the UK and US governments, the ECB has allowed the euro to float freely.

The euro

Since its establishment, the euro appears to have worked, in the sense that over its first five years there have been no major problems. It is argued that those countries adopting the euro have benefited from:

- lower transaction costs

- greater price transparency, leading to more competitive markets

- increased trade between member states

- increased foreign direct investment (FDI) into member states

- stable exchange rates.

However it has been suggested that:

- the ECB has kept interest rates too high

- rates of growth for euro members have been lower than those in the UK

- there is a reluctance to adopt supply-side policies that would increase competitiveness and promote long-term growth in aggregate supply

- UK-based businesses would be faced with transition costs if the UK chose to adopt the euro.

The UK government has set its own convergence criteria that need to be met if it were to consider adopting the euro. These are:

- movement to an economic cycle similar to that of other member states

- flexibility within the euro area for coping with economic changes

- entry to benefit FDI to the UK

- benefits to the UK financial services sector

- employment and economic growth will increase.

It is hard to understand how achievement of some of these criteria can be demonstrated prior to membership of the euro. Currently, the UK government has not shown any enthusiasm to join, perhaps out of fear that any referendum on entry would result in a 'no' vote.

ACTIVITY

Assess the economic validity of arguments in favour of the proposition that the UK should adopt the euro.

Enlargement

At first there were six, now there are 27. In 10 years this figure could double, if former members of the USSR are included. In other words, the EU is getting bigger and bigger. Currently it:

- contains 500 million people, about one-thirteenth of the world population

- produces 31 per cent of the world's GDP

- is the largest trading block in the world

- has the potential to become the largest single market

- encourages political stability in Europe.

This data provides a rationale for the expansion of the EU. Potential members want to join to access what could become the world's largest single market, and existing members have a clear interest in accessing an even wider market. However, enlargement is not without its problems. These include:

- **transition issues** – many of the new and prospective members of the EU were formally part of the USSR and have had varying degrees of success in the transition from command to mixed economies. Neither have all established democratic

traditions, property rights, and more acceptable levels of corruption that would be expected in a well-functioning market economy.

- relatively large and unproductive agricultural sectors in some new member states. The EU cannot afford to extend the level of resources previously available to the agriculture sectors of the original members of the EU.

- ethnic and racial tensions, especially when it comes to the free movement of workers from the relatively poor east to the relatively rich west. There has been particularly strong resistance to accepting the membership of Turkey and this can be seen to be racially motivated and anti-Muslim.

- poor and weak environmental policies, especially in the former communist countries.

- decision making in the smaller earlier versions of the EU was never easy and increases in both scale and diversity are likely to force changes in the EU's institutions.

learning tip

Expect to be asked questions about enlargement such as 'Assess the impact of enlargement of the EU on the performance of the UK economy'.

ACTIVITY

Assess the possible implications for the Russian economy of potential membership of the EU.

Exam Café

Relax, refresh, result!

Relax and prepare

Sally

Our teacher is always going on about the need to 'define terms'. So when I'm writing an essay or a longer data-response answer, whenever I introduce a technical term such as 'elasticity' or 'national income', I always supply a brief definition. But it MUST be brief, otherwise it breaks up the essay too much.

Writing brief but accurate definitions is something that you need to work at, but I have proved that it is worthwhile because my marks have improved no end since I started doing it.

Matthew

I agree with Sally about definitions, and a useful tip, especially in macroeconomics, is to state, before you write the definition, whether an economic concept is a FLOW, a STOCK or a RATIO.

A flow concept, such as income, is measured over a time period, while a stock, like wealth, is measured at a point in time. Remember this, and you'll avoid making basic errors, like saying that GDP is a measure of 'national wealth'. I've seen journalists on the TV making this mistake.

Ratio concepts, like the rate of interest or price elasticity of demand, are neither simple stocks nor flows. They are calculated by dividing or multiplying stocks and flows together. They might be measured over time (like interest rates) or they might have no time period (like the unemployment rate), or they might simply be a number with no units of measurement (like elasticity).

Julia

I have improved my marks in essays and the 'mini essays' you get in the longer parts of data-response questions since I started writing a brief 'essay plan' before starting to write my full answer.

This helps me to make sure that my essay is focused and well structured, with a beginning, a middle and an end. As well as helping to ensure that all the content that I need is there, and that I don't forget to include anything important, I can also make sure that I am displaying all the skills. I make sure there's some analysis, application and evaluation.

I know that examiners have to mark a lot of exam answers, so I try to help them out. I always write the word 'PLAN' very clearly before my plan, and I put a large cross through the plan so that the examiner doesn't waste their time reading it. I also start the actual essay answer on a new page.

Other ways in which I help the examiner are by writing clearly and legibly, and by clearly writing the number or the letter identifying the question in the left hand margin of the answer paper. I also make sure that I have a pencil, ruler and eraser with me in examinations, so that I can draw diagrams neatly and label them clearly.

Refresh your memory

Revision checklist

Can you ... ?	Turn to page ...
Explain how demand-side and supply-side 'shocks' can affect the economic cycle	110–12
Make a list of supply-side factors and explain how they can affect the long-run trend rate of growth	113–16
Assess the costs and benefits of economic growth	117–18
Discuss the main uses and limitations of national income data	119–21
Explain what it is that the Human Development Index attempts to measure	122
Evaluate the causes and consequences of unemployment	131–32
Define 'natural rate of unemployment'	129, 132–33
Use a Phillips Curve to explain possible relationships between inflation and unemployment	128, 132
Explain how index numbers are calculated	122, 124
Describe the main features of the Retail Price Index and the Consumer Price Index	124
Evaluate the causes and consequences of inflation	126–29
Use AD/AS analysis to show why there might be conflicts between government macroeconomic policy objectives	135
Explain 'rules-based' budgetary (fiscal) policy	137
Discuss how interest rates are determined, and explain their likely effects on aggregate demand and inflation	149–52
Define globalisation	160
Explain the law of comparative advantage and the gains from trade	164
Discuss the issue of free trade versus protectionism	163–70
Assess the significance of balance of payments deficits and surpluses	171–74
Evaluate policies aimed at balance of payments equilibrium	172–74
Explain what is meant by a customs union	178–79
Discuss the impact on the UK economy of the widening of European integration (e.g. the accession of new member countries)	179–80
Discuss the impact on the UK economy of the deepening of European integration (e.g. the development of the single market, and the euro)	180–81

Key word quiz

Define:

1. Inflation
2. Unemployment
3. Fiscal policy
4. Monetary policy
5. Globalisation
6. Single market

These are answers to the following part b) essay question:

'Evaluate the policies which could be used to in order to correct a balance of payments deficit on current account.' (25 marks).

Kofi's answer

Examiner comments:
A very good introductory paragraph; it is focused and displays economic awareness. It sets the scene very nicely.

Examiner comments:
These are indeed two 'main' possible policies, but there are other possibilities.

The balance of payments on current account measures payments for exports and imports of goods and services. The figures are usually published on a quarterly basis, and then on an annual basis. It is called 'current' because it tracks day-to-day transactions and does not include long-term movements of capital investment. In recent years the UK has usually had a deficit in the 'balance of trade', which measures payments for goods, and within the balance of trade the UK now has a deficit in manufactured products. In previous decades the balance in service items (insurance, financial services, transport, tourism) has been large enough to more than compensate for a balance of trade deficit, but this has not happened in recent years. Some economists are concerned because the UK is living beyond its means, consuming today and leaving it to future generations to pick up the debt.

Two measures that could be taken to lower the current account deficit are barriers to imports and making UK goods more competitive through reducing the exchange rate of the pound against other major currencies. There are two types of barrier that could be imposed on imports. The first of these is a tariff which is in effect a tax on imported goods, making them more expensive. Tariffs have the advantage of protecting domestic firms by enabling them to charge a higher price, and they also provide useful revenue for the government, but they have the disadvantage of creating a 'welfare loss' because consumers are receiving fewer goods than they want and paying a higher price than necessary. The other type of barrier is a quota. This limits the physical amount of a good allowed into the country. The policy might work faster than a tariff, because unlike the tariff policy there is no need to predict how consumers will react (the goods are immediately made less available rather than more expensive, so price elasticity of demand is less relevant). However, the goods that are allowed in are likely to become more expensive, so there is a welfare loss, and the system needs policing to avoid smuggling, which costs money to the taxpayer.

Both tariffs and quotas have serious disadvantages: they might break international agreements (e.g. the World Trade Organisation), they might encourage retaliation which will hit UK exports and there is also the long-term problem of protecting firms that really need to be encouraged to become more efficient.

A devaluation of the currency, the pound against other currencies such as the dollar and the euro, will in effect make UK exports appear more expensive to overseas buyers, and make imported goods and services appear dearer to UK citizens. Whether this will improve the current account depends on the price elasticity of demand for imports and exports. If our exports are price elastic, then our export earnings will increase. But if our imports are price inelastic (for example because we are importing things that we can't produce ourselves) then total spending on imports might increase by an even greater amount and our balance of payments deficit could actually increase. It might also be difficult these days to deliberately alter the exchange rate, because they are strongly influenced by interest rates, which these days are out of the hands of UK politicians and controlled by the Bank of England to target the inflation rate.

It could be argued that the above policies are short-term 'fixes' and the best way to improve the balance of payments is to have patience and use long-term, supply side measures, such as investment in productive assets and human capital to make the country more productive and competitive. Some economists say that balance of payments deficits do not matter anyway. We do not know what the balance of payments of Lancashire is because we do not measure it, so we do not worry about it. On the other hand, if industries in other parts of the world are 'winning' because they are more efficient, then this will cause problems such as unemployment in the real economy of Lancashire. Many economists argue that what is important is the size of the deficit as a percentage of GDP, because this gives us an idea of how long it would take the country to pay any debts it might be building up.

Lee's answer

The UK has moved from trading manufactured goods to trading services with the rest of the world. Developing countries will work for low wages so costs of production are lower. Also we have more trade within the EU where there is a single market without barriers. Most raw materials come from abroad so it is cheaper to turn them into manufactured products over there, reducing transport costs. Britain has a comparative advantage in services so should specialise on those and forget about selling goods.

The government could respond with embargoes, which are a total ban on foreign goods. This will improve the deficit because the public will have to buy British. Or the government could put tariffs on the imports, so that the British public stop buying them.

Overall, protection does help reduce the current account deficit, but it can also keep the problem the same. If the UK operates protectionism then other countries are going to retaliate, so that UK exports are reduced, so the deficit might reduce only slightly.

Another way that the UK can reduce the deficit is to reduce interest rates.

Hot tips

On each of the two papers ECON-3 and ECON-4 there are three essay questions, and you choose one essay on each paper. The essays are split into two. Part a) is worth 15 marks, and part b) 25 marks. Give each of these essays a beginning, a middle and an end, but be aware that there will be a 'theme' linking both parts together. Obviously, you should spend more time on part b) than a). In part a) you should try to make as many points as you can, because the marking scheme will be organised on a point-by-point basis – and points mean marks. Part b) will be marked using what examiners call a 'Levels of Response' mark scheme. Here you need to pay a great deal of attention to 'higher order' skills, especially evaluation.

Synopticity

Papers ECON-3 and ECON-4 are regarded as 'synoptic'. This means that some of the tasks will assess your understanding of the relationships between different aspects of economics. In practice, this means that you must NOT say 'goodbye' to the work you learned for AS economics when you embark on A2. Economics is not like that anyway: economics tends to link together in a chain quite naturally, and the understanding of one concept will depend on the understanding of a previous concept. The best way to learn economics is therefore step by step and link by link, and the best way to prepare for studying A2 topics is first to recap on AS topics. You will have noticed that this is the approach taken in this book.

Answering essay questions

Some people think that essays are the most difficult of all types of exam question. This is because they are more open-ended, and you have to organise your knowledge to argue a case. You need to practice writing essays under exam conditions in the time allowed. Here are some points to bear in mind:

- Make sure you UNDERSTAND exactly what the question is asking you to do. Just because a question mentions a topic, such as competition or unemployment, this is NOT an invitation to write 'all I know' about the topic. As a lawyer might say:

- … answer THE QUESTION, the WHOLE question, and NOTHING BUT the question.

- Note the COMMAND WORDS used (see below). Examiners have a language all of their own, and you must translate these words so that you understand them BEFORE you start.

- Before you start:
  - ○ Use a highlighter to underline all the KEY WORDS in the question.
  - ○ Make an ESSAY PLAN. Make sure that each key word is addressed somewhere in the plan at least once.

- When you start:
  - ○ Open with an introductory paragraph that
    - ○ sets the scene, and
    - ○ says how you have interpreted the question.

- As you write:
  - ○ Define key terms as you introduce them.
  - ○ Argue logically.
  - ○ Use your awareness of the economy and economic principles.

- ○ Be careful to distinguish fact from opinion.

- ○ Do not pre-judge an issue. Examine different sides of an argument.

- ○ Quote expert opinion where relevant.

- ○ Write in a lively style – show enthusiasm for your subject.

- ○ Do not over-abbreviate ('GDP' is acceptable, as long as 'gross domestic product' is written out in full the first time it is used; 'govt.' for 'government' is simply unacceptable.)

- ○ Do not waffle. Stick to the point.

- ○ Spare a thought for the poor examiner. Write legibly and as neatly as you can.

- As you get to the end:
  - ○ Make sure that you have justified any judgements that you have made.
  - ○ Finish with a concluding paragraph that sums everything up.

Some typical command words

DESCRIBE: show your knowledge of facts and theories.

APPLY: use an economic principle to discuss an issue.

ANALYSE: explain the principles behind an economic issue; refer to facts or data and discuss patterns and relationships between them.

EVALUATE: balance advantages against disadvantages, pros against cons, arguments for and arguments against; discuss several issues and then prioritise them (say which are the most significant and why); come to a conclusion or judgement and justify it.

Essays

1. a) Explain why economic growth is regarded as a major policy objective of governments.

   b) Country A is growing twice as fast as Country B. Does this mean that the citizens of A are better-off than the citizens of B? Justify your answer.

2. a) Why do governments collect taxes?

   b) Evaluate the economic consequences of an unbalanced government budget.

Further reading and references

It always pays to have access to other economics text books, especially when it comes to bits that you find difficult to understand.

Anderton, A. (2006) *Economics*, 4th edition, Causeway Press. A well-written text in a new edition to match the new specifications

Bamford, C. and S. Grant (2000) *The UK Economy in a Global Context*, Heinemann

Bamford, C. and S. Munday (2002) *Markets*, Heinemann

Hale, G. (2001) *Labour Markets*, Heinemann

Powell, R. (2008) *A2 Economics AQA: Student Unit Guide to Unit 2*, Philip Allan Updates. A clearly written revision guide

Sloman, J. (2006) *Essentials of Economics*, 6th edition, Prentice Hall Europe. An introductory text used at university level which is clear and very thorough but written at a higher level than is required for the A2 examination

Smith, D. and S. Grant (2003) *UK Current Economic Policy*, Heinemann

Economics Review. Available by subscription from Philip Allan Updates, four issues a year; includes a very useful update in September

Economics Today. Available by subscription from Anforme, four issues a year; accessible articles about economic issues

Glossary

Absolute advantage: exists when one country can produce goods and services more efficiently than another

Absolute poverty: those living on incomes below a given threshold

Accelerator principle: an explanation of the greater volatility in levels of investment

Actual economic growth: the extent to which economies grow to their potential

Allocative efficiency: theoretical situation in which goods and services are produced to reflect the demands of individual consumers

Asymmetric information: when either buyers or sellers know much more than the other party about the factors affecting the sale of a good or service

Average cost: also known as *unit cost*, refers to the cost of producing each individual good or service

Average revenue (AR): price per unit of sales – usually abbreviated to price

Balance of payments accounts: records of financial transactions between one country and the rest of the world

Barrier to entry: factor limiting ability of new firms to enter a market

Bilateral monopoly: the combination of a *monopsonist* and a single supplier of labour – usually a trade union or professional association

Boom: period of rapid economic growth

Budget deficit: when governments plan to spend more than they plan to raise in revenue

Budget surplus: when governments plan to raise more revenue than they plan to spend

Capital flight: the export, often illegal, of cash and valuable assets from poor countries

Collusive oligopolists: *oligopolists* who try to co-operate with each other

Common market: a group of countries between which the movement of capital, labour and goods is not restricted

Comparative advantage: applies when one country can produce goods and services at lower opportunity costs than another

Concentrated market: a non-competitive market dominated by a small number of firms

Concentration ratio: the market share in the hands of a given number of producers – usually 3 or 5

Contestable markets: markets in which the fear of competition or takeover forces firms with market power to behave competitively

Convergence criteria: in the context of the EU, these are tests that have to be satisfied if an individual member country is to adopt the euro

Cost-benefit analysis: a technique used to assess the relative significance of the *social costs* and *social benefits* of different forms of economic activity

Customs union: a group of countries that trade freely with each other, yet maintain common tariffs in respect of trade with other countries

Deadweight welfare loss: combined welfare losses of both consumers and producers – often associated with *monopoly*

Deflation: falling price levels

Demerger: the splitting up of a large firm into two or more separate entities

Demerit goods: goods producing significant negative externalities and which are likely to be over-produced by the market system

Depression or **slump:** long-term *recession*

Derived demand: when the demand for one good, service or factor depends on the demand for another good, service or factor

Dirty exchange rate: government manipulation of exchange rates

Diseconomies of scale: rising long-run average costs

Downturn: period in which aggregate demand is in relative decline

Dumping: pricing exported goods at less than their cost of production

Dynamic efficiency: long-run increases in efficiency

Economic agent: an individual or institution whose decisions have an impact on economic issues

Economic cycle: cyclical fluctuations above and below the long-run trend rate of economic growth

Economic growth: increases in national output over time, often measured by changes in GNP

Economies of scale: falling long-run average costs

Embargo: prohibition on imports of specified goods or services

Equity: social or judicial 'fairness'; also the value of the shares issued by a company

Exchange control: government intervention to limit the exchange of one currency for another

Exchange rate: what one currency is worth in terms of another

Export subsidies: government subsidies to encourage exports

Fiscal policies: using changes in government revenue and expenditure to achieve macroeconomic policy objectives

Fixed costs: costs which don't change with output

Fixed exchange rate: exchange rate set by government intervention

Floating exchange rate: a system by which market forces are left to determine exchange rates

Game theory: a theory developed by psychologists to model interdependent behaviour and applied to oligopolists

Gini coefficient: a numerical value used to measure the extent of income inequality

Globalisation: production and distribution of goods and services on a global scale

Golden rule: maintaining a balanced budget over the economic cycle

Human capital: the productive capacity of people

Hyperinflation: very rapid rates of inflation

Import quotas: physical restrictions on imports

Income: earnings to the owners of factors of production over time

Infant industries: newly established industries that cannot compete with larger competitors

Interdependence: how decision making between oligopolistic firms can be affected by the decisions of other oligopolistic firms

Interest rates: the cost of borrowing and lending money – always expressed as a percentage

Investment: spending to increase the productive potential of an economy

Law of diminishing marginal returns: applies in the short run: if output is increased by using more and more of a variable factor, a point will be reached beyond which increased factor use will lead to smaller and smaller increases in output

Lender of last resort: role of the central bank in terms of always being prepared to lend to commercial banks – at a price

Lorenz curve: a graph used to measure the extent of income inequality

Margin: the effect of changing one variable by a small amount – usually one unit

Marginal cost: the change in costs brought about by changing production by a given number of units

Marginal revenue (MR): the change in revenue brought about by changing sales of a given number of units

Marginal revenue product: the change in revenue caused by changing a given number of workers employed

Market share: the proportion of market in the hands of a given number of producers

Marshall Learner condition: the requirement that the combined elasticities for imports and exports need to be relatively elastic if a fall in the exchange rate is going to benefit the balance of payments

Maximax strategy: taking greater risks to obtain higher potential profits

Maximin strategy: taking less risks and accepting lower potential profits

Merger: two or more firms joining together to form one larger firm

Merit goods: goods producing significant positive externalities that are likely to be under-produced by the market system

Minimum efficient scale of production: the lowest amount of production consistent with earning significant *economies of scale*

Monetarism: theory or theories explaining inflation in terms of monetary factors

Monetary policies: policies involving changing the interest rate and/or the supply of money to achieve macroeconomic policy objectives

Monopoly: technically speaking, when one firm has a 100 per cent market share

Monopsonist: a monopoly employer of a particular type of labour

Multinational: company producing and selling in a number of different countries

Multiplier effect: the extent to which a change in a component of aggregate demand can lead to a proportionally larger change in national output

NAIRU: the non accelerating inflation rate of unemployment, also known as the *natural rate of unemployment.*

Nationalisation: transfer of ownership from the private to the public sector

Natural rate of unemployment: according to Milton Friedman and others, a rate of unemployment at which inflation is stable and not affected by changes in government policy; another name for *NAIRU*

Negative equity: situation in which debts are greater than the assets that secure them – typically housing

New economic paradigm: suggestion that it is possible for positive economic growth to co-exist with low rates of inflation

Non-collusive oligopolists: oligopolists who compete with each other

Non-price competition: when firms use advertising, branding and other techniques in preference to cutting prices to attract more customers

Normal profit: level of profit required to keep a firm in a given market – neither expanding nor contracting

Objectives: the basic goals that a firm sets itself

Oligopoly: a market dominated by a small number of firms

Overheat: what an economy does when its aggregate demand exceeds its productive potential

Perfect competition: a market consisting of a very large number of small firms

Potential economic growth: growth in the productive potential of an economy

Price discrimination: charging different customers different prices for the same good or service

Price leadership: influential firms whose pricing decisions are copied by others

Price maker: a firm with sufficient market power to have some influence in determining the price of its products or services

Price taker: a perfectly competitive firm has to accept the price set by market forces – hence the phrase price taker

Privatisation: transfer of ownership from the public to the private sector

Product differentiation: the ability of producers to make similar products appear different to consumers

Productive efficiency: production at minimum cost

Profit maximisation: gaining the maximum profit – shown where marginal cost is equal to marginal revenue, usually expressed as MR =MC

Progressive taxation: taxes that take proportionally more from the better-off

Property rights: the clear identification of who owns what

Public ownership: collective ownership of resources

Quantity theory of money: theory that explains changes in the rate of inflation by reference to changes in the money supply

Quasi goods: goods and services that can be viewed as private goods but can be supplied to others without a significant increase in costs

Real income: a measure of income that excludes inflation

Recession: negative economic growth for more than 6 months

Redistribution of income: making one section of society better-off at the expense of another

Regressive tax: a tax taking proportionally more in taxes from the poor than from the rich

Relative poverty: poverty in relationship to average levels of wealth and income in a given economy

Repo rate: the rate of interest charged by the central bank

Revenue: flows of money that are received by a firm

Sales maximisation: gaining maximum sales – shown where the volume of sales is as large as possible without making a loss, i.e. where AC (average cost) cuts AR (average revenue) at the highest possible level of sales

Satisficing: doing the minimum required – usually in the context of keeping dividends to shareholders to an acceptable minimum

Shareholder value: the price at which shares are traded at a given time

Single market: a market with a common currency and economic policies

Social benefit: the full benefits to society of the provision of a good or service

Social cost: the full cost to society of the provision of a good or service

Social needs: needs of society and special interest groups

Soft landing: avoiding *recession* in a time of economic slowdown

Stagflation: the co-existence of low rates of economic growth and relatively high inflation

Sunk costs: non-recoverable fixed costs

Supernormal (or abnormal) profit: anything in excess of *normal profit*

Survival: avoiding bankruptcy

Sustainability: economic growth that does not deplete non-renewable resources

Symmetric information: when buyers and sellers are both reasonably well informed of factors affecting the sales of a good or service

Tariffs: taxes on imports

Technological changes: changes in the ways that goods and services are made or provided

Technological shock: random fluctuation in labour productivity

Total costs: average cost × sales

Total revenue (TR): price × sales

Transition issues: used in the context that countries newly admitted to the EU have to deal with economic and political problems arising from their membership

Triangle model: theory of inflation that combines demand-pull, cost-push and the role of expectations

Upturn: a period in which aggregate demand is increasing

Variable costs: costs that change with output

Wealth: the value of assets at any point in time

Index

Bold page numbers indicate a definition on that page. Italic numbers indicate figures.